My WAR, My LIFE

My WAR, My LIFE

A TRUE STORY BY

K. SOPHIE STALLMAN

MILL CITY PRESS, MINNEAPOLIS

Mill City Press, Inc.
322 First ave N., Fifth floor
Minneapolis, MN 55401
612.455.2294
www.millcitypublishing.com

ISBN-13: 978-1-62652-253-4
LCCN: 2013911842

Cover Design by Sophie Chi
Typeset by Mary Kristin Ross

Printed in the United States of America

DEDICATION

When reading through these pages, please take to heart the words
of the Polish poet Adam Asnyk, whose wisdom still holds true today:

Ale nie depczcie przeszłości ołtarzy,

Choć macie sami doskonalsze wznieść

Na nich sie jeszcze święty ogień żarzy,

I miłość ludzka stoi tam na straży,

I wy winniście im cześć!

Adam Asnyk 1838 – 1896

Do not stomp on the altars of the past,

Even if you should rise to better ones;

On them the sacred fire still glows,

Human love stands there, guarding

And you owe them your honor.

CONTENTS

CONTENTS

INTRODUCTION

It was difficult to start writing about my life. Three generations ago, I was a child in Poland, on the European continent so distant from my current home in California. In those days, automobiles were a novelty; planes were two-seaters with open cockpits, and the privileged traveled comfortably by train at unprecedented speeds of 25 miles per hour. The world was slower then.

How, I asked myself, could I explain the life of a child raised in a traditional Polish family, in a privileged class, the nobility? The privileged class was so proud, and yet compared to our present lives in the twenty-first century, they had only a fraction of the comforts with which we now indulge ourselves. The concept of nobility grows increasingly dim with the passage of time.

And how could I possibly explain my experiences during World War II? For many years I told myself: "Your experiences were no different than those of thousands of others. Why should *you* write?"

Besides, I would have to write in English, which is my fourth language. Would I be able to express myself? The Polish language is one of the most difficult to master, with a grammar more complicated than Latin. As a child, I was fortunate in that my family spoke at the most sophisticated level of expression, and I too was able to master the nuances of my native tongue. Now I use English, which I love. I would never write in another language.

Beyond the difficulties of expression, I had yet another excuse not to start writing. As a child, the Polish culture subliminally taught me that I should be modest, and attempting to write my memoirs seemed somehow presumptuous.

In spite of all these excuses, a gnawing feeling in my heart eventually forced me to face the truth. I always thought of myself as a happy woman, someone who made people laugh. Was this the truth, the whole truth? If so, then why for so many years had I kept my memories bottled up inside? For self-preservation?

Friends and family urged me to put my stories on paper. My visual memory was always very good. Now I realized that my whole life was stored within me in a series of pictures. Some memories took the form of movies, others still images, all vivid in my mind. So I started writing, like a chronicler, pouring out the pictures of my life's stories on paper.

As I wrote, something happened to my cheerful personality. When my stories stared back at me from my computer screen, a strange feeling squeezed my throat and tears welled in my eyes. I began to see myself from a distance and in a different light. Frequently, I was startled by some personal characteristic, familiar but also foreign to me. Where did those traits come from? Some had an obvious source; others were more mysterious. However, I never lacked determination or self-discipline. Once I started writing, I kept on to the end.

In one story after another, I relived the dramas and tragedies that lingered deep inside me. For the first time in my life I was able to grieve. Grieving is never easy, and it does not ever seem to end. I found that I had to give up looking for perfection. Our life on this earth is very far from perfect. Finally, I had to abandon my inherited false modesty and admit that my life story was worth preserving.

I have asked God many times why I was saved. Why did I not perish like most of my friends? There is no answer. So I decided to do what I learned to do so well: stay alive and enjoy the rest of my life. I feel the presence of the strong men and women who raised and inspired me as I write this story. Now, once again, I am among the privileged. Now, at the end of my life, I live in the best place in the world, my beloved United States.

PART I:

CHILDHOOD: OLD WAYS, OLD WARS, HAPPY MEMORIES

Poland, the Coveted Peaceful Land

During the last century, in the 1930s, I was a little child growing up in Poland. It wasn't until the next century that I realized how special my country was—truly the land of milk and honey, with slow-flowing rivers, forests full of animals, and rich soil that provided Poland's people with food, clothing and building materials. People grew to love their land, their wilderness, their children and even their enemies, once those enemies stopped fighting and settled peacefully in Poland.

For we had many enemies over the centuries, who came periodically from all directions. Descendants of vicious Huns invaded from the west, searching for space and food. Cruel Russians, looking for Western culture and civilization, invaded from the east. From further away, Tartars, Turks and other Muslim peoples came during the spring, moving like plagues through the Ukrainian steppes to steal, rape, plunder and burn whatever they could not carry away. Even the northern Swedes invaded us at one time.

Poles did not invade other lands. They did not need or want

to, or perhaps they did not have such aggression in their blood. However, once Poles were attacked, they forcefully defended their land, sending the invaders back home. In the fourteenth century, the Lithuanian Grand Duke Jagiełło asked to be united with the Polish Crown, creating a large Polish Lithuanian commonwealth (we called it the Union) under a common king. Later, Hungary's kings also joined the union, creating a powerful country whose territory under the Jagiellonian dynasty extended from the Baltic Sea to the Black Sea.

It was a long period of peace and prosperity, proving what is perhaps a lesson of history: only a powerful country can secure peace. Later, our country's cultural tradition of peace and integrity was borne out by the Polish King Jan, the third Sobieski. To me, it is only America, centuries later, which has consistently shown the same principles of benevolent power.

In 1683 the Ottoman Empire's Pasha Kara Mustafa marched his Turkish armies, aided by Tartars and other Muslims, outward to conquer Europe. The vast armies overpowered all countries in their path and surrounded Vienna. The Austrian King Leopold fled, leaving his army to defend the city. Pope Innocent XI pleaded with the rulers of all the European countries to unite against the Ottoman threat, fearing that the whole of Europe would be overpowered by Islam.

King Leopold and his German allies had difficulty asking Poland, their traditional enemy, for help. Eventually, in desperation, King Leopold sought out the Polish king. By early September 1683, the situation in Vienna was desperate. On the evening of September 11, King Jan Sobieski arrived in Vienna. From the Kahlenberg Hill above the city, he took command of all the European forces.

Having been besieged by Middle Eastern hordes for years, the

Polish military had learned successful strategies for use against them. The scouts that King Sobieski sent out prior to his arrival told him that the Ottoman troops were suffering from dysentery. Also, the weather had turned cold. Immediately upon arrival, King Sobieski set his forces in formation for the attack. Kara Mustafa prepared his forces below to fight. King Sobieski kept them waiting until the cold morning hours. The southern Ottoman forces, waiting during the cold night in formation, were left weak and disoriented.

Finally, King Sobieski's armies attacked from three directions. The Polish Winged Hussars were their most formidable fighting force. The movement of wind in their artificial metal wings created an uncanny sound which unnerved enemy horses and drove superstitious soldiers into a panic. The battle was over in few hours. The demoralized Turks fled in disarray, abandoning tents, weapons and provisions, which the returning Polish armies brought home to Poland. They can be seen to this day in the museum chambers of Wawel Castle in the city of Krakow.

King Jan III Sobieski saved European civilization. His character and high quality of leadership earned him international respect and the love of his people. The grateful citizens of Vienna erected a chapel in his honor on Kahlenberg Hill. On the ceiling of that chapel are painted the crests of all the lines of Polish aristocracy and nobility who took part in the battle for Vienna. I was proud to find my family's Pomian crest among them.

Austrian and German gratitude to Poland lasted less than a hundred years. By 1772, the three black eagles (Russia, Hapsburg Austria and Prussia, the three countries with eagles as their symbol) organized a takeover of the Polish-Lithuanian Commonwealth. Maria Theresa of Austria invited the representatives of Frederick of Prussia and the Tsarina Katharina of Russia to Vienna to sign the division of Polish land. The Austrian king helped the Russian Tsarina Katharina and the Prussian monarch to overpower and divide a greatly weakened Poland.

This history, which I learned as a young girl, informed my views of my country and my role in Poland's history. I was very proud of our long fight against foreign dominance and of the ways in which Poles had risen to the challenge of aggressive invading armies in the past. Years later, I would find myself and my family thrust into this long tradition by Germany's aggression in World War II.

Christmas and the Old Traditions

Poland received Christianity in 966 A.D. Poles were christened peacefully, but unlike other countries, they did not destroy their pagan relics, and they assimilated many pagan traditions into Polish Christian culture. To many of us, the Polish Christmas celebrations are the epitome of that cultural hybridity and embody a special magic.

What is Poland's Christmas magic? Is it a tradition, a custom, a series of special celebrations, or a set of beliefs? Or is it all our memories, wishes and disappointments combined? Christmas, like a deity, has been and always will be for those of Polish descent. I can recollect my past years through the memory of Christmas Eves.

Yes, Christmas Eves. In my family, only Christmas Eve held the elusive magic of Christmas.

Winter solstice days in Poland, at the fifty-second parallel, were dark by late afternoon. Our salon would be locked for several days, so that the undisturbed "angel" might prepare the tree, decorations, and presents. During those days our whole house was warm and exuded a special Christmas smell: the distant scent of forests, which in my naïve mind did not connect to the locked salon, and sweet wafts of baking honey cakes and yeast dough *struclas*.

The cooking culminated on December 24 with the final preparations for "Vilia," the traditional Polish Christmas Eve supper. During my childhood, the traditional supper meal had already been reduced from the feasts of yesteryear, with the traditional thirteen courses limited to thirteen dishes.

Tradition is a peculiar thing. Most people do not know where their traditions start or how they evolve, but everybody knows that a day or a celebration should stay as it is ... because it is tradition.

Long before Christianity found its way to Poland, the pagan Slavic tribes celebrated the winter solstice and the promise of a new beginning. They knew that the days would grow longer and that Mother Earth would give birth to new crops. That promise allowed them to celebrate by opening the winter storage and delving into their precious food supplies. There were beets, cabbage and potatoes from the root cellars, fish from the lakes, and dried fruits, dried mushrooms, and flour dishes from the pantry.

Eventually the pagan traditions blended perfectly with Christian celebration of Christmas. We tend to revere the old in Poland, and I agree with the words of Adam Asnyk, the Polish poet, who wrote:

"Do not stomp on the altars of the past,

Even if you should rise to better ones;

On them the sacred fire still glows,

Human love stands there, guarding

And you owe them your honor."

To little me, my mother embodied the essence of the Christmas spirit. In the days preceding that precious holiday she was extra calm, smiling and warm, never allowing anything to spoil the special atmosphere. I did hear funny stories about a wooden rod that bad children received instead of presents, but I was never afraid of it. I was good, helpful and cooperative because it felt good to be good, especially around Christmas time.

Our immediate family consisted of only my mother and my two sisters. Our Niania was a servant, but in a way she was also part of our family. However, on every Christmas Eve we were surrounded by guests. These were visiting family members or invited friends who did not have family in town. We were all prettily dressed; I would look out of the window, waiting for the first star in the sky, the necessary signal that our Vilia[1] supper should commence. Since animals gave shelter to the little baby Jesus in a manger, animals were not eaten or hunted during the Christmas Eve day.

As we waited, Mother would tell me about other Polish traditions. For instance, in the country hunters walked through the fields or woods with shotguns, but never shot any animals on Christmas Eve. My father claimed that animals must have known about this practice, because he always saw more wild game on December 24 than on any other day of the year.

When my father walked the fields on Christmas Eve, he had his hunting dogs with him, two German Shorthair Pointers. I loved Mother's stories about those dogs. I had long wanted a dog, but as I grew up and we moved homes, I understood that it would be unfair to make a dog live in our city apartment, and did not include a dog on my future Christmas wish lists.

Another Polish tradition common among our predecessors in

_____

1 Vilia is the traditional Christmas Eve supper, consumed on the day of the Christmas vigil or *"Vigilia"*.

8

the country was inspired by an old saying: "A guest brings God into the house." In memory of the night when Joseph could not find shelter in Bethlehem for Mary to give birth to baby Jesus, lit candles were left in the windows of Polish homes to guide any traveler who might be out in the snow. At every table, one extra plate was laid for a hungry or cold traveler.

Immediately before sitting down to Vilia, we broke bread with our family and friends. Following Christian tradition, we broke pieces of wafer called *opłatek*[2] and exchanged good wishes. This was a special moment, during which each one of us would tell the other something private. We would kiss and hug; our eyes would hold that special glistening. We would also break the *opłatek* and exchange wishes with our animals. Country people knew that on that special Christmas night at midnight even animals were able to talk.

After exchanging wishes, we sat down to eat Vilia. Our dining room furniture was made of dark, heavy oak. On Christmas Eve, the dining room table was covered with a brilliant white tablecloth and napkins. Two big credenzas held brightly polished silver and crystal dishes; their sparkle added to the holiday atmosphere.

As we ate our Vilia supper, the talk around the table would turn to the mystery of Christmas. There was a mood of secretive anticipation and everybody's eyes were on the children, especially me, the youngest. I loved that special supper, but it was hard for me to wait until the end. When the last dish, a compote of stewed dried fruit, was served, I knew that the big moment was near. I waited, looking with anticipation at the dark glass door to the living room.

As I finished my last stewed dry fruit, the sound of a silver bell

---

2 Opłatek is a thin white wafer. A revered Polish custom includes the "breaking of the opłatek" between all guests on Christmas Eve.

announced the angel's arrival. Everybody got up from the table, smiled, and looked at me. Mother went to the glass door, opened it, and pushed aside the curtain inside that had concealed the activities of the last few days.

In the corner of the salon, a Christmas tree covered with lit live candles stretched to the ceiling; presents surrounded its base. I was mesmerized. Mother would pick up each present, read the name the angel had written, and hand the presents to the intended recipients. There was magic in the air. The room smelled of the tree and burning wax candles and each pair of eyes glistened with a special light.

After we opened our presents Mother lit the candelabras on the piano and played Christmas carols called *kolęda*. We all sang; if I had not yet learned the words, Mother would prompt me. I looked at the presents again, played with my toys, and eventually curled up on a sofa and fell asleep.

A Different Christmas: 1890

My father as a boy, with his family.

From left to right: Tadeusz, Władysława, Julian and Ludwik.

On Christmas Eve in 1890, my ten-year-old father was walking with his father in the late afternoon along the snow-covered field roads. It was a special tradition: my grandfather would walk with his eldest son, just the two of them, through their estate, Karwin. The shotguns hanging over their shoulders did not scare the animals; again, nobody would shoot game on Christmas Eve. They were enjoying each other's company, talking quietly as they walked through the fresh snow, their footprints the only mark on a vast swathe of white. The edges of the road were barely visible.

Taking a wrong step, my young father moved a little to the side and tumbled into a ditch full of deep, soft snow. Little Tadeusz had difficulty getting up, so his father reached down to help him.

When my grandfather leaned over my father's head, trying to pull him up, he must have released the trigger on Dad's shotgun. The shots hit Grandfather's head, and he fell on top of his son. My poor petrified father managed to scramble out; terrified, he ran home for help. Neighbors and family members rushed his wounded father home. Grandmother immediately sent a man on a horse several miles to the Złotniki estate, where another line of the Srzednicki family lived. They were able to summon a doctor, but by the time he reached Karwin, Grandfather Leon Ścisław was dead. My 38-year-old grandmother, Paulina, was left alone with her four children. The youngest, Ludwik, was barely a year old. My father, the eldest, was only ten.

Grandpa Ścisław was buried in the little town of Poborowice. Our Srzednicki family was the main benefactor of the parish church where my father and his siblings, all born in Karwin, had been baptized. My grandfather was buried in a family tomb next to his mother Maria.

My grandfather had been able to administer the estate of

Karwin with the help of various employees while simultaneously practicing law in Krakow. But after her husband's death, my grandmother had to manage by herself. When running the estate became too burdensome, Grandma sold Karwin and moved to her other estate, Wieruszów, near the town of Wieluń. Later, she also sold Wieruszów and lived in Krakow, probably to be closer to her children's schools.

While Krakow was under Austrian occupation, the Polish people there enjoyed easier conditions than under the Russian and Prussian occupations. Austrians had no objections to Poles studying, and Grandmother Paulina arranged for all her children to receive higher education at the University of Vienna. My father became an engineer-agronomist; Aunt Wladka studied political science, and Uncle Julian took up mechanical engineering. Grandmother depended on her oldest son, my father, and after his studies, my father also leased the estate of Korytnica using the estate money.

The Importance of My Family

My family was always very important to me. Long before I learned the word "genes," I knew that I was who I was because of my family, and that my future family would be whoever they were because of me. For most of my early childhood, I lived with my mother and two sisters, but the importance of our larger family always entered into our talks and considerations.

Though my grandparents passed away before or very shortly after I was born, they were very real to me. I felt yet closer to my father, in spite of the fact that he was in a grave in the cemetery, which I visited frequently with my mother to say a prayer and plant fresh flowers.

When Mother talked about various members of our family, she did not idealize or criticize them. In her descriptions they became real, some better people than others, some funny, some exciting, all accepted and loved. There were many sad losses. As my mother said, "There were wars in Poland during every generation, and many people unfortunately died younger than necessary."

Every loss tends to increase and intensify the value of that which is endangered. The difficulties and suffering my family endured helped us clarify our moral principles. My love for my country and my family increased with every story I heard about our suffering and our enemies' attempts to annihilate us. I learned to be proud of my forefathers, who worked hard to contribute to my family and to Poland's development and defense.

By contrast, our human nature is unfortunately such that during the times of prosperity and well-being we tend to forget our principles, morals, and patriotism. After the greatness of King Sobieski's reign, during the eighteenth century "too good living" cost Poland her independence and freedom for 150 years. Poland was divided and occupied by its hostile neighbors: Prussia, Russia and Austria.

When my Grandfather Ścisław died, the Polish people had been living under occupation for more than a hundred years. They made their living in spite of occupiers. Finally, in the early 1900s, there was new hope for the poor Poles; a hope for freedom, for liberty, for a chance to have their own country once again.

What was so marvelous? The possibility of a war!

The Polish occupiers—Russia, Prussia and Austria—began to fight with one another. This infighting brought new hope to Polish patriots, who organized military legions, clandestine organizations through which every Pole might ready him or herself for the fight to win our independence. To me, the story of my aunt, my father's sister, is synonymous with this era.

My Aunt Wladka

Since childhood, I have heard stories about my Aunt Wladka[1], my father's younger sister. My mother did not criticize Aunt Władka too much, nor was she overly positive. My mother saw Władka as a very controversial individual.

In retrospect, Aunt Władka lived either ahead of her time or outside any time. She was better educated than most young women of her generation, and was strongly influenced by her own Aunt Anna, the first Polish female doctor. Aunt Władka's was the same age as my mother—both born in 1888. Both completed gymnasium, as high schools were called in those days. But from there, their educations took different paths. Mother studied at a music conservatory and became an excellent piano player, excelling beyond the common level for well-mannered young ladies, who in those days

---

1 I verified the various stories I heard growing up with facts about my aunt, whose full name was Władysława nee Srzednicka, Pawełkiewicz, Długoszowa, Macieszyna, documented in the *Polish Biographical Dictionary* (1974).

were intended to be pianists, fluent in French, and impeccably mannered.

My aunt went a different way. After gymnasium she studied political science. She worked on multiple fields and subjects, and judging by her ability to move through many countries with ease, she must have had a terrific command of language. Her life speaks for itself.

Members of the family, however, liked to describe Aunt Władka as "always extremely mysterious and secretive." It was true. Not because she was pretentious (though she was), but out of necessity. My father and grandmother might have known that Aunt Władka, as a twenty-three year old, studied in the Krakow school of Political Science from 1911 to 1913. But I am certain that my father and his mother knew nothing about Władka's other activities during that time: she joined a society for the independence of academic students and a secret organization called the Polish Army, which later transformed into combat units supporting the Polish Legions during World War I. Nor did Władka share the fact that in 1911, she also formed an organization with another brave young woman called the "Women's Combat Group."

This was three years before the beginning of World War I. Poland was still occupied by Czarist Russia, Prussia and Austria. Polish patriots like my aunt hoped to gain independence for Poland, and prepared to fight for their freedom. The opportunity presented itself with the beginning of WWI. Poles formed clandestine military organizations in every occupied zone. Aunt Władka was living in Krakow, the less oppressive Austrian-occupied region.

"While officially working in hospitals," the *Polish Biographical Dictionary* notes, "she also served the Intelligence Section of 1st Company (later 1st Brigade) of the Polish Legions."

At that time, my mother and father lived in Warsaw. They were falling in love and preparing to be married. Whenever Aunt Władka visited, she must have been on highly secret political missions. Though happy to have a safe *pied a terre* with her mother, this young woman, only twenty-seven, was crossing borders illegally, carrying orders from one military commander to another in the different occupied zones.

My mother's impression of Władka from those days was of an extravagant, controversial and incredibly brave woman. My aunt was beautiful and liked to draw attention to herself, but because of that beauty she was able to do incredible things that nobody would have suspected. She managed to "cross the front lines to Warsaw three times, carrying instructions, money, and publications for Polish military organizations and bringing back to Krakow military and political clandestine news."

Warsaw was then under Russian occupation. In order to move with her contraband from the Russian zone to the Austrian, while avoiding suspicion from the Tsar's police, Aunt Władka had to travel with guns and papers through Kiev, Odessa and Romania. She was arrested several times, but was somehow able to talk herself out of prison.

One such experience is well documented: in December 1914, Sława (as she was known at that time) and another courier received orders to cross a very difficult border between Germany and Russia to deliver a large sum of money to a Warsaw military organization. Sława independently took a large suitcase of contraband literature and guns as well. The ladies managed to contact the Russians near the town of Płock. Sława told them that she was trying to reach her sick, elderly mother. Suspicious, the Russians decided to search them. As they were about to open the suitcase containing the guns

Sława said, "I forgot to tell you that I have a revolver." She opened her purse and handed the gun to the amazed soldiers. The puzzled Russians forgot the suitcase and put both ladies in prison, later delivering them to army headquarters. Sława must have charmed the officers, for they treated her and her companion with typical Russian hospitality: caviar, champagne and flirting. After four days, not knowing what to do with their beautiful prisoners, one of the officers decided to release them, saying to Władysława: "You have eyes too honest to be a spy." He was rewarded with that beautiful smile. As incredible as it sounds, the Russians never looked back into the suitcases.

My aunt formed a close alliance with Jósef Piłsudski, the commander of the Polish legions, who became a marshal of independent Poland after the war. During the war, in 1915, "she met Stanislaus Długosza, a poet and a freedom fighter. They fell in love and became engaged. The next month he was killed in battle by Samoklęski. Władka was devastated. She assumed his name and mourned him for a long time."

But mourning her beloved did not stop Władka from doing political work. Just the opposite: she began traveling through the front lines and borders dressed in black, wearing a widow's veil and other mourning paraphernalia, carrying guns and secret information. Who would have suspected a poor, bereaved woman of being a political agent? In this way, losing her beloved threw Władka into more dangerous political activities. She started to work in a hospital again, this time on the front line. Her ability to cross borders was soon needed, and "she was sent to Kiev at the end of 1915 carrying falsified Austrian documents for imprisoned Polish Legionnaires, who as Russian subjects were threatened with [the] death penalty for treason."

At the end of World War I, Aunt Władka was at work in the Polish Military Organization. During the 1920 Soviet invasion, the *Polish Biographical Dictionary* adds, she worked in camps with prisoners and repatriates in Baranowice-Stolpce-Niechorzele, in eastern Poland, spending time particularly in a hospital for people sick with typhus.In the following years Aunt Władka continued to work closely with Józef Piłsudski. During 1922 and 1923 she traveled frequently, this time to Germany, where she worked with Polish laborers in Bochum, Essen, Dortmund, Stettin, and Berlin. After her return to Poland, she worked in the Headquarters of Unemployment Funds from 1924 to 1934; at the same time, she was active in social and political actions in the Federation of Polish Organizations of Defenders of Homeland, the Organization of Female Military Preparedness for the Defense of the Homeland, and other organizations.

There is no question that my Aunt Władka was among the highest-ranked members of the Polish espionage apparatus. In 1914, Pilsudski created a special operations organization, the *Agencja Bezpieczenstwa wewnetrznego* (Internal Security Agency), which worked alongside the Polish Legions. That organization, the Second Department, was colloquially called "Dwójka" (Two) and had specific tasks in intelligence and counterintelligence. It was further divided into "sections." Section II-B operated in the West. About one million Poles had emigrated to the Ruhr Valley during the 150 years of occupation; though they did not return to Poland, they remained loyal to the homeland and cooperated with independent Poland after 1918. In 1922 and 1923, when my aunt worked in Germany with Polish laborers in the town of Bochum, she established an espionage network in Essen district, gathering intelligence, and becoming familiar with the territory.

This knowledge would prove extremely important for her and Poland—and above all, for Great Britain—during her operations twenty years later. After her return from Germany she was given more free time, which allowed her to make frequent visits to my parents' estate. I doubt my mother knew any of the details of her political actions, which would greatly inspire me later in my life.

World War I

In 1914, World War I broke out after the murder of the Austrian Archduke Franz Ferdinand in Sarajevo. The war was most famous for its "Western Front," a long series of battles fought in the trenches of Belgium and France. Polish patriots battling for the freedom of our land participated vigorously. My aunt was in the middle of this conflict.

During the war, both my parents' families lived in Warsaw, then a principality under Russian governmental control. My mother had already divorced her first husband, Jan Jeziorański, with whom she had had my half-sister Alina (b. January 19, 1911). In April of 1915, my parents traveled to Wilno to wed. Wilno, an old Polish and Lithuanian town, recognized divorce; Warsaw did not. My parents were married there on April 18, 1915.

At the end of WWI, the 1918 Treaty of Versailles awarded Poland independence. After 150 years of oppression and plunder, our patriots started to rebuild our country, but almost immediately were attacked again. The Russian Tsars ceased to exist, but they were replaced in the October Revolution of 1917 by something worse – if that is possible: the Soviet Communist regime. The Soviets disregarded Versailles and invaded Poland again in 1920, marching on Warsaw.

Again, this battle was rightly called a miracle, as the young Polish forces defeated the Russian hordes and remained free. Poland began to rebuild. The Soviets had disregarded and disrespected international agreements for the first time. More such instances would follow. The one in 1939, nineteen years later, would be a sharp knife in Poland's back.

Dębogóra,
My Parents Home

My father Tadeusz Srzednicki and my mother Zofia Gorska Srzednicka. The only pictures of my parents to be recovered after the World War II.

On February 4, 1921, my mother gave birth to my sister Ann in Warsaw. Shortly after, my father succeeded in leasing an estate from the Polish government. He bought the necessary equipment and animals and moved to the Dębogóra estate, whose name means Oak Hill or Oak Mountain,. It was a fairly large estate of 4000 morgas (2.14 square kilometers, or 0.84 square miles). The estate was two-thirds agrarian fields and one-third forests. Since the fields were worked only with horsepower, forty work horses plus other horses for Father and the estate administrators to ride were stabled there. The manor house had no running water, though Father later installed this feature

I loved my mother's stories about life in Dębogóra. Her vivid descriptions, combined with a few surviving photographs, have left lively images in my mind. In Dębogóra, my parents started to build a very happy life. Awash in the glow of Poland's recent independence, they reveled in life together in a free country.

Father was an energetic man. He rode the fields on horseback, supervising the working farmhands and advising his administrative employees. He organized hunting parties in his forests, entertaining large groups of guests who stayed for days at a time. Mother ran the house and directed its many servants. When Father returned from his trips and told her who he had invited for the next hunt, Mother tried to object, telling him that there were not enough beds to host so many. At her words, Father only smiled and assured her that he knew she would manage to accommodate everyone.

"And I did," my mother would say, ending her stories with a reflective smile. To my further inquiries, she admitted that some younger men had to sleep in the barn on piles of hay. It must have been fun, I thought, knowing how much my sister and I loved to play in the hay during summer.

Mother also kept business books for the entire estate. In those days the only adding machine was a contraption called an abacus, made of beads strung on wires; the beads represent different amounts and are moved back and forth to perform calculations. Mother knew how to use the abacus, but she could add much faster in her head. I would watch her shift a pencil in a smooth motion from the top of a page to the bottom, where she would instantly write the total for the two columns. Later in life, I was happy to learn addition and multiplication so that I could play with numbers as my mother did.

My paternal grandmother lived with my parents in Dębogóra and Aunt Władka was a frequent guest. I loved hearing stories about these ladies. They were known for being greatly beautiful—and equally difficult. Mother laughed when she spoke of them. Father›s love and devotion must have made my mother secure enough to find them amusing. Mother too was not only beautiful but charming, a characteristic that hardly applied to the other two ladies. My father's family adored her.

Running an estate was not a simple matter. Besides all the family members, the manor housed fed an administrator, his family and the kitchen workers who lived in adjoining servants' quarters. The field workers and their families had houses in the village. Mother received a great deal of help running the house from her beloved Józia (Yoozia), the cook. During my mother's teenage years, Józia worked for my mother's Gorski family of eight in Warsaw. At some point, however, she quit and announced that when my mother married she would come back to work for her.

Józia kept her promise, coming to work for my parents as soon as she heard about their marriage. Mother claimed many times that everything she knew about cooking she learned from Józia. Józia was legendary, not only in our family, but among many of our friends who were entertained royally at my parents' estate. Niania, who later became my nanny, knew Józia well, for she also worked in my parents' house, sometimes helping in the kitchen. Years later, when she cooked for us in Bydgoszcz, Mother and Niania would check recipes in the Ćwierciakiewiczowa, an old cookbook and reminisce about Józia.

Since I was too small to remember anything from Dębogóra, I

listened to the stories of everybody who lived there. My sister Ann, older than me by five years, lived there till she was almost seven. She often recalls two stories, one of which involved Grandma Paulina putting sugar in Ann's soup. In Ann's story, Grandma claimed that the soup was better that way, but Ann hated it. Mother tried to soften the story by saying that it occurred only once with tomato soup, which happened to be sour, but Ann insisted that it happened to all the soups and that she hated it.

The other story involved Father spanking her for something; because she did not want to apologize, Ann claimed that he had hurt her. To this story Mother added that Ann was quite stubborn and difficult, and possibly deserved a good spanking.

"No, it was Father who beat me," Ann objected. Mother only raised her eyebrows with a smile.

Whenever our half-sister Alinka heard these stories, she repeated a story of her own about Ann. One Easter Sunday, Ann received a big egg box full of candies. She ate one after another, not wanting to share any or cease eating. People tried to persuade Ann to stop to no avail. She finished the whole box and promptly threw up.

"Aunt Władka was also quite stubborn," Mother added, alluding to the well-known fact that Ann resembled my father's sister.

An absence from the stories I heard of Dębogóra is the truth of what caused Józia's illness and subsequent death. Mother did tell me that when Józia's death became imminent, my father was away on one of his frequent business trips. The day Józia started failing, she kept asking when my father would return. Evidently she considered it her duty to say goodbye to her master. Father was due that evening. Józia kept waiting for him.

As soon as my father arrived, Mother rushed him to Józia's

room. Father was able to speak to her briefly; they said goodbye, and then Józia allowed God to take her soul. I have heard this story since my childhood, and it always rang a dear sound in my heart, bearing out the truth that the household workers meant much more to our family than one might expect from the title of "servant".

In the years that followed, my father continued to be energetic, using every minute of his time productively and traveling widely for business. Mother could prepare things for him, but he insisted on packing everything himself at the last minute. Often, the horses had arrived to take him to the station while he was still in the midst of packing.

"No reason to panic," he would say to Mother. He called the railroad station and had the head of traffic hold the train for him. The coachman waited outside, ready to run the horses the instant Dad boarded the coach. Sometimes the horses were even put to a gallop, which is not normally done when horses pull a carriage.

After my mother became pregnant, my parents decided that she should spend the last few days before my birth in the delivery clinic in Poznan, the nearest large town with a good maternity clinic. For that trip, Mother insisted that Dad be ready to depart an unheard of twenty minutes before the deadline. Of course Dad did what Mother wanted, but he teased her, saying that she would wind up like his mother, who went everywhere an hour early and once wound up taking the train in the direction opposite her intended destination.

For several days, Mother stayed in a private room at the clinic. Father went back to Dębogóra to attend to the estate. He did not have to worry about Mother. Several of our good family friends lived in Poznań, and Mother promised to call the moment she went into labor.

I was born on April 14, 1926 at 9 PM. Mother claimed that all nine pounds of me plopped out easily. Later, when I was a teenager, I learned that Mother and Dad were exceptionally happy that the pregnancy and delivery went so well; a few years earlier Mother had been pregnant with twin boys, which ended in a miscarriage.

At the time of my birth, my father, Tadeusz Srzednicki, was 46 years old. My mother, Zofia, was 38. I was lucky to look very much like my mother. We also shared the Zodiac sign of Aries.

The day after my birth, Dad took a train to Poznan to meet his second daughter. According to Mother, her room was full of well-wishers. Foods and spirits flowed abundantly – which was not unusual as Dad and a few other guests had arrived from out of town. In the middle of this party came an official from the registrar's office.

It seemed there was some confusion about my first name. Mother and Father were used to the registrar's rules in central Poland; there, a symbolic "S" for son or "D" for daughter was noted at birth, leaving the choice of the newborn's name and the registration of that name for the time of baptism.

Poznań, however, was previously under Prussian occupation. The city's rules required registration of the first name immediately after the birth. According to the story, the dialogue went something like this (I must add that well-established opinions about Poznań's provincial people held that they were ponderous and lacked any sense of humor—the Prussian occupation having taken its toll).

"Are you the father of this newborn child?" The registrar formally asked Father.

"Yes, my wife gave birth to our daughter Kordula," Father said with a chuckle.

My mother objected to the sound of the name Kordula. "Don't even mention such a horrible name!"

"All right," agreed Father, "I had chosen my favorite name for a son, whom I would have called Kordian, but since it's a girl let's call her Kordianna."

Kordian was my father's favorite drama by the famous Polish Poet Laureate Julian Słowacki.

Everybody liked the story, laughed and probably raised a toast to Kordianna. However, the registrar, who appeared ill at ease in that relaxed social atmosphere, left immediately with the name Kordianna on his books. Nobody realized at the time that, according to the local rules, my name was set in stone.

There was another peculiar controversy connected to my birth. My half -sister Alinka (Jeziorańska) was then fifteen. She was also living in Poznan as a boarder and student at a high school run by the convent of Catholic sisters of St. Ursula. Father called to arrange for Alinka to visit her mother and meet her younger half-sister. The nuns objected to "such an immoral and improper suggestion," claiming that "innocent young girls should not visit maternity wards."

Such prudish hypocrisy did not sit well with my father, but Alinka was allowed to stay with the sisters for a while longer, until they made another blunder that could have caused Alinka's death. When Alinka complained about stomach pain, the sisters accused her of trying to avoid going to morning mass and forced her to get ready. Alinka, who was very meek, complained only to her friends and followed the sisters' orders. Fortunately, one of those friends told her mother about Alinka's problems; the friend's mother promptly called our mother in Dębogóra, and Mother took the next train to Poznań. She rushed Alinka to a hospital and in an emergency operation doctors removed an appendix that ruptured on the table, saving Alinka's life. In those pre-penicillin days, there was no cure for an appendix ruptured in the abdomen. After this near-disaster, Alinka was removed from the convent school.

Several days after my birth, my parents and I traveled back to Dębogora. A date was set for my baptism. My godparents and other family members and friends arrived for the festive occasion. Our parochial town was Kcynia, and everybody traveled to the church in horse-drawn carriages.

The parish priest met the party, showing all due respect to "Dziedzic," which means "master heir." Traditionally, the local estate owner was the best contributor to the church's needs. Besides his respect, the priest greeted everybody with a surprising announcement. The Kordianna *quid pro quo* was long forgotten by my family, but the priest already knew my name as Kordianna and according to local rules, he had to baptize me using that name.

Luckily, there was another rule which my mother hoped would remedy the situation. "You should add another name, the name of a patron saint," the priest agreed. My parents decided to add a middle name, Zofia, like my mother's, and I became Kordianna Zofia, with the middle name underlined to indicate that it was my used name.

If I hadn't known about the connection to the ugly name of Kordula, I probably would have liked the unusual name of Kordianna. Though my sister Ann made certain that I would never forget its origins in "Kordula," as a teenager, I used "Kordianna" in a variety of forms and loved every one of them. As a baby, however, everyone called me little Zosia. Little, because my mother was also diminutively called Zosia by family and close friends.

A Dark Cloud Named Hitler

During the spring of 1939, our idyllic life was upset. I was only thirteen. In movie theaters during the news, we frequently saw reels of film showing Hitler shouting speeches that roused crowds of adoring Germans to frenzy. By contrast, Chamberlain always carried his umbrella, exuding British calm.

I overheard the never-ending discussions among Mother's friends: "Damn Germany will start another war." "No, they won't. Hitler already managed to annex the Austrians and scared the Czechs into letting him have their country without a shot." "Then why he is constantly screaming about the corridor and Gdańsk?"

After one of these big get-togethers, I asked Mother what she thought.

"I know that I don't know, but don't worry; somehow everything will be okay," she told me with a smile. But she did not look sure.

To comfort me, my mother decided that we should visit her friend Eva. I liked Eva more than any of Mother's other friends. She was Mother's favorite bridge partner. This time, we went to find out what her husband, Captain Michael Kamiński, could tell us. Capt. Kamiński was in "Dwójka," the second department for national security and espionage set up by Marshal Piłsudski immediately after WWI.

My Aunt Władka certainly would have known a lot about it …

Mother and I chatted with Eva while waiting for the Captain to come home from work. After he was settled, Eva opened the discussion.

"Zosia—" she pointed at my mother, "is concerned about our political situation and wonders how to prepare for the inevitable."

The captain looked at Mother, nodding his head but remaining silent.

"Michael, I don't expect you to tell me any secrets," Mother interjected.

"Zosia," he stopped Mother. "Most of the news is a public secret. There's no question that the Germans are mobilizing like crazy. Hitler is rallying his Krauts, making speeches demanding a corridor to East Prussia, claiming that Germany needs elbow room; at the same time, he's signing agreements with Chamberlain, who most likely does not know what he's doing or saying."

The captain sat quietly for a while, shaking his head. Then he looked at Mother and Eva and continued speaking.

"Not long ago Chamberlain assured the world that we'd have peace in our time, because he signed the Munich Pact with Germany, Great Britain, France and Italy; last March, he even assured us that Britain would support Poland if our independence was threatened."

"So you think he may not start a war?" Mother asked hopefully.

"I would like to hope so, "Michael said. "But personally I don't trust Germans in general and especially not Hitler, the little Napoleon—ha! He's a big megalomaniac. He is damn dangerous!"

For a time, then, the discussion moved to lighter, more socially acceptable subjects, but as we bid our goodbyes Michael tradition-ally kissed Mother's hand and assured her that he would let her know in plenty of time if it would be necessary to leave Bydgoszcz.

Spring came, and the May 3 holiday commemorating the signing of our National Constitution approached. Our garrison town hummed with preparation for more than the annual military parade.

The adults and the military might have thought about the in-evitability of approaching war. To them, the ominous shadow of the broken cross, the swastika, was visible on the Western horizon—but my still-childish blue eyes could not grasp it. I was too young, too optimistic. Zosia, the little Polish Patriot. I looked forward to the celebrations.

In past years, military parades were held on the main street in the center of town. That year, the military announced a special parade on the outskirts, behind the cavalry and artillery divisions, which were on the main thoroughfare north of Bydgoszcz. Nearby were the Ułans, a mounted division. On the other side of the thor-oughfare, behind the parachute training tower and a little forest, was another division of our young Polish military, the new motor-ized units.

Soon, the big day arrived. We sat with the forest behind us and a large expanse of empty fields in front. Far to our left waited the military units in formation, their colorful standards fluttering in the wind. General Skotnicki[1] arrived and took the stand with other

---

1 Stanisław Grzmot-Skotnicki (1894–1939) was a Polish military commander and a general in the Polish Army. During the invasion of Poland in 1939, he commanded the Czersk Operational Group. He was among the highest-ranking Polish officers to be killed in ac-tion during World War II.

dignitaries to receive the parade. The general's daughter, Stefa, was Ann's best friend. I felt proud that I also knew him.

The parade started with marching bands and various organizations, followed by a military band and an infantry unit, after which one of the bands remained, playing nearby as if waiting for the last unit to get out of the way. The wide road in front of us cleared.

Then came something I have never seen before or after. A large unit of Ułans in extended gallop approached from the far distance. The Ułans' uniforms included woolen capes which flew from their shoulders, their white horses passing in front of us in perfect formation. It was beautiful and thrilling.

When the last of the Ułans disappeared to our right, the cavalry arrived on brown horses, pulling a variety of light and heavy guns. They were also in full gallop, in perfect formation. Then came the heavy artillery, every cannon pulled by six or eight horses with men riding the horse on the left side of three or four horses abreast. The onlookers cheered and applauded enthusiastically, watching the mighty spectacle. When the dust settled at the end of the parade our new motorized division emerged, showing off the troops in cars and tanks.

After the parade, we moved to a nearby area in the forest for refreshments, after which another event was held: pistol shooting from moving tanks. Many of the officers, their wives and children were our friends and frequent guests in our home. Conversation lingered on the perfection of the incredible parade. We learned that all the units had performed equally well during recent military maneuvers. Our patriotism filled us with pride and hope. "We will manage," we told one another, "as we did for centuries."

As we sat on the side of the road waiting for the competition to start, I asked one of our friends to show me his pistol, a Polish VIS made in Radom. Not only did he show me how it worked, he took it apart—dropping one piece in the sand. I felt bad and helped him to clean it well, but he laughed.

"Don't worry," he said, "it really doesn't matter; Radom VIS pistols seldom jam."

This is a truth I learned myself a few years later, while working for Poland's underground army. I still revere that great 9mm pistol, beautifully designed in the style of the American Colt. Whenever I handle it, the memories come back.

As we talked, a little tank appeared on the road to the right of us. The officer stood and started shooting, aiming at plywood figures barely visible among the trees and bushes on the other side of the road. One magazine of nine bullets and less than thirty seconds later, his performance was over. We applauded all the officers who exhibited, but cheered more enthusiastically for the ones we knew and liked.

As the scores were calculated, civilian guests were invited to try. Only a few men volunteered. My excitement gave me away; I could not hide it.

I was the only woman (or rather, only girl) to try, and was given big overalls to protect my dress. When my turn came, I climbed into the tank for the shooting run.

The soldier piloting the tank obviously had fun driving for me. He told me where to look for the next hidden figure and slowed down to allow me to take better aim. Even though these were my first shooting attempts I placed my shots well. The onlookers cheered; my mother was laughing and I was exuberant. I even won a small trophy.

During the next two months—until the end of the school year—the political news steadily worsened. Germany had signed a pact of non-aggression with Poland and had signed many other pacts with the rest of Europe, but there was also news of an enormous German army amassing on the Polish borders.

That was the first summer ever that our family did not leave town for vacation. In June, Mother sent away our last maid. A year earlier, my favorite, Niania, left us to go back to Wilno, her hometown, to take care of her ailing sister. After Niania left, Mother went through an array of maids. In comparison to the faithful and efficient Niania, these maids were either dumb, liars, cheats, unable to cook or all of the above.

We were alone, Mother, Ann and I, without any strangers in the house. Mother could cook – Józia had taught her. Now it was time for Mother to teach Ann, who had recently gotten engaged to a good-looking man, Eva Kamińska's brother.

At this time, Eva and Michael Kamiński started preparing for their evacuation from Bydgoszcz, and kept Mother informed about when we would have to do the same.

War loomed closer by the day. In August, the Germans were massing their troops across the border not far from Bydgoszcz. We dug ditches in the parks preparing for air raids, sang patriotic songs and waited.

The school year was ending. I was in seventh grade. In our school system, we started learning languages after sixth grade. Until the end of sixth grade, I had no difficulty following Ann's example and earning passing grades without studying. I always had A›s in math, physical education and chorus. In the rest of my subjects I earned B's and C's, but never F's.

In seventh grade we started Latin and one foreign language. I chose French. My problems began when I did not memorize the new vocabulary. I don't remember what I was thinking—or if I was thinking at all. I remember claiming that if languages had numerical systems, I would remember everything. "I don't have any linguistic ability" was my standard excuse.

Ann was finishing high school and preparing for graduation exams in close to ten subjects. She was studying more than ever, but still claimed sitting over the books was "not cool." Stupidly, I must have thought that memorizing languages was beneath my dignity. I learned a tough lesson when I received unsatisfactory marks in Latin and French. According to the rules, this meant I had flunked seventh grade and would have to repeat it next year. My shame knew no bounds. I had difficulty even thinking about going to the same grade next year. I felt that the whole town knew about my failure and was laughing at me.

As devastated as I was, more important things quickly drew our attention.

The majority of our family, including my half-sister Alinka, lived in Warsaw. Mother was in constant contact with all of them. John, Alinka's husband, had been drafted as a reserve officer in the army. He was a second lieutenant in an artillery division. Alinka had recently had a baby, Basia, who was nine months old.

The atmosphere in Bydgoszcz grew hotter by the day. Many people in town were of German descent; in the past, they intermingled easily with Poles. Now they became less friendly, seemingly in wait for the arrival of their beloved Fuhrer. In contrast, Polish military families were leaving town.

At the end of August, we packed everything we could send to Warsaw into trunks and suitcases. Things like bedding we sewed into big bags made of heavy blankets. Married couple of our military friends took me with them in their car. Mother and Ann planned to leave two days later, their luggage accompanying them on the train to Warsaw.

The weather was beautiful and warm. We traveled in the car with the top down. The closer we came to Warsaw, the more crowded the roads grew. It was not heavy traffic, but it was a chaotic exodus. There were horse-drawn carriages of all sizes, little horse and buggy carts, even cows pulling farm wagons. All these wagons were heavily loaded; people sat atop their luggage with goats and other small farm animals tied behind. It was almost impossible for cars to pass through the throng. Horns honked, people yelled at each other, and the calls of geese, ducks and chickens in cages added to the cacophony.

We drove for many hours, reaching Warsaw in the evening. Our friends dropped me at Alinka's apartment. Within a day, or two Mother and Ann arrived.

PART II:

WORLD WAR II

The Beginning

On September 1, 1939, Germany declared war by crossing the Polish border and bombing Warsaw. Sirens sounded an alarm whenever the German planes approached. Our days were spent between the cellar and Alinka's apartment on the fourth, top floor. The apartment blocks were newly built by the large insurance company for which John worked as a lawyer, Bank Gospodarstwa Krajowego. They appeared strong enough to withstand all but a direct bomb hit. We prayed for those not to occur.

Alinka had the radio, which blared constantly, providing all the information we might want or need. The Mayor of Warsaw spoke at least once a day, trying to keep spirits up. Between announcements, Chopin's music played.

Radio was still a novelty to me. Back in Bydgoszcz at the tennis club, we listened to music on the radio. Now I listened to everything, trying to figure out this thing called WAR.

What was it? What did it mean? History studies, which I enjoyed in school, were different from reality. Wars started and ended on the same page in the book. There was no sitting in the cellar, wondering where and when the next bomb would fall.

At the first sound of a siren, Ann and I ran down the stairs, jumping two steps at a time, caught up in a peculiar excitement. None of it seemed real, nor did it make any sense. A few air raids later, we "knew" what to expect and were slower in responding to the alarms. Mother and Alinka urged us to hurry.

"Go ahead, we'll catch up with you before you get down," was our smart-alecky response. In the cellar, we heard the bombs exploding and felt the rumbling of the ground. Ann and I tried to figure out how far away the explosion was, but even the bombs were not real, not yet.

During one raid, somebody brought a radio to the cellar, and we gathered in one larger space, in a corridor between individual tenants' stalls. Sefan Starzyński, the mayor, spoke about Britain and France who "will come to our aid, as they signed a common defense pact with Poland in the last week of August." We were told where the enemy was attacking and how our army would defend us. Further information included the names of the streets where buildings had been bombed and were burning or destroyed. Survivors were told where to find shelter.

Though Alinka and John had lived in their apartment for two years, Alinka barely knew her neighbors. Mother, Ann and I were complete strangers. A few raids later, we began to know the people next to whom we stood. Little Basia, with her wavy bronze hair and sweet smile, instantly made friends with everyone. Alinka was only then realizing that she might be pregnant again, which increased her tension and anxiety and inspired protective feelings in many of the women. Mother tried to be helpful and supportive, but her calm was becoming too calm. I noticed that she was not the same charming, gay lady she had once been. A cloud hovered over her demeanor. When people wondered what the next days would bring, Mother started reminiscing about her childhood under the Tsarist Russian occupation and the later sufferings of World War I.

Mother was a beautiful ballroom dancer, but she was never athletic. She always walked on medium high heels, never flat shoes. For years she did walk daily, but not for more than half an hour. Now every time she had to hurry down the stairs to the cellar, she grew visibly tired and bothered. After the air raids she climbed the nine flights of stairs more and more slowly.

In one of the first radio broadcasts, we heard exciting news from Westerplatte, a tiny peninsula near Gdansk where the 1918 Council of the League of Nations in Versailles allowed the Poles to keep a tiny garrison. This was the first place Hitler's forces attacked early on the morning of September 1, since it was on Hitler's way through the proverbial corridor to East Prussia that he kept demanding. The Westerplatte garrison was comprised of less than two hundred Poles. A German battleship started the attack with a salvo of heavy guns, followed by a large troop of Germans soldiers. They were certain that this would put an end to the Polish resistance, but the attack was met by the crossfire of well-placed machine guns. The Germans took their first defeat, with many dead and wounded men. Every morning when we heard the opening announcement, "Westerplatte still fights on," our spirits rose.

Running to the Cellar

Alinka's apartment consisted of two rooms, a small kitchen with a tiny space for a maid and a small but comfortable bathroom with running hot water and a separate toilet, which was a blessing for five women and a child. There were many apartments like Alinka's housing "fugitives" from western Poland. Consequently, there was always a lack of hot water in the evenings. Ann and I started vying for the first chance to take a bath.

One day soon after the first air raid, Alinka decided to stay with little Basia in the sunshine in the garden area between the apartment blocks. Mother was happy to stay with them and avoid an extra trip up the stairs. I saw my chance to get clean.

"I'm going upstairs to shampoo my hair and take a bath," I declared.

"So am I," Ann said.

"Girls, please be ready to come down at the next alarm," Mother and Alinka said in unison.

"Of course," we responded.

Upstairs, Ann and I quickly organized ourselves, determining who would wash her head under the shower, who would use the sink for hand washing, and who would sit in the tub. We enjoyed our "ablutions"; indeed, it was too much fun not to sing as we bathed. The bathroom was in the middle of the apartment. The only daylight came through a little window in the kitchen. We took our time, for there was no reason to rush. There were no sirens, at least none that we could hear.

Finally, dressed and with our hair set, we went downstairs.

Something was wrong. We heard no voices from the garden area. When we arrived, there was nobody there. Ouch!

Suddenly we heard the siren—but it was the siren calling off the alarm. People started coming out of the cellar. Our guilty faces spurred many funny remarks. Finally Alinka emerged, waving her hands in despair.

"*Wariatki*, my lunatic sisters, why?"

Alinka was irritated, but Mother was frantic.

"Mamusiu," I pleaded, "we didn't hear any sirens."

"It must have been that running water and the bathroom being inside the other walls of the apartment," Ann said, trying to prove our innocence. We looked at each other, conveniently forgetting to mention our singing.

"Maybe the Krauts don't intend to throw any bombs outside the town center," one of us said, trying to appease Mother and Alinka.

After the next bombing, we heard: "Westerplatte still fights on." The announcer started calling it Polish Thermopile, in memory of the heroic Greeks who fought against overwhelming Persian forces. Bombs were falling; again we heard distant explosions.

Suddenly, a bomb fell close by. We waited a long, long second or two for the explosion. Everything shook, but our house stood solid. We breathed a sigh relief. It wasn't us!

After our arrival, we learned that all luggage sent to Warsaw by rail had been piled at the Warsaw East station across the Vistula River in the Praga district. We had to get it. That luggage contained everything we owned.

Then—and many times in the years to come—when I was surrounded by confusion I tried to look for something real, something easy to define, something I could *do*. Though I was only thirteen, I decided that I had to recover our luggage or we would have nothing to wear.

This was not an adventure for "normal" people. Mother objected to my going, but she wasn't very convincing. She finally acquiesced and I went with Marysia (Mary), Alinka's live-in maid. I can't remember why we were chosen, but my guess is that Mother knew she herself was not strong enough, nor did she possess know-how for rough situations. Alinka was pregnant; Ann was too smart to volunteer. Marysia thought it was exciting, and she was street-smart and had a big mouth.

For myself? I had all the chutzpah and bravura of a seemingly invincible thirteen-year-old girl.

Shortly after a midday air raid, we ventured in the direction of the Praga district. We walked or took streetcars, one of which crossed the Vistula River. The moment we were on the other side of the bridge, we breathed a sigh of relief—every time the Germans bombed Warsaw, they tried to hit the bridges.

Finally, we arrived at the Warsaw-East station. The station had been bombed for several days. Dead horses lay among overturned *droshkies* (horse-drawn cabs). People searched for their belongings, dragging whatever they could find out of the rubble. The danger of the next alarm and the merciless bombs hung in the air. Somehow, none of it seemed real to me. I knew that I couldn't be hurt. Everybody else could, but not me.

Marysia must have felt the same way. Showing her teeth in a big smile, she flirted incorrigibly with any man nearby. Together, we searched through the mounds of luggage in which a railway official had told us we might find luggage from Bydgoszcz. I spotted a familiar-looking corner of a trunk underneath the big pile. We dug and pulled it out, and then found the second and third pieces.

I kept searching, but Marysia was getting antsy. The time for the next air raid inched closer. Marysia found a free *droshky* and I found the last bundle of luggage. We loaded the droshky; I sat on top of the load. Marysia sat where else, but next to the coachman.

We rode through the bridge traffic and made it home an hour later without an air raid! I felt accomplished and successful. Mother and Ann were relieved to have our meager belongings restored to us. Their gratitude grew a day or two later, when we heard a radio announcement about the railroad station being heavily bombed.

After another air raid, we got a glimpse of two Germans parachuting to safety after their plane was shot down. Even though the parachutes quickly disappeared from sight, people kept talking excitedly about the plummeting plane and the success of the Polish flack. I smiled to myself.

"I bet none of you ever jumped with a parachute," I thought.

Little did they know that I had. Before the age of ten, I belonged to a young group of junior Girl Scouts. Our junior Scouts and the main Girl Scout troop were connected, and we frequently undertook joint activities with the older girls.

When I learned that the older girls could enroll in a program to learn to parachute jump from the training tower, I was desperate to be included. Since I was a strong and independent little girl, the older girls knew that I would not be a burden and allowed me to come along just once, "only to look."

The training tower was in a field behind a nearby town known to me as the cavalry division town. I quietly watched the military instructor telling the Girl Scouts to climb the tower, from which another instructor supervised their jumps. I was fascinated. At the end of the session, I hung around the main instructor.

"How did you like it, young lady"? He asked with a smile.

"Oh, I liked it very much." I answered seriously and immediately, so as not to let him shift his attention. "Do you think I could also learn to jump?"

"Sure, you can join this group, but I need your parents' signed permission."

"I only have a mother."

"Do you think she will sign it?"

"Yes!" I was already thinking about how to approach her.

Strategically, I waited until Mother played bridge at the tennis club. Between games, I asked her to sign the permission slip for me to learn parachute jumping. One of Mother's bridge partners was a pilot and lieutenant in the Air Force. He thought it was a great idea. Startled, Mother began to object, but the lieutenant helped convince her that the parachute was connected to the tower and was safe.

The open-air training tower was about two hundred feet high, and was built with skeleton-like metal bars and a counterweight shaft running up the middle. We had to walk up the metal stairs to the top. On the lower levels it was easy; the tower was wide, and there was plenty of protection from falling.

However, on the final two levels (the sixth and seventh) the ladders were straight up, with nothing but the metal tower's skeleton on the outside. This climb was scarier than the jumping (well, at least after the first jump).

Above, a very big parachute fluttered and made funny noises, waiting for my weight to pull it down and fill it with air. I was told to jump. I wanted to, but it was very scary. The first jump was hard to make ... but the instructor's friendly push was always successful in helping us make up our minds.

For the first few seconds, I was in free fall. Once I fell directly under the center of the chute, the counterbalance slowed me. Now, flying more slowly, I enjoyed everything. I could see for miles: the forest, the fields, the sun above the horizon.

An instant later, I had to prepare for landing. This was more difficult and, I was told, the only dangerous part of the jump. The instructor guided me through the landing: "Hold your feet together ... now gently fall to your back!"

I was on the ground; the girls were applauding. The landing area was soft, made of wood shavings and sand. I rolled back up to my feet, and the instructor detached the straps from the harness I wore, snapping them to the wire. The counterweight pulled the parachute up the tower for the next jump.

After that first jump, I was ready for more. My excitement and fascination knew no bounds, and I didn't need any more pushes from the instructor. Each time we came for a training session, we were allotted only two jumps, rarely three. We learned a variety of ways to jump, the same techniques as jumping from balloons or planes: somersaults, stiff body, or instead of opening the gate on top of the tower, we climbed up the gate to prolong the scary initial free fall. My favorite was the stiff body fall.

After several lessons, the instructor asked me and another younger girl, the instructor's daughter, to come when the military trainees had to do their first jumps. On their first jumps, those trainees were as scared as we had been. The instructor introduced us—two little eight and nine-year-old girls—to the group of burly Air Force cadets. To their surprise, he asked one of us to come up the tower with the small group of trainees. On top of the tower, the cadets had a hard time hiding their uneasiness. The instructor gave the last instructions.

"I told you what to do, but now Zosia will show you how it's done." He told me to jump first.

"What jump do you want me to execute?" I asked with a smile.

"Anything you want."

I'll never forget the expressions on all the big guys' faces. Oh, was it fun!

First Encounters
with Darkness

After the siren calling off the air raid, we all rushed to see where the bomb had fallen. That September day, the bomb fell across the street from our apartment, landing in an open area where people had previously dug trenches to use as shelter during air raids. My curiosity took me there. It was my first real vision of the war.

Near the point of impact, people wandered, covered with dust. Some trenches had been destroyed. The crater where the bomb had fallen was in soft, sandy soil. I walked to a place where one of the trenches was covered with the fresh, newly disrupted soil. In the middle was a flat piece of fabric. I touched it; it was a dead man's back. Other people ran up ready to dig him out. I did not wait to see it. I left, having glimpsed only the man's back. I did not know him, nor did I feel sad. Perhaps I was numb or in shock. But if anything, the rush of events struck me as exciting.

Further down the street, a horse was dying. Somebody shot him to put him out of his misery. That bothered me. What bothered me even more was the sight of people carving the horse's meat from its body, desperate for food. Sirens, bombing, fires burning, radios blaring, people running up and down the stairs to and from the cellar—

I understood what was happening, but the severity was not sinking in, not yet.

On September 7, we heard for the last time: "Westerplatte still fights on." Those brave two hundred men battled for seven days against incomparable odds. Furious, Hitler threw bombs at them, hammered them with heavy artillery and armored cars and tanks. Our brave fellows kept fighting. We knew that at some point they would have to surrender, but their resistance became an inspiration to us, a symbol of the resistance that was approaching.

My memory of those days began to run together. There were more bombs, more fires, and more news of what had been demolished and lost in our country—but no news of the Allies, with whom we had signed the common defense pact. People were upset. "We will be forgotten ... again," was one remark I recall; or another, "I thought the defense pact was an honorable agreement with another country one should keep". At thirteen, I was young and completely ignorant of international law.

"What can France and England do from so far away?" I asked. "Maybe they'll start fighting later."

My optimism aside, "if France or England were attacked we would have sent all our forces to help, because we signed the defense pact," was the unquestionable argument I heard over and over in those days.

The truth of this statement struck me, then and now. Poles always kept their word, always helped their friends, even without being asked. I was proud of my country, and despite the fear surrounding me, I remained optimistic.

During the second week of war, we heard on the radio about the battle of Kutno. It was a major battle or chain of battles west of Warsaw. The radio told us day by day how bravely our soldiers were fighting, but we knew that the inevitable was coming.

Poor Alinka was petrified, thinking about her husband John, who was somewhere on the battlefield. Soon we learned that General Stanisław Grzmot Skotnicki had been killed. Our thoughts went to poor Stefa, Ann's friend, who had lost her father. He was the first person whom we knew to die. As the years passed, we got used to hearing familiar names, the names of friends who had perished.

Warsaw was surrounded. Sirens announcing air raids sounded at the same time as the first explosions. Mother was becoming calmer. Despite the fact that we had enough food, she was losing weight rapidly, her nerves taking their toll.

On September 17, the Soviets invaded Poland from the east. They had the gall to announce that they came as liberators for the oppressed people of eastern Poland. I don't remember who revealed that the Soviets and Germans had a secret agreement to divide Poland ... again. That knife in our back did not matter anymore.

Our liberty was dying.

In his last September radio announcement, Mayor Starzyński assured us that Poland's capitulation and transition would be orderly. There was more Chopin. The radio announcers' and the Mayor's voices broke; we, the listeners, bravely tried not to weep.

September 27. The Mayor's last words: "Thank you for your bravery and—" A long silence. "God save us!"

Warsaw had capitulated.

I don't remember much about those days. Nobody was talking, and everybody was extremely quiet. We stayed in our building.

Somebody told us that the German troops had marched in, but we did not see or hear them. They must have been in the town center. We learned that the Germans were distributing bread from big army trucks, but we were too proud to take it.

Marysia went and brought us the bread we badly needed. She probably also smiled at them broadly.

Occupation became a reality. I went for a walk with little Basia. A few German soldiers walking by offered me candies. I looked at them and shook my head. I was scared to refuse their offer, but I was not going to lower myself by accepting cheap candies from the "Szkop," our demeaning word for the Germans.

Within a few days of the occupation, my mother's older brother, Uncle Wladek, and his wife, Aunt Ziuta, arrived in Alinka's apartment.

"Where have you been?" exclaimed my mother. "We tried to call you several times, but nobody answered!"

"We made a mistake and tried to escape from the German invasion, to ride out the fighting in eastern Poland," Uncle Wladek said.

"Yes, and we almost lost our heads in the process," Aunt Ziuta added.

"Did the Soviets 'liberate' you?" Mother asked facetiously, referring to the Soviets' justification for the invasion.

"No, fortunately, we didn't even see their army. It was the Communist sympathizers, the Ukrainians and Jews, who would have liked to get rid of us—and they'd have succeeded, if it wasn't for Stanisław, our chauffeur."

"The Communists must have sent their agitators early, because our minorities acted horribly. Ukrainians, when in a group, are like a wild mob ... unpredictable." My aunt was visibly shaken, recalling their experiences.

"Ziuta, they *were* predictable. Given a chance they would have robbed us first and killed us later with pleasure," her husband said. Turning to my mother, he continued. "I wasn't surprised that the Ukrainians were so hostile, but why did the Jewish people side with the Communists? Trotsky was a Jew, but the Communists in Russia weren't any better than the Tsars when it came to persecuting Jews."

"They were trying to save their skins from the new occupier. They knew Poland was lost," Aunt Ziuta said sadly.

We talked for a while, commiserating over what had happened during the last three weeks of war. Our Polish radio was silenced, but we spoke of everything we had heard before about the international pacts. Poland had a non-aggression pact with Germany and the USSR, which we tended to be skeptical about, as those two countries had never kept their promises. By contrast, our pacts with Great Britain and France had given us some sense that they would fight with us in case of hostile invasion. Alas!

We already knew about Stalin and Hitler's total disrespect for international law. A week before the war started, they signed the secret Molotov – Ribbentrop[1] agreement dividing Poland between themselves. Knowing our country's history with the Russians, we expected them to commit atrocities in the lands they occupied, as they did under the Tsars, when they carried out arrests and forcible evictions, sent people to Siberia, and allowed thousands of murders. Now Uncle confirmed our fears.

---

1 The Molotov – Ribbentrop Pact, or the "Treaty of Non –Aggression," was signed on August 23, 1939. It remained in effect until June 22, 1941, when Germany invaded the Soviet Union.

"As soon as they crossed our border, the Soviets started arresting and killing Poles, especially the intelligentsia. We talked to several people who barely managed to escape."[2]

The discussions led again to Uncle's memories of their escape.

"The first part of our travel was relatively easy, except for the traffic, which was slowed by people like us trying to avoid battle areas. I'm not talking about the automobiles. It was the little horse-drawn buggies with whole families piled on top of one another, the animals roped to those buggies, even people on bicycles. We heard about several incidents of German planes strafing civilians, but fortunately we didn't experience that."

Uncle smiled at his own thoughts. "We thought that the safest place would be away from the bigger towns, so we drove directly east, past the Bug River, into the less populated poorer areas in the district of Polesie."

We nodded. The area was famous for its marshes, bogs, and natural beauty.

"Our troubles started when we went looking for a gas station. There were very few and all of them were supposedly without gas. Stanisław had a canister with gas in the trunk, but he was saving it for emergencies. People we asked about the situation gave us hostile looks, lowering their heads between their shoulders suspiciously." Uncle imitated the looks he was describing.

"We did not know what to think. I told Stanislaw to try to talk

---

2 During World War II, the Soviets sent 1,500,000 Poles to Siberia, prisons, and forced labor camps. Half of those persons died within a short time. When the Soviets joined the Allied Forces, they signed an agreement with the Polish Government in Exile to form a Polish Army from those Poles in Russian territory; however, General Anders managed to evacuate only 115.000 Poles in 1942.

to them," Aunt interjected, proud of her ability to always find a way out. "He went away from the car; we saw him talking to some people and soon the whole group was laughing and clapping shoulders."

My uncle picked up the story once again.

"Stanislaw came back, started the car and waved to the group, who waved back. We quickly drove out. 'Damned Ukrainian mob,' he muttered angrily. They had told him that in the next village some Jews were selling gasoline. Stanislaw did not trust any of the Ukrainians, who were consumed by their hatred of the Poles, especially the rich ones. It shook us all when he repeated their words to us: '"pretty soon our friends from Russia will finish your fancy rich bosses." This is when I laughed with them to pull their tongues more,' he added. They told him that they knew the Soviets were ready to come over."

"It didn't take us long to decide that we had to turn around fast," my aunt said. "Suddenly the Germans looked better than the Ruskis. The only problem was getting gas."

"We stopped for the night in a run-down hotel with a few travelers and some local people who were neither friendly nor hostile," my uncle said. "The atmosphere was tense. Early in the morning we learned that the Soviets had crossed our border. Stanislaw rushed out to find gasoline. After a while he came back and said that he had managed to talk some Jewish men into selling us some. They were playing a game, saying that they did not know how much gasoline they would be able to sell, nor how much it would cost. We went with Stanislaw, ready to pay whatever they asked."

"We came to a little country store," my aunt said. "Stanislaw went inside. He came out with an Eastern Jew, with *pejsy* and in *hałat.*[3] This man baited and mocked us, saying that if we waited for the Russians they would have more gasoline and it might be even cheaper than his gasoline, which was storied in half-liter bottles and hard to open. He kept talking, all to no end. We knew that he was trying to make us nervous in front of the onlookers who'd come out to watch. We stayed calm, but it was a nightmare!"

"Finally," my uncle said, "Stanislaw took their bluff and reminded them that when the Communists come, they would not need to sell gasoline, because they would be giving it away for free to all poor people. The Jew made some remarks about how helpful he wanted to be, and brought out boxes of those bottles. He started to open one at a time and pour it into our tank. Stanislaw succeeded in getting enough gasoline to get us going, though we paid dearly for it. We rushed to Brześć on the River Bug, desperate to get there before Soviet troops from the south or north arrived to cut us off. "[4]

We sat in silence, transfixed, looking at Aunt and Uncle as they visibly re-lived those harrowing days. Finally Mother said: "We survived the Tsarist occupation, which was awful, but I'm afraid these Russian Communists will be even worse. Russians, Germans ... why don't they leave us alone?"

"This time it will be short. America will join the war and tell the Germans where to go, like the last time."

Optimistic Aunt Ziuta broke into our group's gloomy thoughts. We started speculating about the possibility of British forces landing in France, about America sending help and Poland being free in no time.

"The old wars were slow because infantry moved so slowly, but

---

3 Curly sideburns and a long jacket.
4 The Ribbentrop agreement established the borders between Soviet and German areas of influence.

now it will be an Air Force war! The Americans have many more airplanes than Szkopy."

Within two weeks, John returned wearing civilian clothes he had bought from a farmer after his unit's defeat. John had always had delusions of grandeur. Now he was scared, but talking and acting with his typical self-importance.

We listened eagerly to his descriptions of the fight with the Germans, as until then the only stories of the front we'd heard had come from the radio. John told us that his unit fought only a minor skirmish; they were dispersed, and John and several other soldiers were separated from their unit, forcing them to seek refuge among the local farmers. John traded his pistol and uniform for the civilian outfit in which he walked back to Warsaw.

The Germans had already made an official announcement ordering all Polish military officers and noncommissioned officers to register for prisoner of war (POW) camps. In those early days of occupation, Poles talked to other Poles, comparing ideas about the future and what could be done to manage under occupation. We knew of several other officers, reserve or active; their consensus was that no matter how organized the Germans thought they were, they had no way of learning who was in the army and who wasn't. Consequently, all these men decided to stay with their families.

Except John. He immediately decided to obey the German order.

"I cannot risk my life. I owe it to my family," was the egotistical reason for his decision. The pregnant Alinka begged him to stay with her; since John was not in the active army, she insisted, he could claim that his draft number was never called, that the war ended so quickly he never made it into military service. But John decided to save his own skin and go voluntarily to the "Oflag," the officers' POW camp.

1939 - 1940:
German Occupation

At the end of September, the Russian and German forces met on the Molotov-Ribbentrop line. The whole of Poland was occupied, the Germans moving swiftly. With their ruthless sense of organization, they immediately arrested and executed many leading university professors and several national political leaders.[1]

The moment the German army entered Warsaw, they tried to arrest my Aunt Władysława Macieszyna, who was now a Polish senator. She knew better than to stay in her apartment on Szuch Avenue. The Germans continued to search for her throughout the long years of occupation, never aware that at the end of the war, they had her in their prisons under a different name.

Most of the banks were closed, and the Germans requisitioned

---

1 The German "Generalplan Ost" (or "Master Plan East") outlined the strategic goal of eliminating Poland's intelligentsia, the leadership class. Following this set of objectives, the Germans killed about 60,000 Polish nobles, teachers, priests, judges, and politicians.

everything they could, especially recently harvested food supplies. The Nazis imposed "ordnung" (order), which is best described as complete daily chaos governed by threat, murder and fear.

The Germans issued many official proclamations, demanding that Poles turn in all guns, ammunition, and radios. Their orders were always paired with threats of severe punishment should anyone dare to disobey, and it soon became obvious how sadistic the German administrative policies really were. They issued ration cards, but did not supply food to the stores. In order to live, Poles had to depend on the black market; depending on the day and the occupiers' whims, this market could be raided by soldiers who arrested everyone indiscriminately, whether they were selling goods or buying meager food supplies. At other times, German forces drove up, machine guns ready, closed streets as tightly as they could and herded everybody onto trucks like cattle to send them to German labor camps.

The Polish people began a daily fight for survival. Initially, all schools were closed. Later, the Germans allowed vocational schools to reopen, but academic education at all levels was strictly forbidden. Every order was issued as "streng verboten" (strictly forbidden). Whenever Germans found study teams of professors and students, it was reason for arrest and transportation to a concentration camp or immediate execution.

Life with my Aunt and Uncle

Uncle and Aunt settled back at their villa in Konstancin, the most expensive and beautiful of the Warsaw suburbs. At this time, they were alarmed to see how thin my mother had become. During the last month, she had lost twenty pounds from nerves.

In her childhood, Mother experienced anxiety problems while she endured the Russian occupation and WWI. Now she knew she would have to face another cataclysm alone, without a father or husband. She had lost her home and belongings in Bydgoszcz. Now the security of her capital in Polish banks was at the mercy of German occupiers.

Before the war, Uncle Władysław, my mother's oldest brother, had climbed the corporate ladder at one of Poland's biggest banks, the Warsaw Association of Sugar Factories. Sugar beets grew well in the rich Polish soil and were one of the country's primary exports. Uncle Władek, as we called him, became the bank's director in 1930. Some of Mother's money was also deposited in that bank.

When we saw my uncle and aunt again, one of the first questions Mother asked her brother was, "Do you think the Nazis will let us have our money?"

"So far, so good, but I have no idea what will happen," Uncle responded, visibly worried. "Germans do not respect international laws, and we've already been told that they will impose a 'treuhender' on us."

Mother looked questioningly at Uncle.

"They're assigning their supervisors to every company they intend to keep and control." Uncle saw Mother's worried face and smiled. "Don't worry; they told me that I'm still in charge, and our employees will work to keep the bank open."

"Zosiu, I know that Władek has been thinking about you—let him," Ziuta said, smiling gently at Mother. As she spoke, our whole group relaxed. We knew that Uncle Władek would do anything for us.

When Alinka and John took the children outdoors, Mother had a chance to share her concerns for Alinka with her brother. When my uncle and aunt heard about John's plans to voluntarily commit himself to the POW camp, they were appalled. They could not understand or believe his refusal to stand by his wife.

When John returned, Uncle Władek tried to talk some sense into him, but to no avail. In that moment, we all realized that nobody would be able to make John change his mind. In the past, John was always influenced by Uncle Władek, "the rich director of the big bank," but not now. Poor Alinka!

Mother and I were once more alone with my uncle and aunt when Ziuta assumed a funny presiding posture. "We came here today because we have a project for which we need your agreement," my aunt said, looking directly at me. "As you may remember, we were taking care of little Ryś, Ryszard's son. Ryszard and Mary asked us to take Ryś to our house if we could."

"Ryszard is Uncle Władek's and my youngest brother," Mother said, seeing my confused look.

"If Zosia would like to come and stay with us, she would make it easier on everybody," Uncle said with mock seriousness. Mother was close to tears.

"Do you really mean it?"

Smiling, Aunt Ziuta kept playing. "See, if Zosia would come, she could liven up little Ryś. They are the same age and he needs guidance."

I jumped up, hugging both of them. I could not believe my ears! To be free of occupied Warsaw would be a great blessing.

A few days later, my aunt and uncle picked me up. In half an hour we came to Konstancin, a very pretty town full of one-family houses we called villas.

"At the end of this street is our Boża Wola (God's Will)," Uncle said, pointing at a light grey two-story stucco house ahead. We came to a stop by the rod iron gate, which the chauffeur opened. We drove inside and walked in through the service entrance to a stairway.

Half a flight down stood a woman with a baby, whom my aunt introduced as Czesława, Stanislaw's wife and the cook. She and Stanislaw lived in an apartment in the basement. After exchanging hellos we went up to the main floor. In the hallway, a black Doberman pinscher greeted us. "Good Rex," said Uncle, petting him on the head. As if waiting politely for Uncle's greeting to end, Rex changed his demeanor and began prancing around my aunt. Eventually, he was told to lie down on his bed. Being an animal lover, I immediately reached out to pet him. Rex growled low. Uncle explained that Dobermans were one-man dogs, who did not take easily to new people.

Aunt led me up the round stairway to the room I would share with the teacher Uncle and Aunt were going to hire. In a few days, that teacher, Miss Halina, arrived. Ryś and I would both be taught the seventh grade, which I had to repeat because of my scores in French and Latin. Every morning after breakfast, we went upstairs to our room and had lessons with Miss Halina.

After a few weeks, when Aunt Ziuta learned from our teacher how well I was doing, she repeated the old Polish proverb to me: "You never know what goodness may emerge from the worst circumstances."

"If you had passed to the eighth grade, we would not have been able to let you and Richard study together in our house!"

Aunt Ziuta had a simple, frequently laughing way of saying wise things. In my childhood, years before, wild strawberries had made a special connection between us.

Whenever the memories of my childhood years begin to run together, I separate them by recalling the specifics of our summer vacations. Every July and August, we spent time in the country, traveling to a variety of places. When I was four or five, mother rented a house in Osie. My beloved Niania went with us on this vacation and cooked our meals. That vacation is the first in which I vividly remember the company of Uncle Władek and Aunt Ziuta, who spent several days with us.

One afternoon Niania and I went to the forest to gather wild strawberries. I brought my wooden mushroom box and filled it with the aromatic fresh fruit. When we came home, I surprised Aunt Ziuta with my present. Niania told her that while gathering strawberries I did not eat any, because I wanted to give my aunt the full box of berries.

Aunt Ziuta told me years later that she was so moved by this gesture that she had a hard time eating the strawberries. She tried to insist that I share them with her, but I was determined that she should eat them all. To outsmart me, she said, "I will have only the big ones, but you have to eat the little ones."

The next day Niania and I went for another walk in the forest. I carried my colorful mushroom box. Niania noticed that I walked by many strawberries without picking them.

"Zosia, didn't you see? You've walked past so many strawberries," Niania said, pointing.

"I saw them, but they are too small," I explained. "Aunt Ziuta likes only the big ones."

Niania smiled at my determination.

When I filled the whole mushroom box I was ready to return home. I ran to my aunt, pressed the box into her hands, and said, "Here, only the big ones!" Aunt did not say anything for a while. Then she turned me around and lifted me to her lap. With her face next to my cheek, she whispered "thank you" into my ear and ate one big strawberry after another.

As a girl, I could not quite understand why every time we met she talked about those strawberries.

It took only a few days for me to become Rex's friend. However, Rex continued to ignore poor Ryś. His true name was Richard, like his father, but we all called him diminutively Ryś. Aunt Ziuta knew of my love for animals, especially dogs, and it made her very happy that her pet had accepted me. However, it was hard not to laugh as Rex became selectively deaf whenever poor Richard tried to befriend him.

Rex was a proud resident of the house. Outside was a pen and dog houses for the four beautiful white, bear-like Hungarian shepherds, who served as watch dogs: powerful Alpha dog, Ali, his mate,

Iza, and their pups, Dar and Iskra. Besides Aunt and Uncle, only Stanislaw could let them out of their pen for the night and put them back in the morning. I talked to the Hungarian shepherds but kept my distance, not knowing how they would react if I came too close.

There was animosity between the white penned dogs and the black dandy Rex, who teased the locked-up dogs mercilessly by running along their pen. Since Rex was scolded constantly for this behavior, he learned to tease the dogs whenever he thought nobody could see him. We did not have to see anything, however. Sudden barking and thrashing would sound from the pen; somebody would yell at Rex, and he would trot innocently back to the house, a "who, me?" expression on his doggy face.

We got our revenge on Rex in the evenings, when old Ali and his family ran free in the garden. Uncle or Aunt would ask Rex if he would like to go out. In those moments, Rex fell deaf and absolutely could not hear. The more we laughed, the funnier Rex acted. Feeling sorry for him, I would get down on the rug to console him out of his embarrassment.

"I see Rex has won your heart already," Uncle said, looking at Rex snuggling against me on the rug.

"He must have known how much I love dogs, and how much I always wanted to have one. I've never had a dog," I said.

"That's not true," Uncle said. "You not only had two dogs, but they saved your life when you were a tiny baby."

Ryś's ears perked up; Uncle turned to him.

"I thought you knew about it, as our whole family talked about it for a long time."

Unlike Ryś, I knew that story well. I heard it many, many times and always asked Mother to tell it to me again.

Back in Dębogóra, the area around our home looked like a park, full of old trees with grassy areas around them. During the first few months of my life, my mother would routinely put me under one of the old maple trees for a nap, leaving Dad's two hunting dogs as my guardians. Ryś and Boy were German shorthair pointers.

Having left me in good hands, Mother would return to the house to attend to her duties. She was in the kitchen giving orders for the day when one of the dogs came in suddenly and started barking. Mother scolded him, as it was absolutely forbidden for dogs to enter the kitchen. The dog did not leave, but ran to my mother and started pulling on her skirt. At that moment she realized where the dog was supposed to be, and instantly everybody in the kitchen also realized what the dog was trying to say.

They ran to the park. From a distance they heard the unmistakable sound of a maple bough breaking. The other dog lay with his front paws on top of me, looking fearfully at the big branch cracking above our heads. Mother whisked me away; an instant later, the big branch of the old maple came crashing down. This was the first time my life was saved, and the dogs got extra treats that day.

A few months later, when I started crawling, my mother was still able to leave me with Ryś and Boy. Somehow they learned to keep me on the blanket. If I started crawling off, one of the dogs would lie on the edge, blocking my intended path. Inevitably, I crawled on top of that dog, who would simply get up and plop me back onto the blanket. According to Mother's stories, I enjoyed having those dogs around and they also seemed to enjoy their guardian role. Obviously, I could not remember Ryś and Boy, but my deep love and understanding for dogs remained.

Every afternoon we happily greeted Uncle when he came home. I always hugged him in the hallway. On the day we received the bad news about John, I expected him to go to the bedroom he shared with my aunt to change into more casual attire, but he asked me and Aunt to come to the living room instead. He looked at us, shaking his head as if unsure what to say.

"Poor Alinka," he said. "Your mother came to my office today and told me the news. John is leaving soon to go to the POW camp. He already registered, as if he did not want to leave himself a way out. But—" Uncle took a deep breath. "John picked an argument with your mother and he has ordered her and Ann to leave his house!"

"Now, when Alinka needs her family most?" Aunt Ziuta exclaimed.

In our immediate family, John was known for his less than honorable behavior. He flattered those in positions of power and wealth, like my Uncle Wladek, but took pleasure in being mean to people in difficult situations. He never would have stood up to Mother before the war. Now, Mother was poor and powerless. We shook our heads in disbelief.

"John is not only cruel and arrogant, he's plain stupid, ostracizing the family Alinka will soon need so badly," we all thought.

Mother and Ann moved out of Alinka's apartment, renting a room in Mother's sister Wanda's apartment on Tamka Street in the center of Warsaw. They did not join me in the countryside for a number of reasons: crowding Uncle's house was out of the question; while there, Ann would be unable to look for a job that would keep her out of the forced labor camps in Germany; and if my uncle were to open his house to Mother, the other siblings would also clamor for an invitation. As beautiful and luxurious as their house was, there was simply not enough room for more people.

A few weeks after the incident, John reported for transport to a POW officers' camp in Murnau, leaving Alinka alone with Basia, who was not yet a year old. Mother was worried more about Alinka and John's lack of consideration for his pregnant wife than about herself. We all loved Alinka, but we had a hard time understanding her inability to stand up to her often dishonest, amoral husband. I remember talking with Aunt Ziuta about the whole situation. At this time, I found the courage to tell my aunt about John's attempts to sexually molest me when I visited their six-week-old daughter, my half-niece, during Christmas 1938. Aunt Ziuta told me that at the time she suspected something was wrong.

Now we reached the conclusion that we had to help Alinka, for she obviously did not know how to help herself.

A Winter of Hardship
and Change

"Thrown out of the saddle" is an old Polish saying to describe people who suddenly find themselves out of their element. War threw us all out of the saddle, though some suffered more than others. My mother was one of those people.

Before the war, Mother coped well with the difficulty of being a widow and raising her children alone. Before his death, my father settled her in a comfortable financial situation. Later, she tried to make a few "better" investments, which resulted in some large losses, but even then she was remained well off.

My mother was a true lady, intelligent and witty, which only added to her impeccable social manners. People sought her friendship and were honored to be invited to her home.

In August 1939, when we left our home with only our hand luggage and whatever we were able to send via rail, Mother had no illusions that she would ever see the possessions she left behind. During the air raid alarms in Warsaw, I remember her standing in the cellar, calm and dignified, tightening up or closing her eyes only when the bombs exploded nearby.

And I remember Mother rapidly losing weight.

Moving to Aunt Wanda's apartment had one good result for my mother and Ann. While they were there, Alexander Zaleski, my parents' old friend, contacted my mother with a peculiar business proposition.

In the good old days, Alexander used to hunt with my father on our estate; occasionally, he worked for my father. Now Alexander administered a small area of land and sent farm produce to Warsaw's street market. Like every other little estate, he was under the control of a German *treuhender* and could not help Mother, but he told her he could give her some of the produce if she would help him sell it. Mother agreed, laughing at the peculiar proposition. Alexander's worker drove the horse wagon to Warsaw loaded with millet, big zucchinis, beets and cabbage, which Mother sold at the farmer's market.

Instead of feeling degraded or self-pitying, Mother turned her time at the market into an adventure. She told us stories about her associations with the market people, hucksters and peasants who quickly realized that Mother was not of their element.

Rather than taking advantage of her vulnerability, several of those down-to-earth peasant women protected Mother. They gave her advice on how to sell and behave. Recognizing Mother's fine upbringing, these women tried to speak to her properly without descriptive but improper adjectives, a choice that visibly hampered their ability to express themselves.

Every time Aunt Ziuta and I came to town we eagerly awaited Mother's funny market stories—her narratives made all of us cry with laughter.

In the meantime, Ann had graduated from high school the previous June. She intended to apply to university to study stomatology and become a dentist. Now she too had to adjust to the different laws of war time.

To avoid being sent to a labor camp in Germany, she had to find a job—and quickly. Her first work in occupied Poland was even more humorous than Mother's: Ann became a supervisor of grave diggers in the cemetery.

The lives of our family members and friends who had lived in Warsaw prior to the war were somewhat easier than my mother and Ann's. They had their apartments, furniture and some work, for which they received a salary each month. Our currency was rapidly losing value, but any small monthly income was better than nothing—nothing being the situation for those now trying to find refuge in Warsaw.

In contrast, the lives of refugees from the western part of Poland became doubly difficult. They could not move back to seek out their properties, as their territories were automatically absorbed into the Third Reich. The Polish people were told they had no right to live there. The Poles who stayed in their homes during the invasion were evicted, and their properties, homes and land were confiscated and resettled by Germans.[1]

Living in the luxurious suburban villa with my aunt and uncle, I was protected from the discomfort of Warsaw's inhabitants. As a young man, my uncle had lived through World War I. During the years of Polish independence and prosperity, he decided to prepare for a "rainy day" by buying pieces of jewelry for my aunt. Now I

---

1 During the winter of 1939 – 1940, the Germans forced the resettlement of two million Poles who were forced to leave all of their possessions behind.

shared food bought from the sale of one piece after another. Mother was surviving in the same way, though she had fewer pieces to sell, memorable ones with sentimental value rather than grams of gold or precious karats of diamonds.

In the country, Richard and I felt almost untouched by the hardships of war. Uncle and Aunt's villa, named after the Gorski coat of arms, was called "Boża Wola" or "God's Will." And I felt providence indeed; I knew how lucky I was to live there. We were in the suburbs in a beautiful, warm house, well-fed and able to study with a private teacher, while most people during that first year of the war barely had enough to eat and were denied education.

If there had been no Germans, our lives would have been normal. In the afternoon, with my homework done, I waited for the dog's joyous barking to announce Uncle's arrival. Shortly after he returned home, an early dinner was served by Magda, the maid. Conversation was always light, with lots of laughter. My manners, well taught by my mother, were visibly appreciated; Richard's rough edges were subtly corrected by my uncle or aunt with a raised eyebrow or a quiet clearing of the throat.

But one day, something was different.

When Uncle came home, his normal greetings were less personal and much shorter. We exchanged understanding glances with our aunt.

"Let's leave him alone," I whispered. Dinner included a little superficial conversation. Finally, Uncle looked around the table.

"I have something to tell you. When we finish, let's go to the living room. I have asked Stanisław to make us a fire."

"Oof," I breathed. *At least we'll know.*

I loved that living room. It was big but cozy, with a large door to the veranda and a large window on the other side overlooking a beautifully landscaped garden, now dark. The only light, from the fireplace, reflected in the door.

Uncle's big armchair was on the side of the fireplace, where he sat now. My Aunt sat down on one of the armchairs around the side table. Ryś, Rex and I settled in front of the fire on the Persian rug. After a short silence Uncle began to speak.

"I had a very special visit today. Mister—" Eyes on my aunt, he mentioned a name. "Came." Turning to us, my uncle explained that the gentleman was a director of another big bank, and that he was Jewish. "In the past we've had business meetings and transactions. I always liked and respected him. Today he came with a personal problem."

Uncle looked at us as if trying to make up his mind what to say. "I should tell you the truth as it is," he said. "The Germans are locking Jews in a ghetto and building walls around it. They started by erecting walls, saying that they wanted to separate Jews from Polish people, but now the Jews outside that area are getting notices telling them to move inside the ghetto. Today, this gentleman asked me for a little favor and offered me a big favor in return. When I objected, he told me simply, 'I'm certain that tomorrow we won't be able to get any of our bank's money, for they will repossess it. Jewish property goes first.'"

"Do he and his family have to move out of their beautiful home?" My aunt asked.

"Not yet, but he's sure it won't be long till he gets the order for what the Germans are calling 'resettling.'"

"With all the news from Germany, why didn't they leave Poland before the war?"

"I asked him the same thing, and he said they procrastinated; it was difficult to leave their whole life's work behind. Now they are stuck.

"He also said a very peculiar thing. We talked about our attempt to escape from the Warsaw area, and he asked me point-blank if we had problems with the Jewish men in the east of Poland. When he saw my surprise, he said, 'remember, my friend, when you have a Jewish friend, there is no better friend in the world, but when you have a Jewish enemy – beware, there is nothing worse.'"

Seeing the questions on our faces, my uncle continued speaking.

"He told me that the Germans have already established Jewish police in the ghetto. These men are called 'capos'. They are the worst scoundrels, trying to benefit from the misery of other Jewish persons."

We asked more questions, speaking about the matter until Uncle rose, saying, "Believe me, I learned today how good a Jewish friend can be."

Somehow, I knew not to ask anything more.

Every few weeks, my aunt took Ryś to Warsaw to the orthodontist to correct his teeth, a process that began before the war when Ryś was living with his parents, who either did not care or could not afford the procedure. One day, however, Aunt Ziuta told me that it was my turn to go with her to Warsaw.

My aunt helped me to dress as well as I could, considering that I was outgrowing most of the clothing I had in both height and width. When I questioned her about where we were going, she gave her characteristic smile, narrowing her dark blue eyes and raising her eyebrows in a *who knows?* expression.

We took the narrow gauge railroad to Warsaw. Close to an hour later, we got out and took a streetcar through Ujazdowskie Boulevard to the center of town. On both sides of the street, the trees were golden with fall colors. We rode by places that we knew well. First we passed Belvedere, built in 1920 by the first Polish Marshal, Józef Piłsudski, for his residence. In the big park was the palace where the last ruler, King Stanisław Poniatowski, called Łazienki, amassed objects of art—now locked up and occupied by the Germans. Shortly after, we saw a statue of our beloved romantic composer Frederic Chopin. Seeing Chopin's statue from the streetcar always made people smile, as if seeing his statue we could hear his lovely music.

Eventually, we came to the center of town on Krakowskie Przedmieście.

"We are going to pick up uncle," my aunt said with a smile. I knew something was cooking, and that something was going to be good.

Uncle greeted us in the office, and my aunt exchanged a few sentences with the other bank workers. Then Uncle announced that he was leaving, and we went to Stanisław, who was already waiting in the front of the bank.

"We're going to my favorite restaurant," my uncle said, "for we may not be able to go there much longer."

We walked into a spacious restaurant and were warmly greeted by the *maître'd*, who led us to our table. It had been a long time since I'd been with Mother to a restaurant in Bydgoszcz. This restaurant was bigger and more elegant than the ones in our "provincial" town.

"As my good friend told me in the conversation I mentioned the other day, we should enjoy ourselves as long as we can. This is why we came here today, to share this special place with you," my uncle said, looking at me. I don't remember what I told them, but I suspect that my expression revealed how much I appreciated and liked this gesture.

The waiter was as friendly as he was respectful. He and Uncle talked possibilities and probabilities, wondering how the German occupation would affect the restaurant business. So far, the Germans were allowing Polish restaurateurs to buy necessary food, probably because Germans also frequented these establishments.

As if on command, a group of German officers arrived and were seated in an area far away from us. The waiter laughed and said that they had been told to keep the German area separate from the Polish patrons. And then he added with the chuckle: "because the Poles would lose their appetites if they had to sit near Germans".

After a very delicious and festive dinner we drove home, making sure not to let Richard know where we had been.

With gasoline rationed and difficult to obtain, my uncle sometimes took the train to Warsaw. On one such day, several uniformed Germans came to the villa and requisitioned his car. My poor aunt knew better than to argue with them.

Since Uncle had an official permit to keep his car, he tried to recover it. The Germans were proud of their recordkeeping abilities, but the officials my uncle contacted could not find his Chevrolet, claiming that it must have been a misunderstanding, as they did not know who had taken the car or where they had gone with it. So Uncle Wladek started using the narrow gauge railroad to travel daily to work in Warsaw.

That winter of 1939-1940 was extremely harsh. It started early, with the lowest temperatures and highest snowfall in years. It was a misery for the majority of the Polish population, who did not have heating in their homes, who had poor winter clothing, no work, and a minimal amount of money to buy food on the black market. The Germans were still failing to supply stores with food to be sold in return for the ration cards they issued. I almost felt guilty feeling happy that I could go away from Warsaw, to be back with my aunt and uncle in their home.

Before the war, I remembered very well how I imitated Ann's "cool" way of moving through school with a minimum amount of study. As a result, I'd flunked Latin and French. Now, with the Germans forbidding any academic education, nobody had to explain to me that our enemies wanted us Poles to stay uneducated and ignorant. I got the message quickly, and must have said my typical, "Oh yeah? Try me!"

I realized that, although I did not know where I was going or what life would be like after the war, this was *my life*. Every day started to count. At thirteen years old, I started sponging up all the knowledge I could.

In that first year of war, Christmas came suddenly, like a strange event. Aunt and Uncle invited Mother and Ann to visit for a day. They came by rail shortly after noon. There was no Christmas tree, as the Germans did not allow tree cutting. But as always on the evening of December 24, the Vigil of Christmas Day, we had Vilia.

The house was warm and we were happy to be together, but there was no cheer, no matter how hard we all tried to produce it.

"Zosiu, I am sorry our Vilia is so limited," Aunt Ziuta said to my mother.

"Exactly! I expected the traditional thirteen dishes," Mother joked.

Uncle Władek and Mother reminisced about Christmases from

their childhood, when Poland was under Russian Tsarist occupation. They wondered how different the German treatment would be. Everything was completely unpredictable.

After supper we went to the living room, where the fire burned.

"As I warned you, the angel did not find many presents this year," Uncle said, referring to the traditional belief that a Christmas angel brought presents from the baby Jesus.

"My goodness, Wladek, we could not get anything for you, so please—" Mother objected.

But my uncle's angel must have had good connections, for Mother received an envelope that made tears come to her eyes as she hugged her brother and sister-in-law.

Proud to keep the tradition instilled in me by my old Niania of making gifts for Christmas, I presented my aunt with a delicately-embroidered organdy serviette I had worked on in secrecy. Aunt Ziuta was moved and delighted, and immediately put it on the table where, in my dreams, it had belonged.

Finally, Aunt handed me a soft package. I unwrapped it carefully and slowly, as was our custom. Inside was the softest woolen dark blue fabric for a dress. I was so happy to receive material for a dress, as I did not have any that fit. Last winter's clothing was too tight and too short. I don't remember what I wore in those days, but whenever I had to wash my only sweater, I hung it by the radiator, hoping it would dry by morning.

I gave big thank you kisses and hugs to my dear aunt and uncle for this precious present, and even more kisses for the warm and peaceful Christmas they had created.

Periodically during that cruel winter, I went to Warsaw to see my mother. Late in the evening I took the same narrow gauge railroad back.

One afternoon, it started snowing. The train barely moved. After two hours we were only in Wilanów, a town normally fifteen minutes from the Warsaw station. The snow was getting too deep, too fast. Finally, an announcement told us that the train could not go any further. All the passengers got out and started walking. It must have been eight or nine o'clock. It was pitch dark. People grouped themselves by their destination. I walked with the small group to Konstancin, the last town on that line.

The rushing wind cleared some snow from the road, but it also blew snow into our faces and against our bodies. My coat kept me somewhat protected and we walked fast to keep warm, but my legs in their cotton stockings and low shoes were caked with snow and freezing cold.

The group of passengers diminished with the passing of each little town; when we reached Konstancin, there were only a few of us. Finally, I was alone, walking toward our villa. I must have been barely visible when our four Hungarian sheep dogs started barking a greeting. Their voices said unmistakably that someone they knew and liked was coming. Lights came on in the house and Stanisław opened the gate before I could ring the bell. The dogs' happy voices had convinced him there was no reason to worry.

Even though I had never been in direct contact with them before, the dogs acted as if they expected me to play with them. They jumped up and put their front paws on my shoulders, sniffing my face, their breath warm on my face. The greeting charmed me, but I was so tired and cold I could barely stand.

It must have been long after midnight. Having expected me to arrive for supper, my worried aunt and uncle were relieved to finally see me. I was shaking badly and my hands and legs were numb, to the point that I was unable to undress myself. Hoping to bring blood circulation to my freezing legs my, aunt rubbed them with snow—the only method known to avert frostbite. Uncle made a hot drink with cognac for me, which I enjoyed but had a hard time drinking, as my whole body was shaking and my teeth were chattering. But I was happy to be in their warm home and to be taken care of by them. Happy laughter filled the room, especially when my chattering teeth made my speech incomprehensible.

Finally, my aunt and uncle gave up rubbing my legs and allowed me to get in a warm bath. Slowly, I started warming up. Later that night I got a fever, which felt good, for I was not cold anymore.

The experience left me with frostbite on both legs from the ankles to the knees. At first my legs hurt. Later they itched and turned red. The only time they did not bother me was during the warm summer months. However, for many years the first autumn cold brought back all my symptoms. Only many, many years later would the California sunshine eventually cure my frostbite.

In the spring of 1940, a different tragedy struck my Uncle Wladek, who started having problems with his vocal cords. His cancer, which had been operated on at the University of Sorbonne Hospital in 1928, had come back. Aunt Ziuta remembered the elation of the Parisian doctor after the successful operation; he proclaimed that my uncle might live as many as fifteen more years. It was now twelve years later.

Miss Halina, our teacher, was a graduate of the Convent of the Sisters of Nazareth School. At the end of the school year, I wrote my exams and earned straight As. Richard and I stayed in Konstancin with Aunt and Uncle a little longer, till the end of the summer. But Uncle Władek was suffering more and more as the cancer took its course.

June 14, 1940. The Germans were euphoric. Hitler's army was in Paris.

In my uncle's home, this momentous German victory went almost unnoticed. We were saddened by the display of Germany's might, but as Poles, we also felt vindicated. If France, with English help, could not stop Hitler's armies, how could we have done better?

My uncle's cancer was more important to me than the fall of France. I knew that leaving the oasis of their home would be hard, but I also knew that Uncle Władek's life was coming to a very difficult end, and that truth saddened me beyond compare.

While living with my aunt and uncle, I had met some young people who lived year-round in the surrounding villas. During the summer of 1940, I also met a group who lived in Warsaw during the winter and spent the summers in Konstancin. They became my friends, and I enjoyed their company; we played Ping-Pong, volleyball and spent the long summer days together. With them, I felt secure. I was stronger and fitter than most girls, and the best female volleyball player. At the end of the summer, George Schiele organized a Ping-Pong tournament and I won the girls' championship.

But the situation changed when we all returned to Warsaw. There, they still had beautiful homes and old clothing to rethread into new outfits. I had none of these luxuries. My friends never made me feel ostracized or unfit for their company, but I felt different all the same.

At home, Uncle's voice grew raspier. His visits to doctors were more frequent and the results more frustrating. He was losing his battle with cancer.

The end of summer meant it was time for me to leave my aunt

and uncle's house. It was a painful parting; I loved them both, loved their dogs and the villa, and I dreaded the thought of living in Warsaw.

Now I was thrown out of my saddle, and *my* horse ran away.

Warsaw, a Season of Dance and Song

In September 1940, Mother was still living in a room rented from her sister, Wanda. Ann, however, had gone to stay with Alinka after John's departure. After I left Konstancin, Ann moved in with Mother and I went to live in Alinka's apartment with her two children. Basia (Barbara) was now almost two; little Mathew, who we all called Maciuś, was only four months old.

In Alinka's building, I met a neighbor whose husband had been taken prisoner by the Germans and was also in the POW camp. In the evenings after curfew, we frequently gathered to share the latest news and gossip.

Since the middle of summer, news about Polish fighter pilots fighting in England with the Royal Air Force had been circulating. At first these were short notices from various individual pilots whose news managed to reach their families. Soon it seemed that the whole population of Warsaw was exchanging stories from the London Radio broadcasts, raving about the successes of Polish Kościuszko Squadron 303. The radio repeatedly emphasized the

Polish pilots' bravery, efficiency and superior strategy.

We cherished such news, repeating it endlessly amongst ourselves. We recalled with satisfaction the dark days immediately following our surrender, when the German papers mockingly harped upon the poor performance of the Polish forces, calling them the cavalry of the air, unable to even fight German Luftwaffe.[1] Now we felt vindicated. Not only were the Polish fighter pilots able to shoot many German planes, losing few, if any, of their own craft, but the British RAF had come to consider them the best Allied fliers.

By the end of October, the Battle of Britain had ended. Hitler was unable to annihilate Britain's air defense—thanks to the Polish Squadron, who was credited with a big role in the Allied victory. King George VI personally congratulated the whole Polish Squadron for their success.

In Alinka's little kitchen, we too celebrated the glory of Poland's pilots, fighting and dying for "your freedom and ours," as our patriotic motto had proclaimed for two centuries. On one of those evenings, Alinka told us my father's youngest brother's story:

At the end of World War I, my Grandmother Paulina's youngest son, Ludwig, grew fascinated with the new airplane technology and became a pilot. Unfortunately, he died in an accident in 1919, at the very young age of twenty. As a copilot, Ludwig was removing blocks from under the front wheels of a plane. With its wheels removed, the plane turned slightly and the propeller cut through my uncle's temple, killing him instantly.

On a lighter note, Alinka also told us that Grandma Paulina, while deeply grieving Ludwig's untimely death, was irritated that

---

1 The German propaganda machine was concealing the fact that during the Polish invasion, the Germans suffered far greater losses from engagements with the Polish Air Force than they expected.

Ludwig had carelessly spent most of his inheritance shortly before his death. My father tried to remind his mother that Ludwig would no longer need the funds. "But if he hadn't died?" Grandma complained.

In the midst of war, such stories moved us and drew us closer as a family. Here is another which I cherish.

When I was nine or ten years old, among Mother's bridge partners was a pilot in the Polish Air Force. Lieutenant Sypniewski was a friendly man who liked sports and children. He coached Ann and other young girls and boys in tennis.

As a girl, I was fascinated by planes. One day I gathered the courage to ask Lt. Sypniewski whether he could take me up in a plane. After all, I reminded him, he had helped me convince Mother to sign my parachuting permission slip. His answer was, "maybe"; but I would not let the matter rest until I got a definite "yes."

When the eagerly awaited day arrived, we drove in a military car to the airfield on the outskirts of town. Lt. Sypniewski also took his young son. When we arrived at the airfield, I was overwhelmed with excitement, watching the little planes take off and land on the big grassy field. With no marked lanes, planes seemed to be flying in all directions.

I got dressed in a jacket, cap and goggles—everything a "little" too big. I must have looked like Snoopy in the Sop with Camel. With some assistance, I clambered into the front seat of the RWD-8, an open cockpit, two-seat training bi-plane.

In front of me, I saw instruments identical to those in the pilot's cockpit behind me. They strapped me in, and the lieutenant told me that when we were high up in the air, he would jiggle the stick and I could do whatever I wanted with my stick. We could not talk over the engine's roar, but we saw each other in the side mirrors.

Once in the air, the lieutenant must have seen my happy, laughing face. He knew that I felt no fear. The flight was fabulous. I loved every second of it. He jiggled the stick. I pulled it all the way toward me. The plane went straight up, the Lieutenant rolled his stick to the right and we leveled again. We flew for half an hour or so. After we landed, I remember talking to some other pilots; we then drove home. I could not stop telling Mother, Ann, Niania, and anybody who would listen about my fantastic escapade.

That memory lasted for at least a year or two, at which time the Polish Air Force rules about flying civilian passengers changed. In the tennis club, Lt. Sypniewski announced that he could not take anybody up again. He added that only members with special privileges would be allowed.

"Like who?" I asked, my interest renewed.

"Like doctors, or others attached to the military profession," the lieutenant said.

The Air Force doctor sat nearby. He was new and unaware of the joke being played on him. All the grownups burst out laughing. Everybody must have known about my passion for flying. At the time, I did not feel I could talk to the doctor; I only stared at him with incomparable intensity. I wasn't making a pest of myself, but somehow I made sure that the subject came up again, and the doctor did ask my mother whether she would mind if he took me flying. She must have answered that it was hard to object to my determination.

This time Ann was also invited. That must have been one of the first activities that we shared. Ann seldom, if ever, included me, but this time she joined my activity.

Again, we flew the RWD-8. I had no problem talking our doctor-flier into doing aerobatics. That was even more fun than the first time! He loved flying low, a few yards above the landscape. In Polish it was called "mowing flight," or "*koszący lot.*" With the change of one vowel, pilots called it "*kuszący lot,*" the tempting flight. The excitement was incredible. It felt as if the trees were barely below the plane. For the slightest elevation change, the plane had to lift to drop immediately again.

As I told this story, Alinka and her friend looked at me with strange expressions on their faces. In my exuberance, I could not understand their concern. *How could anybody not be excited about flying in an airplane?* I wondered.

The realities of our lives, however, were hitting close to the skin.

With the exception of the summer months, Alinka's apartment had always been cold. Those big apartment blocks were well-built, but did not dry out fully before being opened for occupation. Consequently, moisture was trapped in the walls. During the long winter months, cold dampness filled the rooms; without enough heating, the rooms stayed moist and cold, and our bedding denied us comfort at night.

I remember going to bed, unable to either warm up or fall asleep, and crying out of desperation. When we got up in the morning, the windows were frozen and opaque, with three or more inches of thick ice accumulated at their base. My hands and heels became frostbitten, in addition to my already suffering legs. There were tile ovens in every room, but the Germans did not supply coal to our buildings. The only coal available was that which appeared sporadically on the black market.

Food was also very scarce. Poor Alinka had a hard time taking care of her two tiny children; without enough money, she had to depend on black market prices. To make matters worse, Alinka was never a good or efficient housekeeper. Various members of the family tried to help, though they did not have enough even for themselves.

We were always undernourished, hungry, and cold. Somehow I was able to avoid thinking about hunger. I wasn't that skinny, but my legs bothered me immensely. In addition to having frostbite, I was still growing; the only shoes I had were too tight, leaving my heels chafed and raw. The only solution was to elevate the back of my shoe so that my heel was above the leather. I walked like that for about a year. The following year we managed to buy me new shoes.

And still, the realities of war hit harder. I went to the Sisters of Nazareth convent school, which was officially registered as a vocational school for seamstresses. Many girls in our school boycotted vocational subjects, implying that they were beneath their dignity. I chose not to. When confronted with such snooty behavior, I would say: "I will learn how to sew so that I can demand good work from my private seamstress after the war."

We had barely started sewing classes when I decided to make warm slippers for my little niece, Basia. Our teacher helped me make a form, and I managed to scrounge an old felt hat and a piece of rabbit pelt. I remember coming home with my surprise gift shortly after Basia woke from her nap. I put the fuzzy slippers on her feet. She was enchanted, and wanted to wear them all of the time. Those slippers lasted through the winter and well into spring, when they finally fell apart.

In school, the Sisters of Nazareth worked extra hard with us. We realized that every day of our schoolwork might be the last opportunity to learn anything for a long time. Increasingly, news reached

us about teams of students and professors who were caught and sent to concentration camps or shot in punishment for the crime of being involved in academic education.

One of those incidents hit home, shaking me up and making my determination stronger. Adam, my good friend and neighbor, had an older sister who was trying to finish high school on the "team," meeting with professors and study groups in various private homes. Though they were careful to vary the location of their classes and to never arrive in a group, the Germans must have spotted them. The whole "team" was arrested and executed. One evening Adam came to visit. The moment I saw his face, I knew something awful had happened. He shared his pain and anger with me. I listened and cried with him. For several days, whenever I met his mother or sister, we only looked at each other without speaking. There was nothing to say.

Grief-stricken as I was, my only reaction was to keep studying more often and harder, if for no other reason than to double cross the damn Germans.

At school, the Sisters had a special drill for German inspections, in which the soldiers tried to surprise and "catch" us. It would have been humorous if the results were not so potentially tragic. To look inconspicuous and to blend in with the Polish people, the Germans wore civilian clothes—but they also wore German riding boots, black leather coats, identical hats and talked in their loud, gargling German language.

The Sister at the outer gate minded the entrance. Whenever the Germans arrived, she opened the little window to ask the reason for their visit. Before she opened the gate, she rang an alarm bell inside the school. The Germans proceeded through the courtyard to the building, where another sister sat in her little office. She inquired further before opening the door to the main building. Both sisters spoke German, but otherwise pretended surprise at the "unexpected" visit to a simple Polish girls' seamstress school.

In the meantime, the instant we heard the first alarm bell, the nuns gathered all the contraband educational materials from our desks and ran with it to their cloister, while inside the classrooms we sewed or designed clothing, our official work.

Sister Ezechiela, our Sister Director, was a very unique person. I once saw her talking to the German inspectors. There was no question of who was in command. She was tall and statuesque in her nun's habit, with her head held high, rimless glasses, and a dignified demeanor. She was well bred and well educated, and it showed. Sister Ezechiela spoke several languages, including German, and she did not hesitate when necessary to call the Catholic Bishops in Germany and request their intervention. She never let the German inspections bring us bad results.

I liked the Sisters and felt comfortable in their charge. To avoid carrying contraband school materials home, I preferred to do my homework fast and leave as much as possible at school, as I could be searched on the way to or from home. That method of doing my homework fast and well helped me earn more straight As.

In Warsaw, the streetcars were functioning, but they frequently broke down or lacked the necessary electricity to run. In order to travel, one had to walk or run and jump to catch any ride one could. When switching lines, we looked ahead to see if the streetcar was coming or already at the stop. We jumped out before it stopped and ran to the next one we wanted to catch, which was usually already moving away.

One day I rode from school, not to Alinka's apartment, but all the way to the center of town. I even managed to get a seat. For every person getting out, crowds fought to get in. People said this was the first streetcar going in that direction in some time. And "some time" did not mean twenty minutes. Other riders claimed they had been waiting for over an hour. It was common for young men to stand on steps or even on the bumpers between cars, scanning the streets for a ride.

We were in the center of town on Nowy Świat, about to cross the large Jerozolimskie Avenue. The streetcar was just pulling away from the stop, gaining speed, when it jerked while crossing another set of lines. There was a commotion in the front and then, incredibly, a man's scream. "Oh my God," several people by the window cried. I stood to look and immediately collapsed back into my seat. A man lay on the street, his bloody leg sticking up in the air, blood gushing from the place where his foot had been.

After a short stop, our streetcar began to move again. The man sitting next to me started talking. "It's awful what happened to him, but he'll be OK," he told me. "They will take him to a hospital, he'll stop bleeding and later, with an artificial foot, he'll be able to walk." I sat, unable to control the tears rolling down my cheeks. Finally, I looked at the man, took a deep breath, and said, "Yah, he will be OK."

I even tried to smile at him.

Eventually I got out and walked to Mother's room in Aunt Wanda's apartment. Mother listened to my story and we talked for a long while, Mother consoling me, but I knew that I would not be able to forget that bloody leg without a foot for a long time.

Shortly after I started attending the school of the Sisters of Nazareth in the fall of 1940, I realized that I missed physical activity. Before the war, I took part in many sports. To move around Warsaw, I did have to walk a lot. It was at least three kilometers from Alinka's apartment to school, which meant half an hour of brisk walking if the streetcar was not coming or running full speed to the next stop if a streetcar appeared.

Still, I missed more involved physical activity. Above everything else, I wanted to learn to dance.

Those were hard times. My desire for something so trivial embarrassed me, but I decided to try. In my typical way I began asking around, letting people know that I wanted to learn to dance. However, in order to be socially proper, I justified it as a need for exercise. I did not want to sound improper. War or no war, I remember how upset our Senator, Aunt Władka, was when she learned that Ann was playing tennis and competing in shorts! Dancing would have been even more bohemian.

In the meantime, according to the rules of our German occupiers, Alinka's two-room apartment was too big for the four of us. She was ordered to sublease the second room, and consequently rented it to an old family friend, Mecenas Dulemba, an elderly, impoverished lawyer, our mother's good friend and frequent bridge partner from our happy days in Bydgoszcz. He could have bettered his existence had he kowtowed to the Germans' demands. But he stubbornly refused to work as a lawyer under our enemy and was thus barely able to make ends meet. Since childhood, I'd been fond of him; now I confided to him my desire to study dancing. Mr. Dulemba told me about Mrs. Wanda Jeżowska, an acquaintance of his who taught modern dance classes.

During the occupation, German rules labeled dance schools vocational training and permitted them to operate. However, any national music—Chopin, Czajkowski, Paderewski, and other Polish and Slavic composers—was strictly forbidden.

I did not know that Mrs. Wanda had been a leading modern dance instructor in Poland before the war. She taught modern dance in the style of Isadora Duncan.

My beloved dance teacher Pani Wanda

Toward the end of winter in 1940, I went to meet Mrs. Wanda in an old building at the Three Crosses Square. The street was dirty and full of melting snow. It was a challenge to walk without stepping into puddles.

From the street, I entered a house that had been bombed. The back side of the building was obviously usable, and I had to find a caretaker to direct me to the floor where Mrs. Wanda rented a big hall for her classes in "rhythmic and plastic dancing."

I must have been early, for there was nobody there when I arrived. Shortly after, however, Mrs. Wanda came in. She was tall and blond with big blue smiling eyes. After I introduced myself and learned that she was Mrs. Wanda Jeżowska, I eagerly started to tell her how much I wanted to learn to dance.

"I am uncoordinated, but I will do my best to learn."

"What makes you think that you are uncoordinated?" She inquired sincerely.

"I know I am."

"Are you sure?" Mrs. Wanda said.

"I have an older sister who is very coordinated," I said. "She's always told me how clumsy I am."

"And you want to learn to dance?" She could not hold back her smile any longer. "I am sure you will do well."

Years later, Mrs. Wanda told me that she could never forget our first meeting. In my eagerness, I explained that I did not have much money but hoped that my mother would find some spare funds to pay for the classes. I met the rest of her students, most of whom were older than me but still in their teens, and one Mrs. Lidka, who was twenty-something and the mother of a little baby. Lidka was Wanda›s student from before the war in Krakow, where Wanda had her formal dancing school.

Lidka danced with us until about 1943, when she received a notice that her husband had died of pneumonia in a concentration camp. In those days many people received notices of death from pneumonia in the camps. The Germans were very careful to give their bullets or gas chambers a "proper" name.

Our dance attire was black, the only color to which an old swimsuit could be uniformly dyed. Dancing slippers were unobtainable in those days; we could dance barefooted, but the floor was cold and not very smooth. I decided that if I could make a pair of fur slippers for Basia, somehow I could make dancing slippers for myself. Luckily, Ann had a pair of knee-high boots made of horse or calf fur, which were the object of my incredible envy. Her feet and legs were always warm and dry! Ann gave me leftover scraps of leather from her boots, and I made myself a pair of slippers.

As the years passed, Mrs. Wanda became my dear friend and mentor. Eventually, she told me that when I first came to her school, she had a hard time not laughing whenever she looked at me. According to her I was all concentration, moving enthusiastically, my arms and legs flying in every direction. I loved music and dance, but at that time I was still convinced I was very awkward. Nonetheless, I was desperate to prove my sister wrong.

Months later, Mrs. Wanda asked me to come and lead other classes of younger children. I still did not realize that I had become her top student. I thought that she was letting me lead other classes so that I could dance more without extra pay.

Dance became my passion. I did not worry about anything except the music, its expression and interpretation through dance. At the end of every school year, depending on the availability of performance facilities, we had a big production with two or three shows. The shows were exciting and satisfying to the ego, but it was those lessons two or three times a week that gave me something to look forward to and carried me through a miserable daily life full of danger and suffering.

I had As in school, I was dancing my heart out, but there was still a part of me that was neglected and unfulfilled: my singing voice.

Alinka husband John's uncle was a renowned opera voice teacher. I had heard about him, but had never met him. I kept hinting to Alinka that maybe he could teach me. By then, Alinka was preparing to leave Warsaw to wait out the war in the country, where survival was easier. I was afraid that she would leave without calling the professor.

"Just ask him to allow me to try, to audition," I nagged.

Finally, Alinka made the call.

I was scared when I went to my appointment in Professor Czesław Zaremba's studio. I wanted to study voice so badly, but I had no money to pay for lessons. I was only fourteen, and I understood that the acceptable age for professional voice training was around fifteen, even sixteen.

At the studio, I waited in a tiny entry hall while a beautiful soprano sang. She passed me on her way out, and I was invited into the room with the big grand piano. A nice looking older lady sat at the piano.

Master Zaremba greeted me. He was a grey-haired man whose straight posture created an appearance of being well-dressed even though his suit looked worn. His manners were impeccable.

His instructions were very specific, but also very kind. He told me to relax, to put my throat into a yawn-like position and let my voice flow. At first, relaxing felt difficult, but somehow that yawning came easily and my voice emerged. Master Zaremba pushed my voice up and down and finally proclaimed, "Your voice timbre is mezzo soprano with a pretty good range for your age. We can start training now, without waiting for another year or more, because your voice appears to be naturally set."

Despite my excitement at being accepted as a student, my heart sank thinking of the amount of money I would have to pay.

"And," he continued, "since you are Alinka's sister, I would not feel right charging you anything."

I was in seventh heaven, my longtime dream nearly fulfilled. From that day on I went to Master Zaremba's studio once a week. Soon, we developed a fun game. Normally, the pianist played the first note to cue the tone. But once when the Master was talking to the pianist, I started looking at the music sheets in front of me and humming. They stopped talking and the pianist cued me for the song. I was perfectly on tune. Master Zaremba smiled; with a slight shake of his head, he said that I must have perfect pitch in addition to a naturally "set" voice, which would also explain why my tone sounded so clear when I sang as a little girl. I was flattered, but I tried to humbly object to the compliment in the way I had been taught was proper.

"Maybe I hit the right note consistently not because I have perfect pitch but because I know the range of my voice, which allows me to find the right tone."

Perfect pitch is God's great gift, so I did not want to take credit for my ability. The Master only smiled.

While I looked forward to my exciting lessons, surviving the second winter of the war was tough. It seemed even harsher than the first. It was obvious that Alinka and her children would not survive in Warsaw much longer.

In 1941, spring came late to Warsaw. By March, dirty snow still lay on the streets. If we had had coals, we would have made fires to heat our houses. As it was, only at the beginning of May did we start to enjoy warmer weather. We opened windows, letting the sun fill our apartment. I especially enjoyed seeing the sun hit the couch on which I slept. I felt that golden light was pushing the moisture and cold out of my bedding.

When the days got longer, the Germans extended the hours of curfew. The moment we turned on the lights, however, we had to remember to pull down black shades to secure the blackout. One evening when I was alone in the house, I walked into the front room and turned on the lights with the windows still open. Yelling outside instantly made me turn off the lights.

The German patrol had seen our lights blinking on and off. I'd barely managed to close the windows and pull down the shades when I heard German boots on the stairs and loud banging on the front door. Using the doorbell would be too civilized for them, I thought.

Three soldiers entered the apartment as if expecting to find criminals and yelled at me in German. I became very calm and stood very straight.

"*Ich verstehe keine Deutch*," I announced in a contrastingly calm voice.

They swung their arms, motioning in the direction from which the light shone. I walked to the room ahead of them and let them look at the windows, now perfectly covered. The more ferocious they acted, the calmer I became. In my indestructible teenage mentality, I almost enjoyed their frustration. They could not tell me anything, because I could not understand German, and there was no longer a problem, because the windows were covered.

One of the soldiers took out papers and started writing. "Name" he barked. Kordianna Zofia Pomian Srzednicka, I answered. I did not have to add Kordianna and Pomian, but I was having fun.

The patrolman must have managed to write the first three names, but as I suspected, "Srzednicka" was too difficult. I knew he would not lower himself by asking me to write it for him. Instead, he shut his folder and fell silent. I stood, calm and tall, and opened the door, motioning to the exit. I barely moved my head, imagining the queen of England in my situation.

That did it. They actually saluted and said "Auf Wiedersehen" as they left. Again, I moved my head slightly without speaking. *Auf Wiedersehen* meant, "I'll see you again." I did not want that.

That was my first lesson in teaching dignity to our barbarous occupiers.

Alinka and the children must have passed the patrolmen on the way up. When she reached the apartment, she looked petrified.

"What did you do?"

"Nothing!" I said, laughing. "It's what I didn't do that brought them here."

"Stop it; it's not funny," Alinka snapped. The children looked confused by their mother's fear and my laughter. To calm her, I told Alinka that I had briefly switched the lights on and immediately turned them off. But she was still shaken, and cried, "Imagine what could have happened!"

"What *could* have happened?" I asked.

Alinka did not understand that the only way to deal with the Germans was to be calm and dignified and never, never let them see fear. I knew that I was acting bold and risky, but playing by ear worked.

Soon after, John's relatives arranged for Alinka and her children to move to Raba Wyżna, a small village in the mountains. There, her distant relatives Zduń- Wyżna Głowiński lived on the remnants of their estate. Alinka would live nearby in a peasant's home. Living in the country would make it easier for her to get food and fuel, not to mention the possibility of getting additional supplies from her relatives.

The snow was barely melting when we packed up Alinka and her children and sent them by train to Raba Wyżna. Ann and Mother moved back into Alinka's apartment, and the three of us started living together again.

I'd had very little contact with Ann during the previous two years of the war. Her friend, Stefa Skotnicka, had also came to Warsaw. Stefa had lost her father, General Skotnicki, during the battle at Kutno in 1939. Like Ann, Stefa was twenty years old and frequently overacted out of a spirit of youthful independence.

Stefa was lucky enough to have a rich uncle, Lolek Wickenhagen, the owner of a big estate where he lived with his wife and handsome eighteen-year-old son. My naïve little self was very impressed with Stefa's father and secretly wished to one day have his son as a boyfriend. I still felt the need to imitate my big sister Ann; now I wished to be like Stefa as well.

Lolek made no secret of the income from his estate. Other land owners had oppressive quotas and were barely able to survive; Lolek had a *treuhender*, who was also getting richer, but Lolek was able to bribe him and "everybody was happy". In general the occupying Germans were very bribable if they felt safe.

Frequently, Lolek journeyed to Warsaw, where Stefa and Ann helped him arrange lodging and fun parties with his lady friends. It bothered me to hear about it, but the girls claimed that if Lolek's wife knew, it must be okay. In Lolek's defense, he was financially helpful to Stefa and used the profits from his estate to aid many other people in difficult situations.

One night Ann, Stefa, Stefa's brother Stach, and a group of their friends were trying to arrange a party. They were all in their twenties. I was almost fifteen. I remember only the beginning of this party, for I tried to act very grown-up, and in the process of showing that I could hold my vodka I got drunk as a skunk.

By the time my mother realized that they were giving me booze it was already too late, so she just watched. I slept it off, and the next day Mother told me simply, "Now you know what alcohol can do. You do not remember anything from yesterday. I hope you will learn to drink like a lady."

In a way, I did; I never got drunk again. I learned to recognize the feeling of having had too much to drink and was always careful to stop in time. Fortunately, I had a strong head or hollow leg and could drink a lot without any effect.

A short time later, we received an official announcement from the German occupiers that the two-room apartment with the little kitchen and bathroom was once more too big for the three of us. We had to take a tenant for our second room, and soon Mrs. Maria Stamm moved in. Mecenas Dulemba had announced, shortly before Alinka left Warsaw, that he too would be leaving. The next day, he disappeared with no further explanation. His manner was always eccentric, a quality the war exacerbated.

1941: Daily Life Under German Occupation

Day after day, we were painfully reminded of Germany's hostility towards Poland. The Germans relentlessly exploited our fertile soil and beautiful agricultural lands and forests.

For centuries, the Germans had been the aggressors; Poles and other Slavic peoples—excepting the Russians—were predominantly peace-loving, gentle people. Our love of freedom consistently stood in the way of Germany's imperial intentions. Since Poles would rather be dead than oppressed, we always tried to defend ourselves.

By the spring of 1941, most of Europe was crushed beneath Hitler's boot. In every occupied country, Hitler managed to find a group of collaborators. Poland had no such group, and for that reason we were frequently called "a country without Quisling." Quisling was the infamous Norwegian traitor who collaborated with the Germans.

When the Germans entered Poland in 1939, many members of the Polish government and military, especially the Air Forces, escaped to London. At home, many national leaders managed to avoid immediate arrest and stayed hidden using false documents. Hitler's fury spilled down to his subordinates, who started governing Poland through fear and oppression.

Hitler and his henchmen had brainwashed their nation and expected to do the same in the countries they occupied. For their propaganda to work, the Germans had to cut off our communication with the world. The only news Poles were allowed was propaganda printed by German newspapers.

Before World War I, Poles had lived under the Prussians for 150 years. Under Hitler, it did not take long for Poland to adapt and get organized once more. Instead of letting the Germans confiscate them, some radios and guns were hidden and kept in the country. Soon Poles had their own clandestine news printed and distributed, most of it information picked up from British radio broadcasts. Military resistance organized under the name *Armia Krajowa*, "The Country's Army" or the AK.

Gradually, the Polish citizenry developed unwritten but uniform rules of behavior. Polish solidarity was unquestionable. We could trust each other, but we also knew that we could not take anything for granted. There was always a very real danger of someone being arrested, interrogated, and disclosing under torture everything the Germans wanted to know. Consequently, we did not talk about things which could do damage to anyone. It was safer not to know specifics.

In addition, many Germans who lived on Polish soil before the war were now serving their beloved *Fuhrer* as spies. As they were able to speak Polish without an accent, they could easily pretend to be Poles. The German Gestapo tried to use these persons to infiltrate the Polish underground. Fortunately, individuals who wanted to get our confidence tended to brag about their AK and underground connections—a dead giveaway that they were enemies.

By 1941, most of Poland's Jews were already crowded into ghettos. Some tried to prolong their questionable "well-being" by serving the Germans as Capos. Others tried to save their lives for a short while by denouncing the Polish people who had hidden them. We had to be quick to learn who to trust ... and who might betray us.

What crimes were the Germans so eager to discover and punish? The most severe punishment, for belonging to the AK resistance army, usually resulted in immediate torture (to find out the names of other conspirators) and death. Involvement in academic education, whether one was a student or a teacher, was also a severe offense. Hiding Jews was highly punishable. Other crimes included possession of anything forbidden, like radios, guns, old Polish literature or the nationally revered music of Chopin.

Farmers had heavy quotas of goods which they were required to deliver to the German authorities. Whether they had a good crop or a bad one, they had to deliver. Businesses were allowed to stay open only if they produced something the Germans needed. They also had material production quotas. Again, bigger land estates and businesses had German supervisors, those so-called *treuhenders*. Many of these men were anything but trustworthy

It was interesting to see how quickly our population adjusted to these living conditions and how we managed to navigate that labyrinth of German rules and adjust to what appeared to be "normal life under occupation."

Though we did not discuss forbidden, dangerous subjects, news circulated with incredible speed nonetheless. Underground newspapers carried updates from around the world, clarification of

German propaganda, and warnings of anticipated German actions. Sometimes we were warned that the Germans would intensify their efforts to "catch" people for labor camps. At those times, whenever we saw a group of German army trucks driving through the city, we fled immediately, for we knew they would stop, block the streets and load everybody caught in the middle onto the trucks for transport.

Similar dangers existed on the trains, whether the passengers were civilians traveling from one town to another or food smugglers transporting their wares from villages to cities to be sold on the black market.

Whoever had a Polish newspaper read it quickly, remembered as much as possible, passed it on to the next safe person, or destroyed it. This was deadly contraband, though the Germans caught such materials relatively seldom. We knew how to play safe.

Warsaw people are known for their witty sense of humor. The harder the Germans pressed us, the more we laughed—though not without sarcasm and contempt directed at our oppressor. While in public, people learned to spread news without incriminating themselves or a friend. There was a common saying, "Jedna pani powiedziała" (one lady said), which was soon abbreviated to JPP. It would have been difficult to arrest somebody for repeating gossip from an unknown lady!

At the same time, the possibility of arrest and interrogation was constantly on our minds. We would rather talk about something risqué to a complete stranger in the streetcar, knowing he or she would not be able to identify us a few minutes later, than talk to someone we knew could later implicate us under interrogation or torture.

Our daily lives frequently sounded grim. Many facts *were* grim, but there was also lots of humor. We needed laughter like medicine. Our humorous heroes were the young newspaper boys who sold the official German-sponsored newspapers. These boys frequently yelled out news—in Polish, of course—which had nothing to do with what was written in the paper. The Germans never admitted to any losses, but whenever the London BBC issued news over the radio that the Germans had suffered a defeat, the newspaper boys would yell: "Cheap mincemeat made of kapusta!" Kapusta means cabbage. The boys preferred not to call out the familiar name for Germans (*kraut*), which the Germans could recognize.

Whenever German soldiers closed city blocks to catch people for the labor camps, the newspaper boys effectively warned people, running in the opposite direction, waving newspapers in the air, yelling, "Lapanka, lapanka! (catching, catching)," and the name of the streets. People would run in the opposite direction, avoiding the German trap.

One afternoon I was walking towards Three Cross Plaza for my dance class. I had only one block to go when a little boy ran in my direction from around the corner, yelling, "ŁAPANKA, ŁAPANKA ON THREE CROSSES!"

In the middle of the street, a streetcar was moving in the opposite direction. Several people had the same reaction as I did. We ran to the middle of the street and jumped into the moving car. Two teenagers and I were aiming at the same back door. One of them moved behind to allow me to jump ahead of him. I was careful to follow the rules: run with the streetcar, grab the handle with your right hand, jump onto the first step and immediately follow to the next step to make space for the next person.

As the streetcar took a corner by the fateful plaza and continued to drive away, everybody in the car was able to catch a glimpse of "the łapanka." Now they excitedly compered their observations. From a distance they all had seen the Germans corralling people from the side streets to the center of the plaza and loading them into trucks. Those of us who had jumped into the streetcar going in the opposite direction at the next corner were lucky to have been late getting to the fateful plaza.

For Poles, the name of the game was to double-cross Germans wherever and whenever we could—and to always rise above their attempts to harass us. On the streets or streetcars, whenever we were face to face, we gave the Germans calm, dignified looks, never smiling or showing fear. On the contrary, it was the Germans who learned not to venture into side streets alone for fear that they would wind up without their guns (if they were Army soldiers) or with holes in their heads if they were SS or Gestapo. The Polish AK respected the Army; SS and Gestapo were not felt to deserve any consideration.

We lived in constant danger of being caught on the streets and sent to a labor camp—if we were lucky—or a concentration camp if there was any suspicion of our political involvement. At the same time, we had to live our daily life, as abnormal as it was, and pretend to ourselves that it was normal.

We hadn't heard from Aunt Władka since the beginning of the war. In September, during the siege of Warsaw, she served as an advisor to President S. Starzyński, but from the start of the occupation all news about her ceased. Since she was a senator and involved in the Polish government, we expected that she would continue her work in the AK command—unless she managed to escape to London.

I had never met my aunt before. During the summer of 1938,

she invited my sister Ann to accompany her to Yugoslavia. I wished I were older and could receive similar recognition, but I did not brood about it. For her high school graduation, Ann also received from Aunt Władka a signet ring bearing our family coat of arms. I was told that I would receive mine when I graduated.

In the spring of 1941, Aunt Władka suddenly contacted us; she wanted to see me and Ann. I remember visiting her several times in an apartment in Mokotów, a southern district of Warsaw. Aunt Władka was an impressive person. I was already 5'5" tall; my aunt was much taller, with very straight posture and a head held high. She was Srzednicka through and through.

"I always loved and respected Tadeusz, your father," she told us, "and I am concerned for you, my brother's daughters."

I appreciated her concern, and felt grateful that she was seeking our company.

During our afternoon gatherings, Aunt Władka would talk about political subjects, obviously attempting to educate us. We expressed our fear that the Germans could have arrested her as soon as they entered Warsaw. She laughed.

"I did not wait for them to come get me. I moved out of my apartment on Szuch Avenue immediately. You may know that Szuch was the avenue where most high government and diplomatic individuals lived." Aunt Władka did not have to be warned by Polish intelligence to know the Germans would try to arrest her upon entering the city. For safety, she decided to leave all her important papers and memorabilia stashed in the apartment. She removed a few bricks from the wall, hid her things inside and mortared the bricks back into place.

At the time when we spoke, that beautiful district of Warsaw was occupied by German dignitaries. My aunt laughed and said that if anything survived the war, it would be that area. Then she looked at us with a smile.

"We do not know what happened to Mrs. Macieszyna, do we? I am glad to have such a difficult name as Srzednicki," she said, implying that her current documents were in her maiden and our family name.

I enjoyed these visits. My aunt prepared a meal for the three of us, and while she was busy in her kitchenette, she gave us clandestine newspapers to read. Seeing my concerned look, she assured me, "Don't worry, I do have my secure hiding places."

During one of those visits she gave us several pieces of clothing, silk nightgowns she'd collected while traveling the world. I received a Yugoslavian mountain man's jacket, which became my prize possession. It was made of heavy white woolen felt with wide red embroidery running along all the edges of the material. I loved wearing that unique and colorful jacket, which covered most of my rather drab clothing.

I wanted to talk to Aunt Władka more, but she chose Ann for closer contact. Besides the fact that they spent several weeks of vacation together, Ann looked more like our father, whereas I was the spitting image of our mother. Hence Ann was closer to Aunt Władka; there was a well-known joke about competition and a certain animosity between these ladies, both so dear to my father.

After several visits, our aunt announced that she might not call us again for a while. She planned to be away. Obviously we did not ask nor did she volunteer any information about where she would be traveling. We bid our goodbyes, telling each other to stay safe.

"Please contact us whenever you will be able to," we pleaded.

But it wasn't until after World War II ended that I learned the rest of her incredible story.

Seemingly overnight, there were more Germans and German transports passing through Warsaw by truck and rail—everything going
east. Rumors started buzzing among the Poles on the streets: "Can
Hitler possibly be so stupid?" "He has a Napoleon complex and delusions of grandeur! "Didn't he learn from history?"

He did not. On June 22, 1941, Hitler attacked Soviet Russia.
Once more the papers were full of glory and claims of quick German
victories. But we Poles were exuberant. We knew a repetition of
1812, when Napoleon was defeated in Russia, was in the offing. We
were certain that this was the beginning of Hitler's end. Besides, we
had learned from history that there is nothing better than watching
two cruel neighbors fight each other. We hoped they would fight as
long and as hard as possible.

Our spirits and hopes were raised.

Summer in Raba Wyżna

Alinka's children Basia and Maciuś pose on the rubble near their apartment in Warsaw. They were happy to escape the ruined, war-torn city for the life in the country

When Alinka and her children left, we promised her that during the summer vacation from school I would visit. In addition to companionship, I would get fresh food, sunshine and experience the relative safety of the mountain countryside.

Traveling by rail was neither comfortable nor safe during the war, but at fifteen years of age it was exciting and adventurous. Early in the afternoon one summer day, I arrived in Raba. Alinka and the children were waiting. We hugged and kissed, happy to be reunited. Alinka brought a little wagon to carry my suitcases, and we walked the two kilometers to the farmer's house where they lived.

From the railroad station, we passed through the village, passing the manor house in the distance. Paved roads grew progressively narrower and gave way to dirt. The few peasants we passed smiled and greeted us warmly.

Finally we came to a house that stood alone on the far side of the village. Through the porch, we entered the spacious kitchen. I met the owner, Mrs. Makowska, and her nine-year-old daughter, Danuta. Alinka's room was to the left of the big kitchen. It was spacious, though it had to serve as a bedroom, dining room and washroom, not to mention a play room for the children.

To the right of the kitchen was another room, rented to a lady that like Alinka lived there with her four-year-old daughter. Mrs. Makowska told us that if I wanted an empty room in the attic, I would be welcome to it; she wouldn't charge me anything, as it was unfurnished but for a bed.

I liked having my own room. It had a pitched roof with a window overlooking a mountain spring and willows. I hung my clothing on a few hangers and the nails in the slanted ceiling and went down to exchange the latest news from Warsaw with Alinka.

115

Alinka told me about the Głowinski family, whom I would soon meet. They were John's distant relatives and the owners of the estate. Like everywhere else in occupied Poland, the Germans left the Głowinskis only a "remnant" of their land and assigned a German administrator who controlled what they could keep and what had to be relinquished. But in spite of this severe oversight and the substantial quotas on farmers, it was still easier to survive and get essential food in the country.

We sat on the stairs of the porch, looking at the mountains, the fields and a big stream running past the Makowskis' property, basking in the afternoon sunshine. During my vacations in Meczyszcze, I learned to love the mountains. Getting out of the flat lands surrounding Warsaw, and escaping the crowded city, its noise and the constantly visible oppressive Germans made the view even more enjoyable.

Alinka told me that in the last few days, several young people had arrived from Warsaw to visit the Głowinski family. Some of them stayed in the manor house and others, like Alinka, in various farmers' houses. Alinka also told me that a few days prior to my arrival she had mentioned to them that her sister was coming. Though I was called Zosia, my real first name was Kordianna. They liked this name so much that they decided to refuse to call me Zosia.

"Zosiu, I hope you don't mind that I told them about Kordianna, do you?" Alinka said, a worried expression on her face.

"Of course not," I said. "The only thing I hated was Ann calling me Kordula and making fun of me. But I was proud that Father wanted me to have the same name as the hero of his favorite Słowacki poem."

"Ann did pounce on you." Alinka shook her head in bewilderment. "I wonder why."

"Who knows? At least she stopped hitting me when I got stronger than her."

Alinka started laughing. "I can imagine how much stronger you are now with all the dancing you do."

We were deep in conversation when we noticed two young men approaching on the pathway. Alinka burst into laughter: "You are going to be looked over by the special delegation."

Felix and Joe were seventeen and fifteen-year-old brothers pretending to have something to ask Alinka. They acted as if my being there was accidental. They would never admit that they had come to meet me.

Alinka introduced us and we exchanged a few sentences. After they left, Alinka teased me that, judging from the expressions on their faces, I had passed the "inspection."

Within a day or two, Andrew, the nephew of the other lady living in the Makowski's house, came to visit. Andrew, whom we called "Andrzej" in Polish, was tall, handsome and looked and acted older than his fourteen years. Within a few days Andrew and I became good friends. We were discreet, and the rest of the group never learned that Andrew and I, besides living in the same house, were also exchanging gossip and secrets.

The manor house and the estate belonging to the Głowinski family were presided over by the matriarch, old Mrs. Zduń. Mr. Głowinski, her son-in-law, had died recently in a horrible tree-cutting accident. The men were carrying a tree on their shoulders, with Mr. Głowiński the last in line. The other men were unaware that when the time came to throw the tree down, Mr. Głowiński had the tree on the wrong shoulder. The weight knocked him down, crushing his head.

There were four Głowiński children. John, the oldest boy, was probably nineteen; Rose, even older than John, was out of our "young" company. Anton, eighteen, and Teresa, who was fifteen like me, had constant chores assigned by Grandmother Zduń. Their cousins, the Zoll family, were also staying in the manor house; they had recently come from Warsaw. Eighteen-year-old Ted was too old to mix with us. Felix and Joe, who initially came to inspect me, also had a younger sister, Jan, who at just thirteen was a barely tolerated "youngster."

Other young visitors arrived in the village: Danuta, the teacher's daughter, and John Erenberg, seventeen, who worked in the local wood mill. His mother, Mrs. Erenberg, was Alinka's dear friend and an intelligent, pleasant child psychiatrist. I loved listening to Mrs. Ehrenberg's child-rearing wisdom.

Within a day or two, I had met everybody. Alinka summarized the situation nicely: I, the newly-arrived Kordianna, was fifteen. Seven of the boys were between fourteen and eighteen. Most girls were younger than thirteen or older than eighteen. Consequently I had all the boys to myself.

Two years earlier, I would have imitated Ann and tried to play grownup by looking for adoring admirers. By the time I came to Raba, however, I treated boys like good companions who were stronger and more fun for me to play with than the girls.

Soon, like all teenagers in the world, special bonds began to develop between individual pairs of boys and girls, what we call in Polish "sympatia". In time, Felix became my sympatia. However, it was the closely-knit group friendship that made our relationships so special. We hiked in the mountains, gathered wild raspberries and strawberries, and sometimes rose very early in the morning to hunt for mushrooms. There was a belief that mushrooms are hard to gather later in the day, because they are difficult to spot. I knew how to distinguish between the kinds of mushrooms that grew in the mountains, and was a good gatherer. Whenever I brought a basket full of Stone, Rydz or Champignon mushrooms home, Alinka was thrilled and would make a delicious meal for us. When we picked wild berries, we ate them right off the bushes, but I would also bring a full container home to Basia, Mathew and Alinka.

There was no ignoring the fact that all of us young ones from Warsaw were malnourished and hungry, hoping to get healthier, better food in the mountains. But getting it was part of the fun. John Erenberg's friend, Jack, taught us how to catch crawfish. He was a good scout who had acquired many survival skills and was willing to teach us his tricks. We would walk into a stream and, in the areas where the water was calmer and darker, use a small piece of stinky bait on a string. When the crawfish grabbed the bait, we would pull out the string and add them to our basket. We only had to ensure that no crawfish mistook our bare toes for the bait.

Jack also knew how to catch trout with his bare hands. I composed myself to try it and managed to catch one fish. Triumphant, I lifted it up—only to drop it the moment it wiggled. I wasn't that steady.

We ate all our meals in our respective homes. After breakfast I usually played with Basia and Mathew or did house chores. After lunch, Andrew and I would often go to the manor house, where Andrew dutifully practiced piano and I danced in the big salon to the sound of his playing. Or in other part of the house, I helped Grandma Zduń take care of villagers who were ill.

As there was no doctor for miles, the villagers came to the "old lady heiress" with a variety of health problems. I do not remember exactly how Grandma Zduń acquired her medical knowledge, but she knew a lot. With a little common sense and an understanding of basic hygiene, I was also able to help. She complimented me behind my back to Alinka, but to my face she was rather curt. She definitely did not like my attractive looks, especially when her grandsons were around. Andrew and I had our laughs about it in private. The boys told him that grandma was adamant about having big dowries come to John and Anton from their future wives. The estate needed a big infusion of capital. To ensure that they are not interested in me, the poor girl, Grandma Zduń constantly found urgent jobs for them. To our gang it did not matter, as they were too old anyway, but poor John and Anton were jealous of our fun times.

In contrast, as my *sympatia*, Felix tried to be around me constantly. Andrew and I teased him whenever it was time to go home for dinner. Andrew would call, "Kordianka, let's go home." If there was extra time, Felix tried to walk with us, but Andrew kept suggesting that he take his sister Jan back for dinner at the manor house. We had fun playing games with these little jealousies.

Poor Danuta, the village teacher's daughter, became the butt of our jokes, for she acted like a doll, desperately trying to be popular with the boys. Whenever the new hay was brought to the barn, we climbed the rafters to jump onto the fresh piles. It was hard to act like a doll with hay in your hair!

One day, we decided to go to the cemetery after dark. The boys included Jan and Danuta. To start with, we told spooky stories. Whenever one of us got an attentive audience, somebody else would sneak out and hide behind the graves. Our repertoire was endless. Making strange noises and jumping out from behind the graves at unsuspecting passersby were the most common tricks.

That night, to their brothers' delight, the poor girls got scared and never came with us after dark again. Why was I okay? I was Felix's *sympatia*, yes, but above all I was their very good friend and buddy. Our friendship was special.

That summer, one special incident influenced my life, certainly for the remainder of the war—and possibly forever.

Our group was occasionally joined by a brother, Anek, and sister, Oluta, who lived in Rabka, a well-known mountain resort located on the other side of the mountain pass. Anek and Oluta visited us, occasionally coming by train or by hiking seven to ten kilometers through the pass. I knew them fairly well and liked them both.

One day, Alinka asked me to get some raspberries for dinner. It was late in the afternoon; with nobody around, I went to pick them alone. I hiked up the mountain to what I knew was a good area for raspberries. I was high above the village, which lay to the south of me. The afternoon sun soaked the whole area with orange rays. I enjoyed being there at the edge of the woods, gathering the juicy wild fruit.

Suddenly, I heard someone whistling the familiar tune of the *Marseillaise*. After the first part of the melody the whistling stopped. I did not hesitate; the game was too good not to pick it up. I whistled the continuation of the melody, stopped, sat down quietly in a thicket, and waited, wondering who would come out.

After a while Anek walked into the clearing. I pretended not to see him. He was startled when he spotted me. After an initial greeting he asked casually if I had heard someone whistle the *Marseillaise*.

"Yes, I did hear something like that," I said, answering as if it was irrelevant.

The poor boy had to keep his secret, but he needed my assistance. Finally, I stopped playing games and made it clear that I realized he was on some kind of mission. Reluctantly, Anek told me he was supposed to meet a Frenchman who'd escaped from a German POW camp and was being smuggled across the border to Czechoslovakia and then farther south. Anek's job was to lead him to the Czech border.

We didn't find the Frenchman, but I told Anek that I would like to join the Polish resistance. Anek promised to take it to his superiors.

Prior to our meeting, I'd struggled with the idea of joining the AK and had decided that there was really no question of whether or not I would enlist. Helping our organization fight the Germans was every Pole's duty, and I felt that I was old and smart enough to fulfill my part. Like many of my actions, my decision to enlist was instinctive and practical. I just had to wait to meet somebody whom I knew without doubt was in the Polish underground.

Years later, when I learned about other German occupations and the conditions those occupied peoples endured, I realized how differently other countries and populations reacted to similar conditions. The Polish spirit, mentality, or temperament was quite specific, perhaps because it was shaped by our past, our history.

Prior to World War I, Poles spent 150 years dealings with hardships imposed by cruel occupiers, and this led my people to develop unique survival methods. Perhaps our strongest characteristic is our incredible loyalty to our country and our people. While we joke that during peacetime, every two Poles form three political parties, during war we are a solid block. There were no denunciations or betrayals.

For myself, I had an intuitive ability to understand people and sense what they were thinking. I could have been fooled by a boy, but not in a political sense. When I met Anek on that mountain, there was no question in my mind that he was in the midst of a political action. And simultaneously, Anek knew that he could trust me. One of the circumstances that reassured us both was not how much we talked, but how little.

Summer vacation drew to a close. Within a few days of one another, my buddies and I traveled back to Warsaw to start a new school year. Our friendships prevailed. In Warsaw we stayed in close contact, eagerly awaiting our next summer in the mountains.

Nobody ever learned about my special connection with Anek; he and the rest of our vacation group did not mix in Warsaw. Nor did any of my friends learn that Anek was a member of the Polish resistance or that I had joined his unit.

Within a short time, however, Anek came by for a chat with me. I introduced him to my mother as a new friend from Rabka. We excused ourselves and went for a walk.

"I described you to my superior, and he agreed to you joining us."

"Thank you; I'll do my best," I promised.

"I'll be your direct contact, and obviously we'll never say anything over the phone," he said.

"I know that much," I said, laughing at the ridiculous idea of trusting anything to the telephones, which were listened in on by the Germans.

Anek did not say anything about how I was investigated prior to approval by AK, though I'm sure I was, and in depth.

I doubt if my mother could have guessed that I was working for the underground, for I never gave her any reasons to suspect me of such activities. Ann always acted secretive, avoiding telling us where she was going or whom she was seeing. In contrast, I was like an open book, except ... not everything you "read" was exactly true.

In AK, the members of the Polish underground did not know each other's true names or any personal facts about one another. We all worked under pseudonyms. Anek was the only person in our unit who knew my real name and address.

How was my name chosen? At home, I said, some friends call me Kora, which is short for Kordianna. I played my girly game – imitating Ann – saying that I would know who was calling the moment I hear them asking for Zosia, Kordianna—or Kora.

Becoming My Own Person at 15

Upon returning from summer vacation in the mountains, I felt energized by my new friendships. I felt so appreciated; more importantly, I knew that each person cherished the closeness between us. Most of them returned to their homes in Warsaw for the school year. Only the Głowiński family stayed in Raba Wyżna year-round. John was learning to administer the estate; Rose had graduated from high school the previous year, and Anton was working on his last year of high school with a private tutor.

My new friends and I kept in touch, getting together as often as our schedules allowed. Occasionally somebody convinced his or her parents to allow us to gather during the weekend and dance to music played on the gramophone. If we were lucky and the parents of a particular friend had extra money, we would even get some refreshments.

I never had parties in our apartment. My friends would frequently stop by, but three extra people made a crowd in our one-room apartment.

After vacation, I once again found myself in the company of Ann and Stefa. I fell back into my earlier inability to be myself and started to imitate Ann and her friends.

Stefa was a smoker. She found it funny when I attempted to smoke as well. Even before the war, whenever she came by and Mother was not at home, Stefa offered me cigarettes. Stupidly, I was too embarrassed to refuse.

In Warsaw, I started showing off my smoking among my summertime buddies. It was already winter, and we'd taken to ice skating. I made a bet with Joe about the weather, a "discretion" or discretionary bet. Such bets are not specific. The winner can ask the losing individual for anything he or she chooses. I lost, and Joe asked me to stop fooling around with cigarettes and to never again put one in my mouth. Secretly, I was elated. Now I could stop pretending that I liked playing with that stinky white tube.

Stopping my play with cigarettes was almost symbolic. For so many years, I'd tried to imitate Ann, to be more like her in order to win her acceptance—to no avail. Now I did not have to play that game anymore. I was no longer her little sister, symbolically and physically. I had become taller in more ways than one. At home, I still responded to Zosia, but I also accepted my real first name, Kordianna. Ann's teasing did not matter anymore. I enjoyed the friendship of all the boys I had met that summer, and our common affection proved more valuable than Ann's unfair playing with her various boyfriends' emotions.

In addition, while I should have known that I was an exceptionally good student at the Sisters of Nazareth school, I did not think about it and the fact was never stated outright. Quietly, I was given special considerations and treatments by the teachers and the Sister Director—not to mention the good grades I earned.

During my dance and voice lessons, I continued to thrive. And my secret work with the Polish underground fulfilled my patriotic duty. I learned the "drill," carrying guns and messages, being at designated places perfectly on time and always blending in with the crowd.

Maybe, just maybe, I was starting to enjoy growing up and being me.

Besides winning the bet and making me stop smoking, Joe initiated another project for all of us. Joe's father had a boathouse by the Vistula River and Joe, with the other boys, decided to build a sailboat. Somehow they scrounged wood and started building.

When the time came to attach the sides, they had to find wood screws, which were scarce and hard to get. During the war, metal objects were impossible to obtain, for the German military took all they could.

The wood screws gave us a perfect outlet for our youthful daring and mischief.

Warsaw's streetcars were operated by the Germans, who made money by collecting fares. To ride a streetcar and not pay was thus seen as a patriotic act. Now we did the Germans one better. Polish street cars seats were made of one-inch wooden slats. Whenever we went to the boat house, we would take screwdrivers with us and remove the screws from the seats while riding the streetcar. By the time we were on the other side of the bridge, we had pockets full of wood screws for Joe's sailboat.

Were we doing wrong? In religion classes in the Sisters of Nazareth school, we had many philosophical discussions with the priest. He was a young man, and I liked his light way of teaching us the otherwise heavy subject of *propedeutyca philosophiae*. He encouraged all kinds of questions.

In our discussions, the Germans were assumed to be an evil force that we would fight in any way we could. Once we asked whether it was a sin to cheat and not pay the streetcar fare. The priest's answer was specific: "If the controller catches you it is a sin."

We all loved our religion lessons. And following this logic, stealing screws from the streetcars was not a sin as we were never caught.

At this time, I also had a nice group of friends from previous years in Warsaw. Joe Stummer was my cousin, whom I befriended when Mother lived in the apartment of his mother, Aunt Wanda. Two of Joe's buddies happened to live in the same apartment block as Alinka. Being our neighbors, Adam and Stefan stopped by often, especially Adam. He had a hard time adjusting after the sudden death of his sister, who was killed by the Germans for daring to be educated.

Open as a book without secrets, I always let my friends know my schedule and the days and times when I was likely to be home. One day I came home from dancing lessons to find Joe, Stefan and Adam playing bridge with my mother. They immediately explained that they had come earlier, hoping to find me home. Seeing their sheepish faces, I knew better than to confront their obvious lie. When I entered, Mother offered to let me replace her. I took one look at the boys' faces and declined, knowing it would have spoiled their fun.

After they left, my mother told me the rest of the story. The three guys had come early in the afternoon, asking for me. Mother told them that I wouldn't be home for quite a while. To her surprise, they asked whether they could wait for me, for they were hoping to play bridge. Mother was known for being a terrific player. She got the message. When she offered to substitute as the fourth, they jumped at the offer so eagerly that Mother had a hard time not laughing.

After that incident, the boys played bridge—or rather, got bridge lessons—from Mother several more times. They gave my mother a sweet nickname and liked her a lot. From that day forth I teased Mother and the boys, saying that I was always afraid that my older sister Ann would snitch my boyfriends, but my mother?

This is my fondest memory of those days.

The foul fall weather of 1941 again made our lives difficult. Rain, cold and the promise of another joyless Christmas was depressing. But then, unexpectedly, we got an early Christmas present.

On December 7, 1941, the German papers burst with victorious tidings after their third Axis partner, Japan, attacked Pearl Harbor. German propaganda claimed this strike had annihilated the American Navy. Hitler's venomous hatred for Americans and the pride the Nazis took in Japan's actions was seemingly endless.

Despite Germany's best efforts, the news of the Pearl Harbor attack thrilled us. We also learned that the Germans had declared war on America; the United States did not even have to declare war on Germany to become involved in the war.

"History will repeat itself," buzzed the conversation in the streets. "It will be just like World War I. This will be the end of World War II."

There was no doubt in our minds and hearts. Thank God for America!

But still, Christmas came and went. The little girl in my heart had no sparkle in her eyes. We were lucky to put an extra bucket of coal in the oven to keep warm while eating our tiny Vilia supper. In those war years our eyes did not glisten, and we had to be stoic and strong to help each other endure.

As the year came to a close, I started to form a group of friends I'd never dreamt of possessing. My dance teacher, Mrs. Wanda, periodically held gatherings in her apartment near the Poniatowski Bridge. One day she invited Ann and me.

I remember two special individuals from those gatherings. One was a musical genius, a pianist who had been performing since the age of nine. To my fifteen-year-old eyes, he was old. From my age today, I realize he was a young man, only in his thirties.

In Mrs. Wanda's apartment, he played piano for us. His virtuosity was fabulous, his interpretations inspiring. He enhanced the performance with tidbits of information about the composers or the pieces he played. Mrs. Wanda's small apartment soaked up his music in its wall hangings and rugs; the sound echoed in our hungry hearts. I loved being there and being able to listen to that great piano player. Only the approaching curfew hour could force us to leave.

There was another individual whose name I do not remember. We called him the "beard-man" because of his unusual beard. He also played piano, but unlike the other virtuoso, he'd never learned to read music and played only by ear. The Beard-Man was an anthropologist who traveled around the world before the war, going to the most primitive of places. He shared with us stories about his travels and the music and customs of people from faraway lands.

Occasionally the Beard-Man substituted for our regular accompanist at the dance studio. On those occasions we danced to satisfy his descriptions of the lands he conjured up in Mrs. Wanda's imagination. We recreated African stomping dances, Tahitian and Hawaiian hulas, and many others.

I felt happy and honored to be included amongst these gifted artists, and never thought of asking why I was so privileged. I knew that Ann was included only because she was my sister and though I did not understand why I was invited, it helped me to feel more secure during those tumultuous war years.

Spring Comes to Warsaw

Early in the spring of 1942, the Germans evicted all residents of modern apartment buildings, including the apartment where we lived, declaring those buildings "German only." The German authorities assigned us a two-room apartment in the center of town on Oboźna Street, and stipulated that we sublease the second room. We chose to keep living with Mrs. Maria Stamm.

Our new apartment was in a perfect location next to the main thoroughfare, called *Krakowskie Przedmieście* (Cracovia Suburb), and across from the church of the Holy Cross. Our apartment was the only building on the block. It was like an island in a triangular intersection, allowing us to walk out into two different streets.

At that time, Ann was working as a waitress in a restaurant called Fregata. Fregata was run by a mysterious middle-aged woman. She was of Ukrainian descent and was collaborating with the Germans; it was well-known that she would employ only waitresses from the higher echelons of society. Lolek Wickenhagen's influence secured Ann the job.

For some reason, the Germans tolerated many restaurants in Warsaw, which they themselves frequented, all of which operated using black market materials and charging high prices. Fregata was one of the better restaurants, and Ann was happy to work there, expecting good tips to be added to the costly meals. Waitresses were also allowed one of the cheaper meals while they were at work. How cheap or how good the meal was depended on the chef's attitude toward that particular waitress. Ann knew how to treat the kitchen staff well and was frequently awarded with a good piece of meat hidden under the blob of potatoes.

One day, a handsome young man came to dinner and was seated in Ann's section. A few days later, he came again and asked to be seated at one of Ann's tables. Doctor George was a very pleasant person, and I was not surprised that eventually he became Ann's new boyfriend.

I liked everything about George. He was handsome, very well-dressed, and had a great sense of humor. He was in his late twenties but walked with a cane; whenever he visited us, he pretended to be a decrepit, coughing old man. Mother laughed at his antics and enjoyed his company as much as I did.

George was a plastic surgeon and worked in one of the Warsaw hospitals, which like all public institutions was under strict German supervision. George spoke fluent German and enjoyed it immensely when he was able to manipulate his German bosses. He told us all kinds of stories, always making fun of the occupying forces.

He lived with his parents in a big apartment house less than a block away from our place. Luckily for him and his parents, their house and all their pre-war possessions remained intact. George also had an apartment near the hospital where he stayed whenever his hospital duties ran into the night. On his free evenings he came to visit us after dinner. He had an all-night pass and could move about freely after curfew.

However, walking on the streets after dark exposed him to a variety of dangers. He was often stopped by the German patrols; occasionally, he encountered drunks or criminals who preferred to move by night. George knew a martial art called jujutsu and could defend himself in close combat, but he claimed he preferred using his cane to keep aggressors at a distance.

Our apartment house, like most other houses, was locked after curfew. Since we lived on the ground floor, George came up with a great idea to avoid walking through the gate, which would have to be opened by the night watchman. Whenever George turned the corner to our street, he whistled a signal, which sounded like a twelve-tone chromatic scale. Immediately, we turned off the lights, lifted the black window shade and opened the window. George climbed in and pulled down the cover. When we turned the lights back on, he would start his funny antics, pretending to be an old man who had difficulty stepping down with his cane from the window sill.

Naturally, George was most interested in Ann, but he seemed to genuinely enjoy my mother's and my company. And Mother needed every bit of laughter and relaxation life could produce. In the years since the war had begun, she had never regained her full health. She was very underweight; her beautiful hands were swollen; she had painful joints and poor circulation. After a time, George asked her if she would allow him to examine her. She acquiesced, appreciating his concern and care.

Her illness, George thought, was caused by nicotine and the narrowing of the blood vessels. He listened to Mother's pulse in various parts of her body; it was delayed between the heart and the hands and the feet. He let Ann and me listen as well, to hear the difference in her pulse. George called Mother's ailment scleroderma.

Unfortunately, in our harsh living conditions we knew Mother would not have the desire or the willpower to stop smoking. George decided to bring some injections and taught me how to perform them; Ann was squeamish at the sight of the needles, and for her to make an injection was out of the question.

From that time on, I sterilized the syringes and the needles each day, boiling them in water for ten minutes in a special container and using denatured alcohol to kill potential germs. When giving Mother her shots, I tried to be as gentle as possible, but I had to move quickly to prick the skin with the needle, which rapidly grew dull.

I felt sorry for Mother and wished I could somehow show more sympathy. Yet, our life situation was too harsh to allow ourselves any softness. We had to act tough, sometimes heartless, to survive. There was no place in life to be sorry for anybody.

By that time Mother did not have any more money from her accounts, which her brother, my Uncle Wladek, had secured for her in his bank; nor did she have any more jewelry to sell. Our only income was the part of her earnings Ann gave Mother to keep the house. It had to be enough.

With the exorbitant black market prices, my mother had a very hard time trying to manage our household. We did not complain, and we did not talk much about the difficulties—the everyday lack of food and warmth, not to mention peace and security.

Daylight curfew made our evenings at home very long. Located on the 52nd parallel, even the month of March—not to mention December—in Warsaw is cold and dark. We rushed home to be off the streets at curfew time. Before supper, Mother made a fire in our room's heating oven. This was the only time we managed to burn our meager supplies of coal. The oven was built with polished, rust-colored tiles we liked to touch to warm our hands. It was only three or four feet high, and Mother put our plates on top to warm them for supper.

After supper, to pass the time, Mother and Ann usually played solitaire while I read and did my homework. Sometimes George came to play bridge. Even if I had homework to do, I felt obliged to make time for bridge. It seemed like a sin to be a potential fourth for three bridge players and not play. I managed to do my homework, play bridge simultaneously—and have fun doing it. I kept my books and papers on my lap and did my homework whenever my partner was playing, while my hand lay on the table as a dummy.

Sometimes we switched partners, but usually George was Mother's partner and Ann was mine. George and Mother talked about Ann's and my playing, using funny words like an "unconventional bridge." They knew they were unquestionably superior players, but for some reason we usually won. Youthful luck? Perhaps. And no, we didn't cheat!

During one of those bridge evenings I prepared a wonderful report on the comparison between Moliere's comedy, "Tartuffe," and the Polish writer Krasicki's Zemsta's "The Revenge." Theatrical plays were always my favorites, and I delivered that report with gusto, quoting many lines from memory. My class applauded and Sister Lauretana, our literature teacher, gave me an A+. I didn't tell her that I prepared such a perfect report while playing several rubbers of bridge!

One day when George arrived, the expression on his face told us he had a good story. He took out his wallet and showed us his night pass, which was signed by the German Warsaw City Commandant.

When we saw his name, we responded: "That's our present commandant."

"Wrong," said George. "He's now our past commandant."

We were aware that some of the German commandants and other Nazi officials were doing their jobs with uncanny, cruel eagerness. AK, the Polish underground organization, had to somehow curb these atrocities, which were ordered by Hitler and overeagerly executed by local German administrators. When these administrators' cruelty and sadism became unbearable, the Polish underground organization put them on notice.

In spite of the fact that all high-ranking Germans were surrounded and protected by police and Gestapo at all times, the so-called "Polish jury," a subdivision of the Polish Army's legal department decided to sentence this particular City Commandant and managed to catch him alone. The German high command was in Warsaw's Old Town, near the hospital where George worked. According to George, three Poles appeared in the City Commandant's office, entering through the balcony. The telephone line on the Commandant's desk was already disconnected. The Polish jury kindly reminded the Commandant that he would be shot if he made any noise.

The Commandant was formally read the list of criminal acts he had committed, followed by the Polish jury's judgment. His death sentence was temporarily suspended pending a change in behavior. So as to leave without problems, the Polish representatives bound and gagged the Commandant, and then left the way they'd come in.

Despite being given a stay of execution by AK, this particular Commandant did not change his modus operandi. The next stage had to follow. Today, George told us, certain events transpired in the Old Town ...

As usual, the Commandant was traveling through Warsaw with

extremely heavy security. His car was usually preceded by motorcycle police and followed by armored cars. After the police and
the Commandant's car passed one of the Old Town's narrow inter-
sections, a farmer's wagon pulled by a horse drove in from a side
street. The wagon was too big to turn the corner and blocked the
whole street, stopping the German armored cars in the rear. A few
blocks and a few turns ahead, there was another problem. After the
motorcycle police passed, in the space of separation between the
front and rear guards and the Commandant's car, a person emerged
from a gate and shot the Commandant and his chauffeur in their
car. When the traffic cleared again there were no witnesses left on
the street. In any situation in which there were gunshots, walkers
learned to disappear as quickly as possible.

That night George showed us many old night permits issued
to him over a period of months. Almost all of them had different
signatures. Evidently the Germans had a hard time learning to respect international laws and treat occupied lands and other human
beings with fairness.

I do not have any knowledge of other circumstances in which
the Polish underground was able to penetrate Nazi security and appear in guarded offices or homes of administrators to read them
their judgments. In spite of the fact that those German administrators were protected by the Gestapo and the police, every single administrator who had his death verdict read was eventually executed
in some way, as with the Commandant about whom George told us.

Many stories of this sort circulated in Warsaw during those
days, and each was more fascinating than the last. In the German
newspapers, however, there was only a notice about the nomina-
tion of a new administrator without notice of what happened to the
previous one.

My Busy Days

In early 1942, Anek called me to meet him at a precise time and particular spot on the street. I knew never to arrive more than three minutes before or three minutes after the appointed time so as to avoid calling attention to us from any Germans that might have been watching suspiciously.

I was on time, and when I saw Anek coming from the opposite direction, I walked toward him. We met and continued walking together. Anek gave me a slip of paper with an address and told me to get as much information about the building, the number of entrances, and the occupant's arrival and departure times as possible.

"It's supposed to be a small building occupied by civilian Germans who are of special interest to our organization. Make a map of the building, the nearest cross streets, and anything else you find important," Anek said. "When you get it, call me."

"Of course I will," I assured him. We parted, mixing into the crowd.

I didn't know what to expect, but I knew that the key to this mission was out there, waiting for me to find it. The next day, after school, I decided to go to the address and do some investigative work. I checked a Warsaw street map. The address was on the far side of the city center.

I took streetcars to the area, passed the street I wanted and got out. There were workers digging on the sidewalk in front of the building. I passed them and walked to the next corner, noting that the workers were repairing pipes in the ground. Behind them, the building was obviously locked, with fencing in both directions. First problem: I couldn't get inside or around. I decided to try befriending the workers, and looked about ostentatiously, as if expecting to meet someone.

"Excuse me," I asked. "Do you know what time it is?"

After the workers replied, I acted upset and said, "Did you happen to see a girl here in the last fifteen minutes or so?"

I described the imaginary friend I was supposed to meet in exact detail. "She told me she would bring a book I need for vocational school."

I was talkative, but very apologetic for bothering the men while they worked. The workers reassured me that I was no bother, but said they had not seen anybody that fit my description. "And believe us, if she was good-looking like you, we would have noticed!" I pretended not to deserve the compliment, and stayed, waiting for my imaginary friend.

The workers did not mind my company and started joking about the job they were doing, complaining that it was taking them too many days.

"But if you don't repair those pipes, the poor people in the house won't have any water," I said.

"Poor people? – the damn Krauts!" one of the workers responded.

"In that case," I said, joking along with them, "why don't you repair everything and pour fresh concrete just before you leave, so that they won't be able to enter?"

Soon I learned what I wanted. The Germans would be back by 6 PM; in the morning, they'd threatened the workers with punishment if they weren't finished by that time. If the workers left wet concrete outside the front door, the Germans could enter the house through the gate in the fence around the corner on the side street or use another door in the back of the house.

"Do you understand German?" I asked.

"I do, some," one of the workers said. "But one of the Krauts speaks Polish so well, he could pass for one of us—except he has that typical German posture and loud voice! They talk and laugh so loudly, they can't be anything else but Krauts."

"You're right! Whenever I see five or six of them, they sound like a whole battalion," I said, hoping they would give me the number of inhabitants in response. My plan worked.

"No, there are only the three of them. Every morning and night, the chauffer picks them up and delivers them back. We can set our watches by the car. Nine AM and 6 PM, it will be here."

I needed only one more detail. "At least this way their wives can have dinner ready on time."

"Oh no, there's been nobody else here for the last five days we've worked."

I was having fun talking with the workers. I asked a few more questions, expressing interest in their job, before thanking them for not minding my talk while I waited for my friend.

"Evidently something happened to her ... I won't get the book I need today."

Bidding goodbye to my friendly informants, I decided to take a walk around the corner back to the streetcar. I easily located the gate in the cyclone fence, which was locked, but I could see where the back door was and located possible hiding places nearby. Mission thus accomplished, I went around the block to the next streetcar stop. I crossed the street—and realized abruptly that I was on the plaza where, several days prior, a Russian plane had dropped a bomb, hitting a streetcar and massacring the people inside. The remains of the disaster were still visible.

Curiosity got the better of me. Two streetcar wagons had been demolished; blood was visible in many places. Bystanders like me meandered around. The bodies had been taken to a nearby mortuary, I learned, where people were meant to identify the dead.

Someone even made a joke, saying how considerate it was of the Russians to hit a spot so close to a mortuary.

A strange impulse made me go inside the mortuary itself. The big hall was poorly lit, cold, and deadly silent. I was alone, looking at rows of dead bodies with their faces uncovered. It was morbid, but impersonal. I felt nothing. *Another part of the war*, I thought absently.

I went outside into the sunny afternoon, found my streetcar and traveled home. Once there, I called Anek. Mother and Ann were not home, and I could freely draw my blueprint of the building. I did not even wonder why this information was needed, but guessed only that it was another action necessary to wartime.

When I was done, I sat at the round table in the middle of our only room and started my homework. Soon Anek arrived. I showed him the drawing and my notes. He said it looked good and left before anybody else came home.

I liked school. As the Germans forbade academic education, being a good student was challenging; however, I enjoyed double-crossing them by excelling in my studies. Getting good grades was fun, and I did it with zest by using my time effectively.

I had my own study methods, and learned the benefits of staying ahead of my school materials. This allowed me to easily assimilate every lecture I heard or memorize new material I read. Since I had relatively little free time after school, I preferred to do as much of my homework as I could between classes or during the "slow" lectures, usually when the math teacher was explaining something I already understood.

Leaving my homework papers at school also kept me safe from possible German street searches. The Germans would randomly accost and search young people in an attempt to catch us carrying forbidden materials, such as Polish literature or history texts. For that reason we almost never carried forbidden books and hid papers on our bodies.

In addition to school, I enjoyed reading. That year, our class read famous Polish historical epics by Jan Sienkiewicz, a beloved nineteenth-century Polish writer. His books were a "must," like the works of Charles Dickens in the English-speaking world. We discussed Sienkiewicz's book, *Quo Vadis*, with our teacher, Sister Lauretana. One day she asked us whether we had all been able to obtain a copy of the book.

"Yes, my aunt gave me the original version of *Quo Vadis*," I said, waiting for the nun's response. After all, in the original *Quo Vadis* contained descriptions of a Roman patrician caressing the "alabaster breasts" of his favorite slave as she sat on his lap. Those parts were cut out of the "youth" version of the book.

Sister Lauretana did not blink an eye. "How did you like the book?" she asked.

"I didn't like the parts about Roman torture," I said. "It bothered me that Nero ordered people burned like torches, while he played on a lyre and recited his poems."

I made my point without saying outright that caressing a pretty slave's alabaster breasts was much less offensive to me than torture, the scenes of which were not excised from the youth version of *Quo Vadis*. Class discussion followed about the Roman Coliseum and Roman enjoyment of *panem et circensem* (bread and spectacle), in which wild animals ripped Christian bodies apart and gladiators killed one another.

Later, we read Sienkiewicz's famous historical trilogy, known to Poles simply as "The Trilogy". In the first book, *With Fire and Sword*, the seventeenth-century Tartars, Turks and Kazaks invade Poland. They plunder and steal whatever they can carry, burn what they cannot take, rape women, and torture and kill men. Their symbol of superiority was to tie a man's legs to horses and pull him into a sharp pole, which would be lifted with the dying man on it and viewed by the cheering, victorious invaders. In Sienkiewicz's books, such descriptions of torture were not prominent, but as a historical reality, he included few of them for authenticity's sake. In my young mind, however, they were seared into my memory as if with a branding iron.

Everybody in Warsaw had to deal with danger constantly. It was all around us, like the air. But we also knew that we could not react with fear. Fear would kill us.

"Don't let fear control you," were common words of wisdom.

I remember a funny story Father Góral told me during one vacation in Raba. Father Góral was a Catholic parish priest in a little mountain town in southern Poland. His only educated friends were a Rabbi and a Protestant minister. The three men met frequently, exchanging meals and teasing each other about their various religious beliefs. Shortly after WWII, when we were both wandering through defeated Germany, Father Góral told me a story he'd heard from his friend the Rabbi.

A young Jew, fearing the draft, went to his Rabbi for advice.

"Don't worry," the Rabbi said. *"There are always two ways out.* There will be a war, or there will be no war. If there is no war, there is nothing to worry about, but if there is a war, there are still two ways out.

"They will kill you, or they won't.

"If they don't kill you, there is nothing to worry about, but if they kill you, there are still two ways out. You go to heaven, or you go to hell. If you go to heaven, there is nothing to worry about, but if you go to hell, there are still two ways out.

"There is a devil, or there is not.

"If there is no devil, there is nothing to worry about, but if there is a devil, there are still two ways out. The devil will eat you, or he won't. If he doesn't eat you, there is nothing to worry about, but if he eats you, there is ... there is–" The Rabbi hesitated, "only one way out."

Thus encouraged, the young Jew went home and faced the draft bravely.

This exchange happened, Father Goral said, in the innocent years before the 1939 invasion. Shortly after, the Germans entered the little town and the Rabbi disappeared. His friends prayed that he'd managed to escape through the mountains to Romania. For German law did not allow *any* way out but death.

Suddenly the possibility of my own capture and torture became a reality. Whenever the Germans managed to find and arrest a member of the AK, his or her closest associates had to hide. Under torture, some prisoners did not disclose any names; however, many gave up at least some information before being killed. The thought of being caught and interrogated consumed me. I knew that I would not be able to withstand broken bones or any of the other special techniques the Gestapo was famous for using.

My youthful optimism and feelings of invincibility forced me to find an escape from this fear, which I could not share with anybody. My mother and Ann might have noticed that I had a peculiar group of friends who called me Kora. But they did not know, nor did they want to know, that I belonged to the Polish resistance. I could raise this subject only during George's visits, when we talked about current political events. George told us about people who carried poison when they were in danger of being caught. As a doctor, George knew about cyanide capsules that could be planted in a person's teeth, to be bitten when interrogation became unbearable.

I formed my own plan of escape, visualizing a situation where I would first play insane and then attack one of the interrogators, provoking him to shoot me. I knew that I could not foresee all the details, but my conviction that I could always kill myself became my salvation. I relaxed and stopped being afraid of interrogation and torture.

As a free spirit, I enjoyed helping my compatriots and felt eager to do any work to double-cross the German occupiers. But strangely, my plan to resist torture somehow foresaw the concurrent fate of my Aunt Władka.

At least a year later, my Aunt Władysława Macieszyna saved her life by doing exactly what I had planned: having been sentenced to death by the Gestapo, she bit through the veins in her wrist before she could be interrogated. The Germans found her bleeding in her cell, stopped the bleeding, subdued her and—in their contrary way—preserved her life. German prisoners were not allowed to decide when they would die.

Schoolwork, underground resistance activities, and my varied groups of friends were all important to me, but dancing fell into a special category. I measured the days of the week and the hours of the day by the time I could spend in dancing school. Singing lessons were a close second. Everything else became the rest.

By this time, I had been dancing for almost two years. The previous winter, I danced for the first time in a theater as part of a special program for children. The typical Polish folk dances like Krakowiak, Kujawiak and Trojak were very easy for us, and we were able to prepare them in one or two sessions. We danced in original folk costumes, which we rented for the occasion.

Being onstage in the theater was exciting and fun, but Mrs. Wanda was almost apologetic when she asked us to perform. It was not up to our usual, much finer style of dancing, which also used folk motifs and expressions, but in a stylized modern dance form. That children's show was the only time we performed original village folk dances,

Nevertheless, we enjoyed performing in the theater. Like everybody else, I applied makeup that could withstand the hot theater lights. But in dancing several dances, the lights, costumes and fast motion made me hot. I had to change costumes quickly, and while changing I dried the perspiration off my face. With the perspiration went the makeup. However, it did not make much difference for my cheeks were more than rosy.

After the show, my mother gently remarked that I had "a little too much makeup on." We all started laughing, for my own mother did not realize that my red glow was not artificial. "It's not my fault that you gave me a face like that," I teased.

We started preparing a real show for June, the end of the school year. Every class level prepared at least one dance. Our top class prepared the most items on the program. We were working on several group compositions. To appease German censorship, one of them was called a "folk dance," concealing the fact that it was performed to the forbidden piece, "Mazurka," by our Polish patriot and strictly forbidden by Germans Chopin. The dance had three main themes, and we differentiated those danced by the characters of "boys," "girls," and "babas". This dance was so well choreographed that it became a staple of many future shows. Mrs. Wanda also decided that Ann and I were now good enough to dance a duet, entitled "Animals" and performed to Debussy's "Cakewalk".

Since there were no materials available to make costumes, we used swimming suits dyed black as a base, with minimal character-producing accents made of paper fabric. To obtain that paper fabric, Mrs. Wanda had to jump through the hoops of German bureaucracy. Somehow Mrs. Wanda's genius always succeeded to making our costumes comfortable to move in, aesthetically appealing, and in character.

Our shows were held in the school hall, which did not have enough space for all the spectators. We thus had to repeat the show two or three times. There was only one other dancing school of the same level as ours in Warsaw. Our two schools competed for acclaim. Mrs. Wanda invited Mrs. Mieczyńska, the other dancing school teacher, to our performance. When the first performance ended, Mrs. Wanda introduced me to Mrs. Mieczyńska, who told me that she had taken special notice of my ability and expression. I could not have asked for more. I was in seventh heaven.

Jabłonna (Applewood)

Anek was my only contact with the Polish resistance forces. Whenever someone called me asking for Kora, I knew it would be Anek. Kora, my pseudonym, was known only to him and possibly a few of his superiors. However, at home everybody thought it was only a variation of Kordianna, which so many friends had called me since my last vacation.

When speaking on the phone, we always anticipated German eavesdropping. One day Anek called, sounding as if he was my boyfriend.

"Kora, how would you like to spend most of the day on a picnic?"

I played along with his act, replying, "I'd love that; when?"

Anek mentioned a day. I told him I would be able to disappear for the whole day and was going to meet him. Anek asked me to pick him up on the way to the narrow gauge railroad station.

That day at 8:30 AM sharp, I walked to his apartment. He was already by the door. Inside, he gave me two Radom Vis pistols and several magazines to carry. Anticipating this development, I had brought a big purse; when I heard that we would be going somewhere out of town, I knew it would be my duty to carry the guns. I put the guns and magazines in my purse and put some money and my Kenkarte, or German identification card, in the pocket of my trench coat. It was late in the spring of 1942, hence my decision to dress for unpredictable weather.

"We will meet two men at the station," Anek told me while we walked.

They were already waiting for us, milling around amongst the crowd. We walked into a dark corner where, unobserved, I passed two guns to each of the young men. Since we were going by train, in case of a search they would shoot or jump out, probably both. They told me to act as though I did not know them.

In less than an hour we reached *Jabłonna* (Applewood), a tiny station north of Warsaw. We disembarked and started walking. I stayed with Anek while the two men walked some distance ahead. Within a few minutes, we were beyond the town, traveling on a country road between fields.

Anek told me we were going to the "Forestry on the Marshes," and that Dick—the pseudonym of one of the men—had a sketch of how to get there. We came to the forest, where "Dick and Harry" stopped to allow us to catch up. Dick complained that the map did not make sense. In fact, he admitted, nothing seemed to make sense: the map, the man's verbal description and the road we were on all seemed wrong.

We continued walking. Anek recalled the last time I'd been on reconnaissance and prepared a map for action. It was perfect, he told me.

"We could have walked to the building blindfolded. You marked everything, all the possible escape routes, so well. Once we were there, everything went like a charm."

But it was becoming obvious that the surveyor for our action had not done his job so well. We walked in the forest far enough away from Dick and Harry that they could not hear us. "Anek, should I know what we are trying to accomplish?" I asked.

"Yes, I can tell you what I know," Anek said. "Two young Jewish women are being kept in this forest. They escaped from the ghetto and were hiding among Poles. Not long ago the Germans arrested them. Since then, there have been several arrests among Polish people who were connected with these Jewish women."

"Do you think the Germans tortured them?" I asked.

"No, it appears that they are being kept here by their captors in good conditions with good food, as long as they divulge the names of the Polish people they knew."

"Are you supposed to silence them forever?" I asked, worried about what might be coming.

"No, not yet. We will try to find out how much they told the Germans and if there is anything else they still know; if so, we will scare the hell out of them to keep them silent."

"It won't work," I said, "they will always be more scared of the Germans. And Anek, it does not make sense—three guys with pistols to scare two poor Jewish girls?"

"Kora ..."Anek was getting impatient. "We may not find anybody else there, but God only knows."

After a long time, Dick decided to ask for directions. Dick was in command and Anek refrained from complaining, but I could see that he was getting increasingly upset. Asking for directions was foolish—like leaving a trail.

We were supposed to be in a forestry building within two kilometers of the station, but we had walked at least six kilometers by the time we reached the place Dick was told was a forestry building on the marshes.

I stayed in a thicket of woods while the men went to the building. A few minutes later they reemerged, furious. This was the wrong forestry on the marshes. Yes, there were marshes around, but the men had been told that the so-called "Forestry on the Marshes" was less than two kilometers from town. The men inside the forestry spoke Polish, but anybody working for a public office like forestry could be of questionable loyalties, and the entry of three young Polish men could have raised suspicion.

Anek suggested that we scrap the action and go back to Warsaw. Dick decided to finish our mission. Anek and I only looked at each other. Dick was in command and we followed his lead.

Forty-five minutes or so later, we found the real Forestry on the Marshes. I once more hid in a thicket. Again, the men left toward the house. I waited in the thicket for only a few minutes. The men were approaching the building when they spotted several policemen on bicycles approaching from the opposite direction. Though the police wore navy-colored Polish uniforms, the German gendarmes usually followed on their heels.

Seeing the police, my fellows stepped back into the forest; hiding among the trees, they worked their way back to me.

"Kora, you will have to take the guns and ammunition," Dick said, softly speaking the obvious. "The roads will be patrolled. We have passes from work which should take us through the checkpoints. You have to manage on your own."

Simple, I thought. *All I have to do is get to the railroad station without being searched.*

Anek and I quickly determined that I would hide the guns in my purse. The Vis, which was in the best condition, was loaded with an extra bullet in the chamber. I placed that pistol upside down on top of the other two loaded pistols, and then tried reaching for the gun several times to assure myself I could make a quick draw.

The boys left. I was on my own.

I carried the purse on my left arm with my coat hanging over it and my other belongings in my coat pockets. The only reason for me to reach into my purse would be to grab the Vis to shoot my way out of trouble.

Squaring my shoulders, I walked through the forest toward the main road. The men took the only other road to the railroad station. The danger was obvious to me, but so was my duty. I was tense, very alert and mentally "programmed" to deal with whatever might come. I knew what I had to do.

I had walked few minutes when I heard the sounds of truck engines and loud German voices. My heart jumped. I stopped and listened; I was almost out of the woods and the sounds of the area were reaching me, I realized. I must have been passing military installations.

The forest thinned; soon I saw fences around German military barracks. I kept walking, approaching a crossing via another small path. At that moment, two young soldiers on bicycles came toward me. They were not armed, and I realized that they were not regular German army soldiers. Something was different.

Reaching me, the two men got off their bicycles and started talking. They were Russians from the Vlasoff army, speaking broken Polish, trying their luck with me, the Polish girl. The Vlasoff army was comprised of Russians who collaborated with Germans and now served their new masters. I was definitely not interested in talking to them and easily brushed them off. They went their way and I went mine.

The reality of my situation hit me hard as I emerged from the woods and reached the main road. In the distance, in the direction of the railroad station, were two checkpoints with German gendarmerie on the sidewalks on both sides of the road. There were no side streets to go around. The sparse houses and the fields on either side were fenced off. There were only two alternatives visible: go forward, or turn back.

I cast my eyes around for side streets where I might exit in case of emergency, but there were none. As I write this some sixty years later, I wonder why it never occurred to me that the easiest way to get out of this incredible danger would have been to dump the guns and ammunition somewhere in the forest and walk out clean. But the guns were too valuable to our Polish Country Army. The thought was unthinkable.

Instead, I decided to take my chances. I had no idea what to do, but I had to look for some opportunity. I walked forward, toward the town. My foot hurt; I wore sandals not meant for walking all day long. On the right side of the road was an *Apteka* (drug store). I decided to get a Band-Aid and perhaps learn something from the people inside. It would buy me time to think.

The store was empty, with only one man behind the counter, a nice-looking middle aged fellow. I made some remark about checkpoints on the road. He said that there was an unusual air of apprehension among the Germans.

"Something must have happened that they did not like," he said.

I felt as though he suspected me of being part of that something. I asked him for two Band-Aids. He handed them to me and I paid, taking my wallet from my coat's side pocket. I walked to the wooden bench to take off my shoes and put the Band-Aids on my heels.

As I sat and put my purse on the wooden bench beside me, the guns inside made an unmistakable loud sound of metal hitting against metal. I looked up at the man. Our eyes met. He knew. He started speaking.

"I am the last Pole living in this town. I'm tolerated because this German community needs a drug store. Otherwise, I would have been kicked out long ago with all the other members of the Polish community. If there is any problem in town, this is the first place they always come." He looked at me with deep concern in his eyes and added, "but come back here if you have to."

He did not have to say anything more. We understood each other perfectly. If I had to come back to him, he would risk his life by trying to hide me.

"I'll see what I can do. Thank you so much," I said.

I walked out. To the right there were still two German search and check points, with several people standing on each side of the street, waiting their turn. Behind the checkpoint was the railway station I had to reach. To my immediate left was a little bar with tables outside, where three fat, noisy Germans were having their evening beers. Near the bar, a little white dog played. From the direction I had just come, the two Russian soldiers were approaching on their bicycles. Suddenly, I had a plan. The Russian soldiers would be my saviors.

I walked closer to the road and started playing with the little dog. The dog was cooperative, and I was able to make myself as charming as possible to the oncoming soldiers. They swallowed the bait, stopped by me, and again tried to strike up conversation. This time I was more than willing. I cuddled with the dog, making sure they wished they could take its place.

Kissing the dog, I straightened up and started walking with my new boyfriends to the railroad station. The men offered to walk with me on the sidewalk. "No, no," I said, "let's walk on the road. It's more comfortable for you two."

I stepped between them, making sure we were in the middle of the road, as far as possible from both sidewalks. We kept walking, getting closer to the checkpoints. My test inched closer. I had to play my role perfectly or lose my life.

The checkpoint on our left was closer, so I turned and flirted with the guy on my right. The gendarmes on the left sidewalk were busy searching and checking documents, and paid no attention to the Fräulein with two soldiers in the middle of the street. One more to go! I switched my attention to the guy on my left. He was delighted to hear that I would come tomorrow with my girlfriend to have a date with both of them. He beamed, a broad smile on his face, as I described the beautiful blonde I would bring.

A loud voice from the second checkpoint on my right shattered the teasing mood.

"Hey Fraulein!"

My heart pounded, but I turned to face the German with my cheapest look of surprise, the words, "What could you possibly want from me" written on my face. Reaching into the pocket of my coat, I waved the Kenkarte at him. The gendarme looked at me, gave me a smile, and after a moment of hesitation dismissed me with a wave of his arm. I maintained my dumb smile and quickly looked back at the soldier walking on my left to make sure that the gendarme wouldn't change his mind.

I talked with my saviors, laughing, trying not to overdo it, but also making sure that my legs, which suddenly felt like Jell-O, did not collapse under me. I had to catch my emotional equilibrium. The realization hit that I was the only person in the whole town the Germans wanted—and I had just slipped through their net. I wanted to dance and sing. To cover my excitement, I told my saviors everything they wanted to hear. A date tomorrow? – Certainly - With another blond girl, or a brunette? What else?

We were still two to three hundred yards from the railroad station when I spotted my anxious comrades watching me and my escorts. In my exuberant mood, I decided to give them their money's worth of entertainment. When we stopped near the station I bade the Russians goodbye, but to add a little excitement for my conspirators, I told the soldiers that, according to Polish custom, when men say goodbye to a lady they should kiss her hand. I raised my hand in a queenly manner and let them take turns kissing it. My three fellows, looking on from a distance, doubled over in hysterical laughter.

My saviors left and I joined my fellows. They told me that when they walked to the railroad station on another road, they were checked and searched by German gendarmes like everybody else. At the railroad station, they wondered how I would manage to get through. When they spotted me from afar, walking between the two soldiers, they were certain I had been arrested and was being escorted to prison. They began planning how to jump my escorts and fight to free me. Only after several long moments did they realize that I was having too much fun to be in any trouble.

When we got on the train, we did our standard procedure in reverse. I gave the guns to the guys and felt lighter in weight and spirit. We arrived in Warsaw after curfew and at the train station were issued certificates stating that the train had arrived late. If we had been stopped by the police after the curfew, that railroad station certificates could have kept us out of trouble.

Back in Warsaw, I again took two guns and walked with Anek to his house. At the gate, I gave him the guns and made my way home. It was already dark and the streets were empty. I walked quietly uphill, keeping close to the buildings.

In the instant that I finally saw the outline of our house, I heard the noise of German boots on the pavement from the cross street to my left. The only light on the streets was from the moon. If I stepped into the cross street the Germans would see me. I decided not to give them a chance to interrogate me. I stopped in the cover of the last building and whistled our home signal. Ann heard, and the barely-visible inside light was turned off immediately. She pulled up the blackout shade and opened the window. I ran quietly across the street. The German patrol spotted me, yelled and started running in my direction. I climbed through the window, closed it, pulled down the shade and Ann turned on the light, all in less than ten seconds. We heard the Germans running around the corner and under our windows.

I was still standing on the windowsill when Ann nonchalantly spoke the words of a famous Polish poem: "And where are the Lithuanians coming from?"

"They are coming from a night journey," I said, following the poem, and threw my purse on the couch in a jokingly dramatic gesture. The joke was on me; out of the purse came a spare magazine, which fell to the floor with a loud knock. Without missing a beat, I jumped off the sill and kicked the magazine under the couch. Mother and Ann saw it but did not say a word. They continued playing Solitaire.

The German patrol started banging on the gate of our house. The night watchman opened the gate, which made an incredible screeching noise. We heard the patrolmen shouting at the watchman, asking if somebody had just come in. At this point Mrs. Maria, the lady subleasing the second room from us, came to our room. "Zosinka," she called, "where have you been? We were so worried."

"Oh, I came quite a while ago; I was on a picnic. Didn't you see me when you were walking from the kitchen before?" I said, implying that she could have seen me through the glass door to our room. I was trying to confuse her, to make sure she *knew* I had been home for quite a while and that there was no connection between me and the noisy German patrol outside.

The gatekeeper evidently convinced the gendarmes that they would have heard the gate squeaking if anybody had come in. My mother's and Ann's suspicions had been confirmed, but by this time the rules of war and conspiracy were ingrained in all of us. They knew better than to ask and I offered no explanation.

Before falling asleep, I did say an extra thank you prayer to God. My whole experience seemed like a miracle. I thanked God for it, but wondered: why did He do it?

Second Summer in Raba Wyżna

Shortly after the dance show and the end of the school year, I readied myself to travel back to Raba Wyżna to see Alinka and spend my vacation with last year's buddies. The problem was securing safe passage, for at that time the Germans were exceptionally active in seizing people from trains and sending them to labor camps.

Ann had continued to work as a waitress at the Fregata restaurant. During her work, Ann learned that one of her regular gentlemen customers often traveled on business trips between Warsaw and Krakow. Ann asked him if he could take her sister under his protection while traveling on the German-sanctioned business trips. I was happy to travel with him first class in a sleeper; I did not have to worry about my safety from the Germans... or from him. He was very nice and proper. In Krakow he made sure that I transferred safely to the next train, leaving shortly for the mountains.

I was happy to see Alinka, Barbara and Mathew again. After spending two months with them the previous year, we felt happily close once more. Basia and Maciuś, as I called them, were good children and easy to get along with. I had known and loved them since they were tiny. Now Mathew was two and Barbara three and a half years old.

Prior to my departure from Warsaw, Alinka wrote to tell us that Basia was suffering from a string of boils that had appeared all over her little body. Grandma Zduń, the estate owner and the only village medic, tried several remedies, with no success. When a worried Alinka described all the symptoms in her letter, Dr. George took action and figured out what to do. He gathered several kinds of medication and wrote meticulous instructions about how to administer it. From the moment we started applying the treatments to Basia, the old boils disappeared and no new ones appeared.

Unknown as an individual to Alinka and others in Raba, George became known as a famous magician doctor. Even Grandma Zduń shook her head in disbelief.

Felix continued to be my *sympatia*, but his Grandma's two grandsons also started joining our group more often than they had the year before. Anton was now eighteen and his brother John around twenty. Our age differences felt less important that summer. We had great times together, hiking in the mountains, playing with animals, and jumping from the hay loft without "rolling in it," as other people might have done. Sex had no place there, between us. One girl who attempted to work her feminine wiles on the boys was instantly ostracized.

We had fun, but while I enjoyed fresher food than I did in Warsaw, I was having an adverse reaction to something. My chin started developing pimple-like blotches; soon, pus-like moisture began to ooze from them. Alinka suggested that I go to Grandma Zduń to see if she could help. In the meantime, I covered my face by wearing a little scarf like a girl in a Turkish harem. The boys told me that Grandma overheard them joking about my eyes looking more interesting now. It was enough to set Grandma in a panic. She must have decided that she would be safest if I disappeared. When I came to see her, she took one look and told me that I had a very serious problem and the nearest doctor who could help was in Warsaw. I bit my tongue and did not mention that I knew at least one surgeon who had helped little Basia. How thinly veiled was her desire to remove me from her grandsons!

After my "consultation," the gang walked with me to tell Alinka about Grandma's diagnosis. Alinka was initially bothered, for one should not make jokes about Grandma, but Anton or John reminded her that she was their grandmother—and that she made a joke of herself. We decided that I should take a train to one of the two towns nearby and see a doctor in Rabka, to the north, or Nowy Targ, to the east.

Later, Alinka and I talked about the whole silly situation. We suspected that my band of friends, having no other outlet for their mischief, had caused my problems, playing on Grandma's anxiety by glorifying my smarts and general attractiveness.

The final straw or *coup d'état* was delivered by John. Some kind of estate business required him to take a horse carriage to Rabka, a few kilometers away. John offered to take me with him instead of sending me on a train by myself. Going by horse was easier and safer; as I loved to guide the horses, it was also more fun.

In Rabka, I saw a doctor, got medicine, and was good as new in a few days' time. I begged John and Anton not to rub Grandma's nose in her statement that the closest doctor who could help me was in Warsaw.

At the end of August, with summer vacation coming to an end and everybody planning trips back to Warsaw, I developed a very high fever and was confined to bed. I remember reading Tolstoy's "Resurrection"—as if I could not get a simpler piece of literature! My fever hovered above 100 degrees. I do not remember particulars, but I know that in a few days I wound up in the hospital in Nowy Targ (New Market).

There, the immediate suspicion was typhus. They put me in an empty ward with at least six beds. As my blood tests were inconclusive, the doctors decided to keep me separated from the other patients, leaving all the beds in my ward empty. To complicate matters, in addition to the fever I'd developed peculiar problems. Wherever I suffered an insect bite, the bite became large, red, and swollen, which made the doctors suspect I might have a general blood infection. A few weeks later they thought I had both typhus and a blood infection. But they were not sure and consequently I had to stay out of both the infectious and the regular wards.

I stayed in a big room at the end of the hospital wing. Occasionally nurses came to check on me or bring me food. The room was big, with all the empty beds to one side. Since I was able to choose, I chose the bed next to the wall of windows overlooking the Tatra Mountains. The view was spectacular, especially on sunny days. I remember staring at those peaks for hours.

Finally, my boils disappeared and my temperature dropped to normal, but I had to stay until the blood test showed that my blood was free of whatever had been wrong with it. The nurses took pity on me and brought in another girl who was also alone, isolated in a single room nearby with a medical problem similar to mine. We had plenty of time to talk. The nurses told us that one of us could walk to the other's doorway, stand there and speak, but we should never touch or come closer. We enjoyed the company and never disobeyed the friendly nurses' instructions.

Thus began my friendship with Aldonka, who was also from Warsaw. She told me that her father was a Swedish citizen, which in Nazi-occupied Poland gave Aldonka and her mother special privileges.

Finally, in October, my mother came from Warsaw and picked me up from the hospital. We rejoined Alinka, and after few days spent getting organized, Mother and I left for Warsaw. I came back to school around the beginning of November. As usual, the school year had started in early September. When I came to school two month late for tenth grade, I decided to concentrate first on the subjects with which I could not progress further without catching up. Math abilities ran in our family; with Ann's help, I caught up with algebra and geometry in three days.

On my first Monday back, Sister Beata came to give our class a geometry test. When she saw me opening my papers, she started laughing and told me she absolutely did not expect me to be able to take the test. I said that I would like to try. The class chimed in, urging Sister to let me take the test and grade me a point higher.

A few days later, Sister Beata came to class with a pile of corrected tests. She distributed them one by one, and I had to wait. Mine was on the dead bottom. All the girls enjoyed the suspense; Sister Beata liked playing with us.

Finally, she showed me my paper and the big red A+. I hadn't made a single mistake. I repeated the same perfect performance on an algebra test. But I knew that the other subjects would not be so easy.

All the teachers were as helpful to me as they could be, with one exception. For some reason, the lay teacher of geography decided to pressure me to catch up with the past material. Soon she started to belittle me and threatened to fail me.

Many girls in my class were from out of town, living in dormitories. Other girls, like me, commuted daily to school. I did not develop any deeper friendships there, though I liked many of my classmates. When in school, I took notes and studied, frequently doing my homework during lunchtime or breaks. Looking back at my relationships with the girls in my school, I realize that I was a very private person then, extremely busy and more focused on my studies than on the other girls—something of an "old soul," perhaps.

As a result, when the lay geography teacher singled me out, I was surprised by how many girls rose to my defense. They encouraged me to go to the Sister Director. Nervous as I was, I decided to ask Sister Ezechiela for an appointment.

At her door, I could swear that my heartbeat was louder than my knock. When I entered, she was seated at her desk. Her demeanor was dignified but friendly. She asked what was bothering me.

I presented my case, explaining that even our home room teacher, Sister Lauretana, had excused me for a while from the past material and allowed me to start with the material the other students were currently studying. I felt that I first had to catch up with Latin and French if I hoped to progress. I was flustered, frustrated, and hurt. I did not expect what came next.

Sister Ezechiela, the revered director, smiled, walked up to me, and gave me a hug. "I've heard how long it took you to get caught up on your math subjects," she said with a smile. "I will talk to your geography teacher and gain you some time."

I felt relieved. Sister Ezechiela knew I was trying to catch up. In retrospect, I am surprised at my own ignorance. This was my third year at the Sisters of Nazareth School. In the preceding two, I competed for first place in a class of almost fifty with one other girl. How could I doubt that the Sister Director would know what kind of student I was? Evidently I saw her job as overwhelming, what with the welfare of the whole school hanging over her head. With several hundred students to worry about, I didn't think she knew I existed.

In retrospect, I realize that while I liked the teachers—with the exception of the geography instructor—the nuns, and the girls, I was so involved in doing my own things that I was oblivious to what others were thinking about me.

Some time later, I was called to the Sister Director's office. That scared me. It was unusual for her to call anybody in, unless a girl was in trouble.

"I have to ask you for a big favor," Sister Ezechiela began. I could not believe what I was hearing. "Two girls are bringing underground newspapers to school. If the Germans catch them with that contraband, the whole school will be closed."

The Sister Director did not want the girls to know she was aware of their actions. She could not trust their maturity. In that instant, I realized how much she trusted me. Those girls were only a year younger than me, yet she left me to my own devices to handle them.

I decided to talk some sense into them quickly. I did not tell them how I learned what they were doing, but I made them realize that bringing illicit news to school might be exciting, but it was also dumb and dangerous.

I was only sixteen years old, a teenager trying to do what I thought was right. I still did not know where I was going or what was most important to me. I had some hopes and wishes for the good days coming once the war ended, but for a while the most important thing was to stay alive.

Hostages

My contact with friends from Konstancin was slowly dissolving, but we did call each other occasionally. One day I read the name "George Schiele" on the list of German hostages. The impact was unbelievable: my seventeen-year-old friend was going to be executed.

Shortly before, the Germans had issued a proclamation announcing that for every German killed by the resistance, they would execute ten prominent Polish citizens. After the execution of the first ten hostages, the Polish underground put out the order to stop the killings of Germans.

But while the Poles stopped all actions, the Germans decided to continue claiming the deaths of soldiers—deaths that had not occurred. With characteristic German pedantry, they announced the exact locations at which the dead bodies of German soldiers had been found, enabling our organization to verify that their words were lies.

Yet, the Germans took ten hostages nonetheless. The place and time of the first ten hostages' executions was advertised in German papers and in a multitude of posters. In addition to that, to make sure the killings were properly witnessed by a reluctant crowd, German soldiers rounded up people from several streets, forcing everybody to come and watch.

And then the unpredictable happened.

One of the hostages, a prominent Polish citizen, spoke very good German. In the process of the execution, the presiding German officer asked some questions. The Polish hostage delivered a speech in German. The effect on the execution squad was so great that the officer had to repeat the command to shoot. The first ten hostages were killed.

After that incident, the hostages were silenced prior to the execution by having their mouths filled with cement. All they could do was stare at the executioners. This turned out to be too uncomfortable for the shooting squad, so for the next execution the Germans covered their victims' faces. The German executioners were becoming too sensitive, I thought angrily. I dreaded the possibility of being forced to watch one of these executions.

Thus, when my friend George Schiele's name came up, I tried to read and listen to all the gossip circulating in Warsaw, hoping that somehow George would be saved. George's father and uncle were well-known owners of a soft drink factory called Haberbusch and Schiele. In years past they were pushed by the Germans to sign the *Reichsdeutch*, or *Volksdeutch* list, admitting that they were of German nationality. Both Schiele brothers refused. They had a German name, but for generations they were Polish and proud. And the Germans tolerated them for a while. Their factory produced soft drinks, which the Germans were happy to consume.

When George was taken hostage, his father tried to pull all the strings he could to save him. Finally he offered a bribe of a million zloty. Unfortunately the news filtered out and became too well-known, leading whoever was going to take the bribe to chicken out. George was executed alongside the nine other hostages.

Losing George was an awful shock. Our group of friends stopped seeing each other after his death. We had heard horror stories for three years, but when one of our own was killed, we could not deal with it.

Ghetto - Mignon

Jewish Warsaw Ghetto workers. The Germans annihilated these Jewish girls before forcing us to replace them in the uniforms factory. Photo courtesy of the Jewish Historical Institute (the Żydowski Instytut Historyczny ŻIH) in Warsaw.

March 1943 is a time I wish I could forget. I was sixteen, still attending the Sisters of Nazareth School in Warsaw. The school continued to operate under the noses of the German authorities. We
existed officially as a seamstress school, but studied the full high
school curriculum. We were in constant danger. Literature, history,
even math was forbidden. Whenever Germans caught Poles in educational pursuits, they punished everyone equally. Students, teachers and everybody in the apartment or building where the forbidden study took place were sent to concentration camps or executed
outright.

The Polish reaction was uniform. The more Germans sup-
pressed Polish thought, knowledge, and culture, the more intensely
we studied.

One day, the Germans announced that tenth-grade students
from all seamstress schools in Warsaw were to report to the Jewish
ghetto to work. We were supposed to replace the Jewish workers,
who were being "resettled."

We knew exactly what this resettlement implied. Oświecim's cre-
matoriums were sending more smoke than ever into the skies. The day
was set for us to start working in the ghetto, and the consequences for
not reporting were spelled out thusly: "Failure to report would bring
arrest not only of the missing girl but of her entire family."

Our Sister Director tried to intervene through her connections
to the higher German Catholic hierarchy. She spoke to several German Bishops and told our parents that they had promised her there
would be no danger to us as long as we reported for work. We had
no options but to hope for the best.

The day came for us to report. I took a streetcar to an area in
Warsaw I barely knew. The whole "Little Ghetto" was surrounded
by a tall wall with barbed wire and broken glass on top.

The moment I got out of the streetcar, I saw the gate in the walls across the street. Uniformed Germans, shouting noisily, were everywhere. Everything looked grey and dirty. The melting piles of snow were as grey as the sky.

We were directed to a side gate where German soldiers checked our names and school affiliation, and then I entered the Little Ghetto.

At that point, the Germans had been occupying Poland for three and a half years. We knew how much the Jews were suffering, but we tried hopelessly to put their pain out of our minds, for we could do nothing about it.

Yet, I'll never forget the sights I saw inside the ghetto walls. In the middle of the dirty, muddy street, a column of Jews was lined up in orderly rows of eight people across. Everyone held a little bundle of precious possessions.

The Nazis did not have to hunt out Jews in their houses any more. In their systematic manner, they'd printed a list of names, dates and times to report for transport—and the required group of Jews appeared, lining up quietly in an orderly manner.

This was the first time I had seen the Jews who lived in the ghetto up close. I could not stand it. They were so obedient and passive. My whole being was crying out for them to at least try to fight and take some Nazis with them before they died. There were men, women, and children of all ages lined up, all looking grey and pale with their little satchels in their hands, waiting for their transport to death.

Shouting soldiers ordered me to hurry, to keep walking to the factory building. Upon entering, I was hit by a sickening smell from the factory kitchen. They were probably cooking some woody turnip soup, but the smell was sickening. We were told that we would be given lunch. *Over my dead body I'll eat it,* I thought.

I must have gotten overwhelmed by the situation, for I missed the other girls from my school. I was assigned to a huge hall with some two hundred girls. I did not know anybody, but it didn't seem to matter. Big tables with benches on both sides were lined up perpendicular to a wall with big windows. There are many details I cannot recall, but I remember that the whole room was eerily quiet most of the time.

Piles of uniforms were rolled into our hall, and a beautiful young Jewish woman distributed work among the tables, telling us what to do. The loud, uniformed Nazi supervisor, horse whip in hand, strode in and out, shouting orders to our Jewish girl while hitting his boots with the whip. The Jewish woman cringed every time he came close. Obviously, the whip landed on her skin with devastating frequency.

We were given unfinished German uniforms on which to sew buttons and various military insignia. The fabric from which the uniforms were made was thick and stiff, and sewing it was hard. But nobody complained. The Jewish girl told us what to do in a low, cultured tone, never having to raise her voice.

I sat at the edge of one table in the middle of the hall. Our Jewish lady stood next to me when distributing the work or talking. Within a day or two, a sort of understanding formed between us.

She told me that her name was Helen. Before the war, she was a fashion designer, and this was the reason the Germans made her a slave laborer in the position of factory foreman. She was probably in her late twenties. She had the most beautiful auburn hair, fine features, gentle manners, and a cultured demeanor that made her seem incredibly out of place in her rough surroundings. Her younger sister, equally beautiful, was in charge of the adjoining hall where more of our girls worked. We were not allowed to walk to the other halls. The Nazi with his whip made sure of that!

During our little conversations, Helen told me that the people in the ghetto were being ordered to report for "relocation" in reverse order of importance to the work force. "Once the work is done, useless people are disposed of," Helen said. She pointed at the uniforms on the table and told me that as soon as the workers who cut the uniforms used up all the available fabric, they had to report for transport.

"Workers who are sewing the uniforms now will go as soon as they finish their work," Helen said.

Her parents were in that group.

I did not ask any more. Helen knew that she would be among the last transported away to be murdered. She had difficulty dealing with the fact that some members of her family still believed they were only going to be resettled.

I do not remember how many days I spent working in the ghetto. It could not have been more than three or four weeks. Every day we arrived before eight in the morning and left after 3 or 4 PM. Our hall was high, on the third or fourth floor. We frequently heard the gargling sound of German shouting in the courtyard.

We worked like robots, speaking in hushed tones. Our own situation seemed irrelevant. Our whole being was violated by forced labor, intimidated by the surroundings, frightened by the horror around us—but it did not matter. At the end of the day we were free to go home to our families, and eventually the factory was going to run out of the uniforms. The whole ghetto experience would become only a nightmarish memory—except for people like Helen.

People in Poland sing a lot. They sing when they are sad or happy, when they pray or when they work. During one of those long, oppressive days, one of the girls started humming and the rest of the hall joined in. At this point my mezzo-soprano voice had been trained professionally for two years. When we ran out of group songs I sang alone. I remember singing several versions of "Ave Maria" and other classical songs, which the girls and Helen found soothing.

One day the shouts coming from the courtyard below made us run to the windows, where we saw a morbid scene unfold. Soldiers with guns were prodding an old woman and a little boy across the courtyard. When they reached the center of the courtyard, one soldier raised his gun and shot them in the back of their heads. Blood splattered first on the woman's white hair and then onto the dirty white snow on the ground. The little boy collapsed. We were glued to the window, watching in horror as the two soldiers collected the dead bodies, dragging them by the hair across the courtyard.

Suddenly, the German supervisor burst into our hall, whip in hand, and started yelling at us to get back to our tables and keep working.

We had difficulty dealing with the inevitable. Every morning a new column of ghost-like people lined up on command and walked to their death. We knew that every day fewer and fewer Jewish workers came to the factory. The end was coming.

Finally, the morning came when Helen entered with very red eyes. Her parents had been ordered to report to the convoy that morning. She and her sister were the last to leave—tomorrow.

I was beside myself. I did not know what to say. I felt so very desperate for her. When she came close to me again, I asked if there was anything I could do for her.

"Nothing."

"Can I take a message for anybody, anywhere?"

"No."

"Maybe you have somebody in America." I was almost pleading.

"No. There is nobody left."

"You must hate them," I said to her in a whisper of utter frustration. How could she not despise the Nazis for what they had done to her and her family?

"No," Helen replied. "I will die tomorrow, or the day after but they ... for generations, they will live with the burden of their crimes."

For an instant we were silent.

"Can I do anything for you, anything at all?" I was desperate.

After a while, she came back to me and said, "Yes, you can do one thing for me. Could you please sing once more the aria from 'Mignon'?"

I started singing. The hall fell silent. I sang that aria in French, and at that time, when I wanted to sing for Helen as beautifully as possible, I realized that the words of the song described a beautiful land with the scent of flowering lemons and birds flying in a gentle breeze.

"Do you know that land with the golden fruit, the fragrant roses, and the sweet soft breeze?" I sang.

Helen stood near me, her eyes half-closed. As I came to the strongest part of the aria, the door burst open. I stopped singing abruptly. The damn Nazi with the whip entered. The hall was in complete silence.

"Don't stop, keep singing!" He yelled at me in German. Though I understood what he said, I'd be damned before I'd acknowledge that I understood.

"He wants you to sing," Helen translated.

"Tell him that the song has ended," I said.

There were more gargling shouts from the little man. The whip hit his boots, hard.

"He says he knows that it is the aria from 'Mignon,' and he wants you to finish it," Helen said softly.

"No," was my answer. It seemed sacrilegious to let that sadistic turd of a man share Helen's last song. I was not afraid. I was angry and sad and he was an insult to the dignity of Helen's approaching death.

He grew angry and spoke furiously to her. She turned to me, tears in her eyes. "He says that if you won't sing, he will whip me here, in front of you."

I looked at that son of a bitch and said, "All right. I will finish the song." Taking a deep breath, I sang the most beautiful part of the aria: "It's there that I would like to live, to live, to love, and to die."

From that moment on, my memory is fuzzy. I vaguely remember still working in the ghetto after Helen was gone. There was complete chaos without anybody to distribute the work. There were more shouts from the soldiers outside. Our little supervisor disappeared for a while, and without anything to do, several girls and I started to wander through the other rooms in the factory. In one, we spotted a little Jewish boy trying to hide. When he saw us, he started running away. I called out to him to wait. When he realized we were Polish, he stopped, and we brought him our lunches. Thanking us, he disappeared like a shadow.

At home I became ill. I had horrible chest pains and could not stop crying. One day I was lying on my couch, sobbing uncontrollably, when Dr. George stopped by. He knew very well what I was going through. Mother asked him what she could do for me. I remember his answer well.

"Let her cry. She lived through more than she can take."

I did not go back to work in the ghetto. One of Ann's friends worked in the German offices and found out that the German files had misspelled my name; the name of the street where we lived was also wrong, adding an additional measure of protection. Ann's friend promised to arrange for my records to disappear altogether.

It was over seventy years ago, yet I will never forget those days and the beautiful Jewish girl named Helen. As I write, I am still crying.

The Aftermath

The end of the big Jewish ghetto in Warsaw. Photo courtesy of the
Jewish Historical Institute (the Żydowski Instytut Historyczny ŻIH)
in Warsaw.

After the liquidation of a small ghetto in March, the Germans continued to send transports of Jews to the Oświęcim - Auschwitz cremation ovens. Now they were liquidating the "Big Ghetto". Finally, the desperate Jews in the Big Ghetto decided to fight. In response, the German machine guns shot whomever they could kill while soldiers set fires throughout the ghetto, burning alive those who were left inside.

The Germans ordered Polish firemen to stand guard around the ghetto walls to protect the houses outside from catching fire. Some of the firemen could not stand idly by, watching this inhuman massacre, and they committed suicide. The horror of the situation drew Warsaw residents to the walls to watch. People saw desperate Jewish couples embracing in upper-story windows before jumping to their deaths. I had difficulty even hearing about it.

Suddenly the German newspapers started harping upon stories about the discovery of Russian atrocities in Katyń Forest: "Soviets massacre thousands of Polish officers in Katyń[1] forests!" "German army finds bestial proof of Soviet crimes!"

As Poles, our first reaction was: "Are you sure it was Russians, not Germans?" and, "Are you trying to make us forget your crimes in the Jewish ghettos?" But soon the horrid truth emerged.

After September 1939, thousands of families were left searching for missing sons and husbands. Now they learned the truth. Their lost menfolk were victims of the largest simultaneous execu-

---

1 In March 1940, Lavrentiy Beria, chief of the NKVD, suggested executing all members of the Polish Officer Corps. Stalin signed the order. There were about 22,000 victims. Of the total killed, about 8,000 were officers taken prisoner during the 1939 Soviet invasion of Poland; another 6,000 were police officers, with the rest being Polish intelligentsia.

tion of prisoners of war in history. Katyń was the first mass grave discovered. There were later discoveries of NKVD prisons in Belarus and the Ukraine.

Unfortunately, the Polish people were not surprised. We had learned long ago that the only thing we could expect from the Russian occupiers of our country was wild, primitive bestiality. We were stoic and cynical, asking ourselves, "Who is worse, the Germans with their concentration camps and gas chambers, or the Russians with their machine gun executions?"

I had to accept the facts and try to put it out of my mind ... or at least bury it deep inside me. Hitler and Stalin were trying to annihilate the Poles; hence, I had to stay alive.

The same individuals who were instrumental in eliminating my name from the ghetto workers roll had helped me get work in order to secure a Kenkarte, the official ID that protected me from being sent to a forced labor camp. It was the same ID that saved my life on our botched forestry mission. I could not go to school anymore, though we did notify the Sisters about what had happened in the ghetto.

At my job, I sat in an office answering the telephone and doing little else. There were three partners in the company for which I worked. During the duration of the war, the economy imposed by the Germans was corrupt and chaotic. The Germans stole everything Poles were allowed to produce, leaving only scraps for the producers. My bosses traded in grain and had to provide high quotas for the Germans. The remaining grain they sold on the black market, the only existing food market in the country.

The first day I came to work, I learned my bosses' names: Szabłowski, Pawłowski and Szymanowski—simple for a Polish girl to remember. I was told that if Mrs. Pawłoska called, I should tell her that her husband would be home after 5 PM. If Mrs. Szymanowska called, I should tell her that they were at dinner at a particular restaurant and that they expected her to come there. However, if Mrs. Szabłowska called, I was to tell her that I had no idea where her husband was.

As expected, all three ladies called and I mixed up everything. I told the wrong wife where they were dining and refused to reveal their location to Mrs. Szymanowska. When I learned about my gaffe, I was afraid I would be fired. But I was not, and I never mixed up the messages again. As a matter of fact, once I got a feel for the manipulations with which my bosses had to deal, I enjoyed playing secretary. They liked me, especially my ability to recognize caller's voices and respond without first verifying the caller's identity. How genuine it seemed!

My bosses took good care of me; frequently, at around 1 PM a waiter would come with a good dinner for me at the office. Or on other occasions, they would call and tell me to close the office and bring something for them to the restaurant, where they also fed me dinner. With the scarcity of good food, I greatly appreciated this gesture.

On the other hand, if I ever had a time conflict, all I had to do was ask for time off. When I needed extra time for my classes, I would tell them outright. When I had to do something for the underground organization, I would only say that I had a personal problem; they never asked anything more. They were good guys.

A New Muse: Drama

Outside my office hours, I devoted my whole being to singing and dance. I continued my work as Mrs. Wanda's assistant for her growing dance classes, and started replacing her occasionally as a teacher. I felt honored and tried to do the best job I could. I loved it. As my workload increased, I stayed overnight in Mrs. Wanda's apartment more often to accommodate the curfew imposed by the Germans.

During these visits, we were frequently joined by Mrs. Gula Buczynska, an accomplished and fabulous character actress. She was "older," close to fifty. She had a great knowledge of theater, music, dance, and drama. Prior to WWI, she studied in Moscow's best drama schools. Her diction was marvelous. She could whisper and be heard at the end of the long hall. She was heavy, but when she moved one could swear she was suspended in the air. Whenever she talked about the theater I listened intently to every word. Several of Mrs. Wanda's students tried to talk Mrs. Buczynska into teaching us, but she had very little time—and neither did we.

In the meantime, our dance school moved from the building on

Krowoderska Street to the Sewerynów, less than five minutes' walk from the apartment where I lived with Mother and Ann. From February or March forward, we began preparing the end-of-year dance show. Our team, the top level group, choreographed several new dances and perfected old performances. As in previous years, every class prepared at least one new performance; as Mrs. Wanda's assistant, this demanding schedule kept me in the dance school for whole afternoons.

In the center of Warsaw, next to the Napoleon Plaza, stood a little bar heavily patronized by uniformed and civilian Germans. Frank, the owner, was a frequent guest at Fregata restaurant, where Ann worked. He spoke fluent Polish and German. To my sister and the other waitresses, he claimed he "had" to cooperate with the Germans, but he insisted that he was Polish and implied he was working for the Polish underground. In the previous six months, Frank had started dining at Ann's station, tipping her more generously, and talking more and more to her, as if he were trying to gain her confidence.

At home, Ann told us about him. His behavior and stories did not make sense. He was very friendly and told her that he needed an apartment in the center of the city; he asked if we could possibly sublet our second room to him? Ann told him that we were allowed only one room for the three of us, and that we had to sublet the second room to Mrs. Maria Stamm. Frank insisted that it would be no problem; through his German connections, he could arrange another place for Mrs. Stamm. A few extra drinks with his customers from the quartermaster's office and they would find her another room!

Ann played dumb and did not ask him why he could not find a

room for himself if he knew a quartermaster. After I had come home late and dropped a pistol magazine on the floor, Ann knew I was involved in the underground and that I would know how to use the information she was giving me.

I would not have done anything were it not for the stories Frank was telling Ann about his work for the underground. This was such a "no-no." He had to be a *Reichsdeutch* or *Volksdeuch* to run his bar the way he did, but if he were in the underground he would never, never say a word about it to anybody—especially not a waitress. I told Ann to keep talking to him, to play dumb and cute and enjoy his tips getting bigger.

I reported the story to Anek, who said he would send my suspicions along the underground channels. A few days later, Anek told me my "report" had gone up the ladder. I stopped worrying about Frank and his desire to rent a room from us—I had enough to worry about as it was.

I was busy dividing my time between work and dance, limiting even my singing lessons, when I got a telephone call from Anek. He did not want to come to our apartment, instead insisting that I meet him somewhere outside. I knew immediately that something was wrong.

When we met, he told me to leave the city for several weeks.

"This is not my idea," he said. "This is a strong suggestion from above." He added that I was being watched, along with everyone in our apartment, by three different groups. Our telephone, he added, was most likely also bugged.

The German group to which Frank belonged – probably Gestapo – was very easy to spot, Anek said. But while watching the German agents, the Polish watch realized that I was also being followed by some other men. Since the Polish watch had no idea who they were, they were protecting me from a distance, making sure that the other two organizations would not realize our fellows were there. In the meantime, I had to act oblivious to what was going on and fake complete ignorance of the situation.

At that time, city streetcars frequently broke down and ran on chaotic schedules. With the war and German occupation reaching four years in duration, I had developed a foolproof system of moving around by streetcar. Whenever I saw a car going in the direction I needed, I ran to catch it, frequently jumping into the moving car. Streetcars had to slow at corners, making it the easiest place for me to climb aboard. I also jumped out of the moving streetcars whenever a location was more comfortable than the regular stop. When Anek told me I was regularly followed by "watchers," we both laughed, imagining the difficulty my followers had with my habit of jumping in and out of moving streetcars. Both groups must have had real fun following me.

After learning I was being followed, I began jumping into the last wagon of any streetcar to prevent anyone following me from boarding the same streetcar. I had fun thinking about their frustration, whoever they were.

I told Anek we were preparing a dance recital and that under no circumstances could I leave the city prior to the end of June. We decided that I would continue my regular schedule and make sure I acted ignorant of my "guardian angels." I would not watch any men walking around or try to recognize their faces. Following these instructions carefully, I did not bother to even look for my "guardian angels," whatever their political affiliation might have been. But I sure had fun taking different routes everywhere I went and making my schedule less predictable.

I devoted myself intensely to the preparations for our dance show. Our work was progressing smoothly when I contracted pneumonia shortly before the performance. I was a very sick girl with a high fever every afternoon that dropped to a minimum temperature in the mornings. Prostrate on my couch in our ground-floor apartment, I watched people on the street walking past my window. In the afternoon I could see the tops of the heads of girls going to rehearsals.

Mrs. Wanda would stop by the open window to ask how I was feeling. She worried about the group dances, of which I was the center. If I could not dance, she told me, she would be the only one who could balance out those dances. I reassured her that I would be okay, and pleaded with my friend, Dr. George, to put me back on my feet. He hesitated, deciding finally to ask my mother for permission to give me stronger medication. Mother was worried, and I greatly respect her for letting him take the risk. She knew how much my recovery meant to me and to the dance school.

George went to work and started giving me what he called "horse" pills. He managed to knock down my fever and keep my heart beating as strongly as possible.

We gave three performances: Saturday afternoon, Sunday matinee, and Sunday evening. On Saturday I danced all my dances and went straight home to bed, but started to get a fever again. George administered more medicine, worrying now about my heart.

The Sunday matinee was primarily for children, and Mrs. Wanda cut out some of my more strenuous dances to give me a chance to rest for the evening. I don't remember much from the evening show and I absolutely don't remember getting back to bed. George was still feeding me medicine, and as a result I recovered without any visible scars. He eventually asked me to come to his hospital, where he wanted to show me off to the doctors with whom he had conferred about me dancing with pneumonia.

I do not remember whether I went back to work or simply convinced my bosses that I needed to recuperate in the country. Whichever way it occurred, they did let me go and I left for the country home of my cousin, Tadea Srzednicka - Chrzanowska who lived near Radomsko, at a place called "Rzeki," which means "The Rivers".

An Enforced Vacation

Tadea and Alexander were struggling to keep up the remnant of their estate. Remnant, for the majority of the land had been taken away by Germans and was now administered by the *treuhender* (trustee). Their estate house was smaller than the *treuhender's*, but still nice to live in. They had enough villagers to work the fields, and several women to work in the kitchen and around the house. There were no springs or rivers in the area, so we used the water from the well near the kitchen.

There was a little compartment with a bucket for times when we could not go outside because of rain, but generally we used an outhouse a short distance from the building. It was locked with a key and nobody except the family and the head administrator were allowed to go in, because that outhouse was also a storage place for valuable clothing and other items. The food supplies also had to be hidden and were locked in two different places. One was a pantry, which was kept locked to ensure that employees weren't tempted to "borrow." The other locked area was better hidden and held bigger items, like a whole pig or other slaughtered animals, sacks of flour, and other supplies necessary for eating.

Occasionally Germans approached during the day and demanded food or valuables. In situations like that, Tadea innocently led them to the pantry and showed them the small amount of food we had for the next several weeks or months.

At night there were different unwanted guests, young partisans who came from the forest. As much as Tadea and Alexander sympathized with them, they would have emptied Tadea and Alexander's supplies if given a chance.

During my stay, Alexander's niece Klara was also visiting. Both of us slept in a little room in the attic. Luckily, the stairs to our room were tucked away inconspicuously behind the kitchen. Once when the partisans came, I made the mistake of leaving my beige wool Burberry coat, which we'd brought to Warsaw from Bydgoszcz, in the hall downstairs. One of the boys saw it and put it on, claiming it would keep him warm at night. The next day Tadea gave me one of her coats, but we kept it in the outhouse for safety with the rest of the desirable clothing.

That night, when "the boys from the forests" came, as was usual in such situations, they approached the building and knocked on the windows of rooms they thought were bedrooms. Indeed, they had found the master bedroom, and Alexander immediately told them that he would open the door as soon as he put something on. The first thing he and Tadea put on were their high boots, the items most desired by those in the forest. Tadea did not have any socks handy, and she simply pulled her boots on her bare feet, where they were concealed by her nightgown and a robe.

That day the partisans got some flour and schmaltz and my Burberry coat. After they left, however, Tadea could not manage to take her boots off. If I remember correctly, she slept the rest of the night with the boots on and the next morning poured talcum inside. Eventually Alexander was able to pull them off. From that day on, the riding boots were kept in the outhouse as well.

I enjoyed being in the country. One day Alexander's brother, his fiancé, Klara, and I went to gather blackberries in the nearby forest. Arriving home, we put our trophies in the kitchen. Later that day, Tadea's cook wanted to guess who'd gathered which container of fruit. Alexander's brother picked the smallest number of berries, a tiny bit more than Klara. The cook knew that only I would have filled the whole container. She had seen me working in the garden when I had nothing else to do and realized that, "Miss Sophie does not like to waste her time."

I also enjoyed helping to set the table, but it was not proper for me to help in the kitchen. However, when they were making bread, which was done at least twice a week, I made sure that I got the heel as soon as it was considered cool enough. I will never forget the smell of that rye bread being removed from the open hearth, the bread-baking oven, with a long-handled paddle.

While I enjoyed my vacation, I did not think much about the problems in Warsaw. However, several weeks later I got a letter from Ann telling me that Frank was not there anymore and that Anek would like to see me. It was an obvious signal that all was clear and I could come back home.

In the meantime, travel by rail had once more become dangerous. The Germans were merciless, arresting people on trains and shipping them to labor camps. I decided not to risk it. My cousin sent word to the neighboring estates; soon we found a truck going to Warsaw that had a place for me. There, I learned the rest of the story.

It seemed Frank had been instrumental in sending many Poles from the AK to their deaths. Evidently he'd managed to infiltrate the Polish underground, and many of our people were arrested in a string of denunciations. When Anek passed on my suspicions to the higher-ups, everything became clear: Frank was a German infiltrator.

The rest was a necessary consequence. One day in his bar, Frank and a group of his German cronies were executed. The Polish squad entered, sprayed the bar and everybody inside with machine gun fire, and left before the Germans could react.

Who were the other people following me? Polish AL (*Armia Ludowa*, the Folks' Army), a communist organization that functioned without any connection to the AK. I had no idea how they traced me until Anek told me that our group was also spying on the movements of the communist organization. In this way, they must have gotten on our tracks. But now, as I returned from vacation, all was clear. I was able to resume my "normal life" for a while—whatever "normal" meant.

Politically, it was a difficult time. Through the Potsdam and Yalta agreements the Molotov–Ribbentrop line dividing Poland into east/west spheres became official under the new name: the Curzon Line. A third of Poland was assigned to Soviet Russia.

"Could Roosevelt be that naïve?" We asked one another in disbelief. We prayed that Churchill and Roosevelt would not forget their Atlantic Charter agreement, which guaranteed basic freedoms for the post-World War II world. The first point of that agreement stipulated that territorial adjustments could be made only through the wishes of the affected people. Wasn't it obvious to Roosevelt that Stalin's talk about the Curzon Line infringed on that agreement?

Though I was still young and inexperienced, I felt Stalin's devil-ish tentacles reaching out toward our defenseless land. I knew that I didn't know or understand the world's political machinations, the deceits, the treasons, the evils. But I had to believe that one day virtue and truth would conquer all. For me that virtue and truth could exist only in America. For my own self-preservation I tried to think of excuses for Roosevelt's dealings with Stalin. I had to trust and believe in America. I needed at least that one belief for my own emotional survival.

Ivo Gall's Drama School

"I Diana..." The author as young woman beginning drama school
under the tutelage of Ivo Gall

Mother, Ann and I decided not to contact my beloved Sisters of Nazareth School again. Should the Germans be looking for me, it would be easier if the school did not know where I was. That fall, I maintained my phony work schedule, going every morning to the office, where my main job was to answer the telephones and keep my bosses connected with one another and with other businesses in town. I could not have had better employers. They even raised my pay, not by a large sum, but in those times even a small amount was helpful.

Through Anek I received words of praise from the AK: "Thank you," they told me, "your message helped us solve a great many problems!" These brief words comforted me greatly; in the AK organization, the less we said, the safer we were.

Mrs. Gula Buczynska started coming more often to the dance school and to the gatherings at Mrs. Wanda's; I felt lucky to see so much of her. Gula was highly respected by everybody. On several occasions I heard her recite theatrical pieces, and I was overwhelmed by her ability to create a perfect atmosphere and project anything she desired. Whenever she talked about the theater, I listened to every word.

When I initially told Mrs. Gula that I wanted to learn drama and recitation, she must have thought it was only an infatuation with theater work and did not take me seriously. But I was persistent and recruited several more girls. We convinced Mrs. Gula and Mrs. Wanda that we were serious, determined students.

Having found time to work with a few of us, Mrs. Gula gave us each a poem to memorize. I was to learn a poem by Brown describing the personification of the Greek god Poseidon. It was a powerful piece of verse and I memorized it quickly, but good recitation was a different matter. Mrs. Gula taught us that we had to shed all our reservations and expose our souls and emotions in any recitation or declamation.

One day, after some activity at Mrs. Wanda's apartment, Mrs. Gula and I were left alone in to work on my poem. I hoped to make a breakthrough; having finished reciting, I stood and waited for the judgment. Mrs. Gula raised her eyebrows and said, "You pretended to be the god Poseidon very well. You memorized the poem perfectly; your voice and diction are very good ... *but*. You were pretending to be Poseidon. You were still Zosia talking about Poseidon instead of being Poseidon talking about himself."

After a moment of silence, she added, "Well, maybe you do not yet have what it takes. It is getting late and we have to leave soon to be home before curfew."

I was desperate. I knew I had it what it took, and I wanted to prove it to her. But it was so hard to expose myself to the point at which I might become Poseidon. I pleaded with Mrs. Gula to let me try one more time. "Once more," she agreed. "In order to be true, you cannot worry how you look or whether anybody will laugh at you. For better or worse, shed your fears and self-criticism. Be Poseidon. He does not worry about anything; he is god of the seas."

In a corner of the room, I stood and started thinking. I visualized the oceans, the animals, the winds, the skies ... I started reciting. Mrs. Gula disappeared, the room disappeared; I shed my inhibitions and stopped pretending. I became Poseidon.

I finished. I was back in the room, looking at Mrs. Gula. She had tears in her eyes, but she was laughing with happiness. "You made it," she cried. "You won, and you will never have to go back."

I understood what she meant. I was not afraid to be true anymore.

Shortly thereafter, a private concert took place in a big villa in a suburb of Warsaw. Mrs. Wanda's top team performed several dances. We had to choose only those that could fit into a relatively small area. There were some major artists present whom I had never met before. For the first time, I heard Wanda Maliszewska, a beautiful soprano, sing Mimi's aria from *La Boheme*. I will never forget my goose bumps upon listening to her beautiful voice. Her husband, Poldek Maliszewski, played trumpet, nursing great melodies from it. It felt magnificent to be in the company of such artists. I danced a few dances and Mrs. Gula allowed me to recite my "Poseidon" for the first time in public. I must have done a good job, for the applause was long and loud.

A few days later, Mrs. Wanda greeted me with a big smile and even bigger news: Ivo Gall, the famous dramaturge, had asked for me. Other artists at the concert, Ivo Gall's close associates and students among them, had heard my recitation and recommended that he include me in his student drama group.

Before WWII, Ivo Gall and Janusz Osterwa were the most respected theatrical directors/producers in Poland. They organized and ran a famous experimental theater called Reduta. During the German occupation, Ivo Gall lived in Warsaw and Osterwa in Krakow. Both men risked their lives by teaching handpicked drama students, waiting for the war to end so that they could open theaters again. Among Osterwa's students in Krakow was young Karol Wojtyła, later Pope John Paul II.

Though I danced and sang constantly and had recently begun learning declamation and recitation, I was still hesitant to admit that my young life's desire was to be in the theater. I feared this dream would be seen as too bohemian, and I still remembered the time before the war when my Aunt Wladyslawa Macieszyna was beside herself to learn that Ann was a competitive tennis player.

"How gauche, and what is she wearing?" was her first question. Her second remark: "Shorts? Simply disgusting."

My mother found it funny considering the source of the remarks. Aunt Władka must have forgotten that in her own youth she was quite a controversial lady.

But now, at seventeen, I did admit that drama and theater were my dreams. Ivo Gall's invitation to join his theater study group reinforced my wishes. The possibility of my dreams coming true and my being able to study drama made me excited and elated beyond description.

Finally the day came when I went to meet the famous master. Ivo Gall lived with his wife on Tamka Street, not far from the Vistula River, in a quiet part of the city. When I arrived, Ivo opened the door himself and led me through a dark corridor. Ivo's desk stood near a window in a big bedroom, which also served as his study. Against one wall were benches for his students, upon which I later spent many hours listening to his teaching or watching other students as they practiced various scenes.

That first day, I was very nervous, afraid that Ivo would find me unworthy. He was an ageless, grey-haired man with a kind smile and the peaceful demeanor of a philosopher. Early in our conversation, I told him that though everybody called me Sophie, my true name was Kordianna. He picked up on this detail immediately and declared that the name Diana fit me much better than Sophie.

"Who knows?" he said. "One day I may cast you as Diana in an ancient drama." He told me that Poldek and the others had raved about my dancing and my delivery of "Poseidon." That day, for Mr. Ivo and all those around him, I became Diana.

At first I came for lessons alone or with a few other new students. For security reasons, we never arrived as a big group or entered the building through the same gate; our actions were restricted by the ever-present fear of German discovery, concentration camps, and death. In occupied Poland, drama studies were *streng verboten* (strongly forbidden).

My first role was "Jewdocha" from Wyspiański's classic drama, *Sędziowie* (*The Judges*). In a way, Ivo apologized for the difficult and tragic nature of the role, but he claimed that in spite of my being so young and romantic, he had seen my potential for tragedy. I did not see his words' prophetic possibility, but studied hard anyway. I also had a few lighter scenes to work on with other students.

I was the rookie in a group of already accomplished performers. My reaction was the same as when, three years earlier, I entered Mrs. Wanda's modern dance school. I listened to every word of instruction, tried to apply everything I heard and saw, and like my mother used to say, "jumped in with all four feet." Then as now, whenever I get immersed in a project that interests me, I lose sight of everything and everybody else around me. I can only see my goal.

Ivo's teaching was gentle, descriptive and memorable. When he analyzed characters, he had a very deep feeling for each of them. He told us that he wished he could play all the roles himself. He coached us to learn, to feel, and to absorb the emotions of the characters we portrayed and—this is much, much more difficult—to give away those emotions as our own.

"It is easier to strip off your clothes and stand naked in a crowded place than to expose all your feelings," Ivo reminded us repeatedly. I had broken that barrier with Mrs. Gula when reciting Poseidon's verse; in different roles, I struggled to do it again.

We all loved Ivo, who said that he had some favorite students. To be specific: all of us.

Shortly before Christmas, a party was planned for all Ivo's students at his apartment. I wondered what to wear from my extremely limited wardrobe; I considered the black rayon dress I had stolen from the ghetto the last day I worked there, but was unsure, as I had never worn black before. Traditionally, only older Polish ladies wore black. My mother, however, encouraged me to try it. With the addition of a little corsage made of silk sweet pea flowers, the dress did not look too old for my seventeen years.

Our party was on a Sunday afternoon a few days before Christmas. The weather was frosty, and I arrived at Mr. Ivo's apartment excited, my cheeks more flushed than ever. I was happy to see Poldek, my promoter; soon after came Włodek Kwasniewski, whom I had also met before and who was a very pleasant lady's man. Another younger, very handsome man accompanied him.

Włodek led him to me and made a special introduction. "Bohdan, please meet Diana, but remember that's not just her name. I saw her perform and I can vouch that she is *the* Diana, a Greek goddess."

I must have flushed even more, if that was possible, for Włodek pointed at my cheeks and gently kissed me. I smiled, pleased to hear the compliments, and did not object when the new colleague asked if he could also kiss me, following Włodek's example.

And so I met Bohdan.

Shortly after the New Year of 1944, my studies at Ivo Gall's intensified. I remember being involved in more classes and included in more of the other students' studies. Besides continuing work on the tragic role of Jewdocha, I was assigned Marysia from *The Wedding*, a famous 1901 drama, also by Wyspiański. To change the mood, I also learned the role of Klara in Fredro's comedy *The Maidens' Vow*. Fredro's Polish comedies were as entertaining and delightful as his contemporary, the French playwright Moliere. I had written a report on them at school, for which I was much praised by Sister Lauretana.

During this time, the Eastern Front of the war was drawing near. The Germans tried to hide the news of their disastrous campaign in Russia, but it filtered through to the Polish population nonetheless. Railroad transports through Warsaw carried thousands of wounded and frostbitten German soldiers back from the Russian front. As if to make up for their losses, the German occupying forces exerted even more cruelty, making Poles' lives as difficult as they could. We were hungry, cold, and frequently afraid, but I, Diana, was starting to live the happiest times of my life.

Bohdan

My love Bohdan Fidziński

We all had schedules, coming at different times and on different days as life allowed. As people dribbled in, Ivo usually did not interrupt what we were doing; the newcomer simply slipped in and sat down. One day, however, when Bohdan came in and sat in an empty spot next to me, Ivo stopped his lecture and exclaimed with relief, "Bohdan, where have you been?"

"They interrogated me," Bohdan answered quietly. As was usual in such a situation, nobody asked anything more about why or where. The answers were obvious. Yet Ivo, painful concern clear in his eyes, kept asking: "Are you really okay?"

"I'm almost all right now," Bohdan said, "but I did have to take care of my kidneys for a few days." The damn Gestapo must have beaten him to force him to talk, I thought. I did not say anything, but the expression on my face made him smile and reassure me: "Don't worry, Diana, I'll live."

The first time I met Bohdan at Ivo's Christmas party, I liked him. At only twenty-three years old, he was younger than most of Ivo's male students. Włodek and the others were close to, or older than, thirty. Bohdan was very handsome and, more importantly, very talented. Ivo relied on him to stand in for various scenes with other students.

Later, I realized that Ivo also had deep feelings for Bohdan. He wrote in his memoir, *Mój Teatr* (My Theater) that Bohdan was a "young man with a great future, very handsome, gifted with incredible grace, well built, with a silky baritone voice, great charm and physical coordination. In other words, he was one of the very few born not only with great physical attributes, but with seldom-seen talent and intelligence. Besides all these attributes, he was a man of great nobility of character, humble, simple and deserving of infinite trust."

Whenever somebody rang the bell at the front door of Ivo's apartment, one of us had to go open it. Since we lived fairly close, I was often able to come early in the afternoon and when the doorbell rang, I jumped up and went to the entry hall. However, once Bohdan was in, I was happy to let the other students take turns opening the door.

Like me, Bohdan was studying opera. He had the smoothest, softest baritone I had ever heard. While many singers, especially tenors, strain their voices when delivering a song, Bohdan never had to. His voice could be powerful or soft without effort. He studied with Mr. Kazuro, a well-known voice teacher. Mr. Kazuro's school gave concerts, which I started attending regularly. "Figaro" was one of Bohdan's favorite arias. He liked the funny words: "Oh, there won't be any cooing during the war, nor pleading for help under the ladies' windows ..."

I started liking Bohdan more and more. He came to classes and ran away, like most of us, hurrying home in order not to miss curfew. When Bohdan and I talked, we spoke of drama or singing. He was very private and I knew nothing about his personal life. He was an accomplished drama student and I was a rookie. He was twenty-three and appeared quite mature; I was barely eighteen, but felt like I was thirteen. He was nice to me, but I could see him being very nice to all the other students as well.

By that time I had a pretty good idea of how I affected the men around me. With Bohdan, though, I lost all my self-assurance. I did not know what to think, but I could not stop thinking about him. I hid my fondness for Bohdan with difficulty and I intended to keep it that way, no matter how frustrated I felt.

I'll never forget the day in Ivo's study when there were only the two of us, Bohdan and me. Ivo asked us to perform the scene from Fredro's comedy, *The Maidens' Vows*.

I had worked on Klara's comical role for a while, usually with somebody else. This time Bohdan played Gustav. In Fredro's comedy, Gustav is in love with Aniela, Klara's good friend. In the scene we performed, Klara promises Gustav to speak to Aniela and arrange a meeting for them. I enjoyed playing the tease to the poor gullible young man—except this time, the gullible young man was Bohdan. When I, as Klara, promised to arrange the meeting for Gustav with Aniela, Bohdan came close to me and took hold of my hands, thanking me excitedly.

At that point, I lost it! Bohdan's closeness and his hands holding mine was more than I could bear. I continued reciting Klara's lines to Gustav, but emotionally it was me, Diana, revealing her true feelings to Bohdan.

I must have been speaking too fast and portraying anything but the teasing personality of Klara. When our scene ended, I hid my face in my hands and apologized. Ivo was laughing, saying something about the speed of my speech. Bohdan was smiling. I felt like a fool; I was crushed, and I did not know what Ivo, or more importantly, Bohdan was thinking.

Shortly after this incident, Ivo and Mrs. Wanda started new classes for all drama students, with Mrs. Wanda teaching movement study in her apartment. My ego began to feel slightly more secure. I was Mrs. Wanda's best student and assistant, and they, the drama students, were on my turf now.

Bohdan acted the same way as always: nice. Whenever he looked at me, though, there was that special smile in his eyes. Finally I gathered my courage and told him that I would like to talk to him—alone.

After class at Mrs. Wanda's, we left quickly and passed through the courtyard. Instead of going to the street, we went to an adjoining empty area to be alone. The houses there had been bombed and flattened at the beginning of the war. We walked through the rubble. When we had gone far enough that the rest of the departing students could not hear, Bohdan stopped and turned to me.

"What is it that you want to talk about?" His face was serious but his eyes held that smile I was afraid to interpret. I felt vulnerable, unsure what he was thinking, but I was determined. I'd rehearsed my lines for several days, but now nothing seemed right.

"Bohdan, do you have somebody?" I asked, looking into the distance.

"Yes." I looked at him, an obvious expression of panic on my face. He burst out laughing. "I live with my mother."

I felt helpless and hopeless—and he was teasing me!

"Are you blind?" I blurted. "Can't you guess how I feel about you?"

"Well," he said, "that's encouraging, because I don't like to stand in line."

I didn't understand. Bohdan began mocking Włodek's introduction at the Christmas party: "This is Diana, the Greek goddess." I did not consider it funny, and in my confusion I blurted out: "Diana was Roman; Artemis was Greek, and besides, what does that have to do with me?"

"You don't appear to be the most available girl," Bohdan countered.

"Me? I'm not the most available?" I was getting angry. "What about you?"

In my frustration I felt Bohdan was implying I was like Helen of Troy, surrounded by admirers. Other students leaving Mrs. Wanda's were calling to us now. Confused and ready to quit, I said something like, "I shouldn't have bothered you." But Bohdan stopped me and got serious.

"Yes, there is a problem," he said. "Between my work and Ivo's and Kazuro's classes, I have no free time for myself or anybody else."

"What about the weekends?" I asked.

"Diana, please. I have other obligations."

I knew instantly what he meant – the Polish underground.

"Under these circumstances, it wouldn't be right to tie myself to anybody, no matter what I feel," he said. An expression of sorrow washed across his face. "I wish I did not have to live with my mother. I worry about her constantly. The Germans are snooping around me; I hope they won't try to interrogate her. She's suffered enough." The question in my eyes led to further explanations. "You probably don't know that they killed my father and brother."

I did not know.

He was right: there were so many reasons we should stay apart. Yet, the more Bohdan talked, the more I wished I could be a part of his life.

"I'm not demanding; I'm patient; I promise not to complain," I said, realizing belatedly that I was almost begging. Disarmed by my directness, Bohdan started smiling.

"Besides," he assumed the *Figaro* pose and sang, "there won't be cooing during the war."

Finally, he admitted that I'd cracked his armor long ago. We laughed happily, and I told him that I would be satisfied if I knew that he liked me just a little more than everybody else. "Just a little," he agreed.

From that day on, we stopped pretending. For better or worse, we admitted to each other that we cared, and cared a lot. Outwardly nothing changed. We never held hands or kissed when other students were around. Only Mrs. Wanda knew how I felt. She joked that every time she stepped between the two of us, she felt that the flowing current could electrocute her.

In dance school, we prepared intensely for our annual June show, which was going to be bigger and better than ever before. Our advanced team had studied and danced together for more than three years, and this unity and professionalism was visible in our performances. The other classes were not far behind.

Mrs. Wanda asked Bohdan to be the Master of Ceremonies for the show. She liked Bohdan a lot and believed that with his sense of humor and ability to perform, he would make a perfect MC. Bohdan was happy to be complimented in this way, but accused me of twisting Mrs. Wanda's arm. I swore to him that I had nothing to do with it. The fact that he doubted his own abilities and people's opinions of him endeared Bohdan to me even more.

In preparation, I often stayed in Mrs. Wanda's apartment to work past curfew. On one of those days, Bohdan also stayed to work out the details of his job as MC. Surprisingly, in spite of the fact that Bohdan and I were overwhelmed with happiness at the extra time together, we all managed to do our work. Mrs. Wanda was understanding and fond of both of us, and we did not have to pretend in front of her.

Poland's spring weather is unpredictable. It can be clear and warm, cold, raining, and windy or everything in between. Finally June exploded with the long awaited summer warmth. In June 1944, Warsaw's atmosphere mirrored the weather...

Suddenly, big news had electrified Warsaw: American troops, landed in Normandy! Walking the streets, we could tell who had heard the news, for their eyes were smiling. The German newspapers obviously kept mute, but the underground news hit Warsaw's streets like a storm. People's faces held smiles and a glimmer of hope for the end of German occupation, the Nazis, Hitler and all the cruelty and hardship their repressive regime represented.

The next time I saw Bohdan, I was exuberant: "Now the Americans will push the Krauts to the end!" Looking at Bohdan, I found myself imagining the day when we would be able to live normal lives.

"Dianka—" Whenever he addressed me using the diminutive, a special tenderness came into Bohdan's voice. "Yes, the Americans are in Paris, but that's still far away. In the meantime, we have to survive."

"Bohdan, let me transfer to your unit," I said, determined to try

"Diana, please don't even talk about it. It would never work." He was upset, frustration in his eyes. I did not want to anger him.

"I'm sorry. I know I'm silly, but I feel like I can protect you from bullets because I love you so much."

If nothing else, my logic succeeded in changing Bohdan's expression from sorrow to warmth; he gave me his winning argument with a smile.

"If your love can protect me from bullets, you can do it as well from a distance. In the meantime, let's go home. Your streetcar is coming." Bohdan gave me a quick warm hug, guided me to the stop, and watched me get in. As much as I resented the curfew, I never tried to break it. Staying out on the streets unnecessarily late would only give the Germans more chances to exercise their repression.

"See you tomorrow, Dianka," Bohdan called. He waved at me, walking slowly across the street to catch his streetcar in opposite direction.

Our upcoming dance show was planned for a 2 PM matinee on Saturday at Mały Teatr, the "little theater" across the street from my family's apartment house. When the big day arrived, the younger girls readied themselves for the beginning of the program. I was backstage in the theater with them. It grew late, the theater was full, and we were waiting—but we weren't starting. Something was wrong.

I learned that Bohdan hadn't arrived. Such lateness was unlike him. Despite my fear, I hoped, prayed, and stayed calm.

Finally he arrived, running down the aisle to the front of the stage where Mrs. Wanda was standing. We all breathed a sigh of relief.

Bohdan walked to the front of the curtain and said something. I heard the roar of the audience's laughter. He did not have to tell them that he had been detained by the German police, but he did, making a joke of it.

The show started. Bohdan announced dances, told little stories, and sang. I learned later that the audience had a hard time deciding whether they liked him or our dances more! The energy and atmosphere in the theater were fantastic. The audience's appreciation stimulated our dancing and Bohdan's performance, and our performances fed that energy still further.

By the time my solo arrived, all I heard Bohdan say was: "Next, Diana, dancing out." I did dance it out. I no longer remember the choreography, but I know I soared.

The show was an incredible success. We were all flying high, higher than the proverbial Cloud Nine.

After, many people in the audience hung around talking to Mrs. Wanda and Bohdan. Mrs. Wanda liked my mother a lot and introduced many people to her. Ivo Gall, his wife, and most of his drama students paid her great compliments, making her even more happy and proud. However, the girls and I did not mingle with the audience. We were cleaning up, exuberant after a job well done.

When Bohdan came to talk to me, I congratulated him on a superb job.

"The audience loved you more than us, you stinker," I exclaimed. He smiled, but he wasn't happy.

"Diana, I hoped we could spend at least an hour together, but with me being interrogated and the show going long, I have to leave right now. I'm already late." He looked very concerned, knowing he was disappointing me. As much as I wished that I could have celebrated our success, I accepted our duties calmly.

"I understand," I told him. "Please don't worry. I'll be okay."

Backstage, people milled about, packing up costumes and preparing to leave. To those girls, I was a big star. I helped choreograph and teach many of their dances, but above all, I danced lead, or center, in every performance by our top ensemble.

The irony was cruel—in that moment I, the star, felt all alone.

Bohdan and I stood a proper distance apart, not even allowing our hands to touch, speaking softly. I was torn. Every cell in my body yearned to melt into his arms. I saw in his eyes that he knew exactly how I felt, which made it harder for him to follow his duty and leave. At the same time I did not want him to worry.

Finally he made me promise that in order to unwind I'd call some old friends and spend the rest of the afternoon with them. We barely touched hands, and then he ran away.

It was a pretty, warm, and sunny day. I came home alone. Our room was peaceful; the sun shone through the windows, and I felt incredibly satisfied. Not only was my personal performance my best ever, but the rest of the school and all the groups I'd helped train had reached a higher level. My greatest pleasure, however, derived from the public's appreciation of Bohdan. I enjoyed sharing the talents of the man I loved.

I could not help but think how strange it was that my own sister hadn't invited me to spend the rest of the afternoon with her and the girls. As I left, Ann and several of the younger girls were talking excitedly about going somewhere. Mrs. Wanda expressed her concern for me, having seen Bohdan leave alone, but I reassured her that it was all right. But as Bohdan had suggested, being alone that afternoon turned out to be too difficult. I decided to call old friends from vacations in the mountains, people I had not seen for many months.

When I called, they were delighted to have me join them at a get together that afternoon. They were genuinely happy to see me again; it felt good to be with old friends. We played records, danced, and talked about this and that. As we spoke, it became clear to me how much older we were than the last time we'd been together. Was it less than a year ago that we were still carefree youngsters?

We did not talk about the war and the military situation. However, it was painfully obvious that we were all aware of the encroaching German/Russian front, which would run over us soon with unpredictable results. Two years earlier, when we had fun together, we were indestructible teenagers. That afternoon we were so much older, worried about what was coming for each of us. I guessed that we were all involved in the Polish underground, though this was a forbidden subject.

It was the end of spring. In less than four months, by the beginning of October, I would be the only person in that group to emerge alive from the uprising in Warsaw.

During classes, Bohdan and I saw each other a lot; however, the only time we were able to be alone together was after class. We would take a streetcar to a point halfway between our homes. We joked about how great it was to be in the overcrowded streetcars, where we could hug each other discretely.

Frequently, we perched on rubble on street corners, waiting until we had to take the last streetcars in opposite directions directly to our homes, which we reached seconds before curfew. In June, we ate cherries bought from street vendors as we enjoyed these precious moments together.

In those cherished days, I learned more details about Bohdan's family. Two years earlier, the Germans had murdered his father and older brother. I remember vividly my reaction when he told me that painful story.

"Aren't you waiting for the end of this war to get even?" I asked, feeling his pain. He looked at me with a serious expression.

"Their lowly actions aren't worthy of our hate. Hate and revenge would only do us damage," he said, deeply held conviction in his voice. "I am waiting for every single German to go back to Germany and leave our country alone, so that we can build our own lives anew."

He looked at me, a smile returning to his eyes. He made me feel included in his dream of a better life. His words made sense to me. He was so young, but so very wise.

At that time, we did not talk about our work in the Polish underground, though it was obvious that the reason Bohdan had no time on the weekends was because, as I learned later, he was training his platoon for action.

During one of our meetings that beautiful summer, Bohdan was unusually apprehensive. When we parted, he asked me to give him something for good luck. Following our underground principles, he said only that he was going on an extremely dangerous assignment.

I had a little silver chain bracelet which I always wore on my left wrist. It was the only precious item I had, so I took it off and handed it to Bohdan. I knew what extreme danger meant. Bohdan could be killed, or worse, caught, imprisoned and inevitably tortured during interrogation. I did not have to say anything; I looked at him and he knew that my thoughts and prayers were with him, that I hoped for a good angel to guide him to safety. My bracelet made a tiny pile in his hand. He let it slip into his left chest pocket, his hand further covering his chest, as if to make sure that his talisman was secure.

"Please call me as soon as you can," I pleaded.

"I will," he said.

Our silence was more eloquent than any words. I prayed that my love would shield him from harm. And shortly after that incident, I decided to once again say the unmentionable.

"Bohdan, we mustn't talk about the details, but let's stop pretending. We are both doing our patriotic duty in separate places. I'd like to transfer to your unit. Whatever I am doing now, I can do as well in your company. Either of us can initiate my transfer."

Even the possibility of our working together in AK made me happy. However, this plan was the furthest thing from Bohdan's own aims.

"Yes, and if something should happen to me," he said sarcastically. "You'd be very careful not to risk your life."

I knew how right he was, but I wasn't about to give up. "If we fight close to each other, I could save your life, or you could save mine."

My arguments were logical to me, but not to Bohdan. He reassured me that he would always try to take care of me, but he wouldn't let me move to his company. I knew that I would have walked through fire for him, but I also knew that he was determined and I wouldn't win this argument, no matter how hard I tried. Bohdan knew the position assigned to his company, which made his judgment final.

Like all our compatriots in Warsaw, the two of us had been living in constant danger for four years. Every day we heard about somebody being arrested, disappeared. or murdered. We hoped and tried not to fear. We did not talk about our anxieties. Rather, in those precious times that we were together, we felt very peaceful, almost tranquil, as if the horrors outside could not touch us.

The end of the war drew near. One day, Bohdan told me that he wanted to supply me and my family with some fabric. "God only knows what the situation will be when the Germans leave and the Russians come," he said darkly. He wanted me to have something of value to barter with, and he was working in a textile warehouse where well-known Polish textiles from Bielsko-Biala were stored before being sent to Germany. Bohdan arranged to have an order go my way, asking that Ann come pick up the textiles. Taking a droshky, Ann brought several bolts of valuable fabric home.

Bohdan decided to secure me still further. He came to our apartment unexpectedly and handed me a pile of Polish zlotys. I was completely flummoxed.

"Bohdan, what is this?"

"Don't you recognize it? It's money!"

War made for unusual circumstances, but to me, receiving

money from a man, no matter how much we loved each other, was unthinkable. I didn't know what to say.

"Dianka." Bohdan looked at me with his patient smile. "Just put it in a safe place for a rainy day. You know as well as I do that there will be more than a little rain soon."

His concern overwhelmed me. "Thank you, dear; I'll keep it safe for both of us."

"You cannot imagine how much I hope so," he said, almost to himself.

In the next moment he kissed me and told me that he had to run. *What else is new?* I thought.

Under the occupation, our Polish currency was badly devalued, but the amount Bohdan gave me still had substantial value. I was happy he was trying to provide me with some security, but it worried me. Was he able to anticipate the unpredictable future?

July 1944. Our nation was between a rock and a hard place. The Germans were withdrawing from the Russian front. The approaching Soviet "liberators" seemed ominous. It was obvious to every Pole that between the departing German army and the descending Soviet Communist machinery, we would soon have to battle for our capital city.

Bohdan managed to get one Sunday free and we left the city for a picnic, taking the narrow gauge train to a small town north of Warsaw. There, the river Vistula is very wide with many sandy beaches. The day was sunny and warm. We walked through a little forest where many people like us were enjoying the beautiful summer weather and taking respite from the difficulties of everyday life.

We found a sandy island a short swim away and changed in the privacy of the willows. Bohdan was a strong swimmer and carried our picnic and clothing across. We lay on the warm sand, alone on the island, separated from other people by water and willows. I remember how incredibly peaceful I felt, which surprised even Bohdan, who was used to me being anything but quiet. I was happy; I had everything I wanted that day. I was close to my love, able to touch and kiss him, and neither of us had to go anywhere. The sand was warm, the water cool, the breeze refreshing, but above all, Bohdan was looking at me with loving eyes. What else could I have wanted?

In the late afternoon, rested and happy with well-roasted skins, we started back toward the railroad station. In the forest, we encountered five Don Kazak conscripts from the German army. They were walking and singing in the most beautifully harmonized way. We listened and waited for them to come closer. These were very young men, nearly boys, obviously enjoying themselves and singing like only Don Kazaks could. Bohdan complimented their singing. They returned the compliment by calling me "krasawica." Bohdan translated, explaining that "krasawica" means a beauty.

"They could have talked about anything, but they had to talk about you. Do you understand now why I considered you so unavailable?" That subject remained our favorite topic of teasing banter.

Those last two weeks of July, we lived a day at a time. Daily military transports rolled through Warsaw's thoroughfares. I did not know what was coming; I only knew that I hoped we would survive the deluge. Today, I do not remember anything specific except the last Friday, July 28.

Late in the afternoon, somebody called and asked me to deliver two bottles of Mountain Ash vodka, which I was trading at the time on the black market. The drop-off point was only a few blocks from where we lived, so I walked. The individual lived in a *cul-de-sac* off Novy Świat. I made my delivery and turned for home, walking slowly in the middle of the street against the traffic of residents rushing home before curfew.

Suddenly, I saw a commotion on the sidewalk ahead of me and an individual running in my direction.

It was Bohdan. At first I did not recognize him. He wore some kind of cap on his head, baggy pants, and high boots, an outfit I'd never seen. He ran up to me with strange urgency. We embraced in the middle of the street; he held me tight, repeating, "I thought I'd never see you again," in a whisper.

Bohdan sounded desperate, near tears. I held him, waiting for him to regain his composure. I did not have to speak. Shortly, Bohdan told me that he would let me know what had happened, but we had to find a place off the streets before curfew.

I was beside myself, standing in a daze. I loved Bohdan with all my heart and I knew that he loved me, but in that moment I was overwhelmed by our love and its power.

Our apartment was nearby, but in the one room with Mother and Ann, we would not be able to talk, nor was there an extra place for Bohdan to sleep. Mrs. Wanda's apartment was big but too far away; I did not even know if she was in town. A nearby hotel seemed like the only solution, but Bohdan was concerned about the impropriety and, to a lesser degree, the danger of German police, who habitually raided the hotels.

It took me no time to make up my mind. With the recent movements of the German armies, I doubted they would bother to raid us. As far as my reputation was concerned, Bohdan's opinion was the only one I cared about.

To ensure that my mother and Ann did not worry, I called home and told a white lie about meeting a girlfriend and deciding to stay with her for the night. In the hotel room, we checked for listening devices, which were frequently installed in hotel fixtures. Finding nothing, we settled in a corner of the room, staying away from all light fixtures just in case. I settled in Bohdan's arms and he told me what had happened.

That morning, the Polish underground army headquarters received a radio message, ostensibly from London, giving the order to start the uprising. Polish troops were mobilized and called to their positions. However, the underground army headquarters had doubts about the order. Over the last few days, Warsaw's Polish High Command had been sending messages to London with specific information about German troops amassing inside the city. On that Friday, there was a very high concentration of German military units in Warsaw. They were coming from the east and staying in the city instead of moving farther west.

However, while they awaited further orders from London, Polish headquarters in Warsaw kept all units in their assigned attack positions, and Bohdan's unit was fully mobilized. I asked him where his position was.

"In Mokotów (Warsaw's southern district), across from the SS barracks."

To me, the SS barracks sounded like a death sentence.

"Yes," Bohdan admitted, "we were preparing to attack them." My heart sank. "In the afternoon," Bohdan continued, "Polish Warsaw High Command finally managed to reestablish contact with HQ in London. London never sent any orders."

The instructions to start the uprising had been sent by Moscow, the underground officers quickly realized. Bohdan's unit was dismissed and told to go home. Bohdan took a streetcar from the far end of town, rushing against logic and safety, not knowing if he could find me before curfew, nor where he would be able to spend the night to get off the streets. He kept repeating: "I was afraid I wouldn't be able to see you again."

I'd never seen him so desperate. I cherished his love and felt his anxiety. We knew that while the uprising had been called off that afternoon, it would be on again soon, this time by order of London. We tried not to talk about the dangers we would face. We only told each other to be careful and promised to survive the next few weeks. There were no tears. We cherished our short time together, enjoying loving each other and being loved. We sat for the longest time in the security of one another's arms. Finally, emotionally exhausted, we fell asleep.

Early morning city noises woke us. We dressed with heavy hearts and embraced for the last time. Bohdan held my face in his hands, as if trying to remember it forever. We walked out of the hotel and back toward the main street. On the corner we touched hands for a second and parted, going in different directions.

I could not bear it. I stopped at a store window to look back. Bohdan was getting into a streetcar. He stayed on the steps of the moving streetcar, looking back. Our gaze held until the streetcar took him away.

I went home. Telephone orders instructed Kora to stay close to home. I knew what that meant: as soon as some of the German troops moved west, the next order would come from London.

August 1, 1944:
Warsaw Uprising

Thor missiles and bombs strike Napoleon Plaza during the Warsaw Uprising, August 1945. We moved past this site daily. Photo by Sylvester Braun, pseudonym "Kris" courtesy of Historical Museum of Warsaw.

For the next two days I stayed home, as ordered, waiting for the courier with whom I would travel to our unit's battle position. For obvious security reasons, the exact place was unknown to me.

The whole of Warsaw felt as if it was sitting on a keg of dynamite. For five long years, we had told one another: "Till the end of the war." Now that end was visible.

The Germans had been beaten on the eastern and western fronts. In the last several weeks, special observation points had been erected to watch and count German troops entering and leaving Warsaw. These observers also reported many hospital transports from the Russian front, bearing German soldiers who were literarily in pieces. That alone was reason for us to rejoice—except for the fact that behind the German retreat was an advancing Soviet Army. Poland's history with Russia was well-ingrained in our brains and hearts.

In September 1939, as part of their pact with Germany, Soviet troops invaded Poland from the east, claiming they were there to liberate us. Five years later, we knew all about the Communists and their intentions toward Poland and the Poles. Russians, whether Communists or White Tsarists, were never friendly to Poland. Even in 1920, shortly after the signing of the WWI peace treaty, they invaded us again, unsuccessfully. Prior to that, Tsarist Russia occupied Poland for almost two centuries.

World War II was drawing to an end, but not for Poland. We knew we could not avoid occupation, but we could lessen its effects if we could win control of our capital before the Soviet arrival. A military uprising was the only logical solution.

It was set to begin on August 1 at 4 PM in the afternoon, but in several places shooting broke out earlier. Around 3 PM we heard the first shots on the streets and saw people running past our house in all directions.

Our house, six stories high, was like an island surrounded by a triangle of streets. We were set back slightly from Krakowskie Przedmieście, one of Warsaw's big thoroughfares. From the lower part of town, near the Vistula River, our street, Oboźna, ran into Krakowskie Przedmieście directly across from Police Command and the Holy Cross Church. From Police Command, two streets ran like two arms on either side of our house. Immediately behind, the third street, Karaś, closed the triangle. Karaś was a very short street ending at the side entry to the University of Warsaw. On this street there was a big building, a theater called Mały (Small), with an entryway directly across from the back entrance to our building.

At the first sound of shots, some people ran away from the big thoroughfare and stopped for shelter at our gate. Soon after, machine guns from Police Command began shooting down our street.

Behind our house, some Polish soldiers ran out of the theater and proceeded toward the university. As they crossed our street, a machine gun cut two of them in half. From our window, we saw one man seemingly stretched into an eight-foot long body.

After the initial wave of passersby ran into our gate and the two soldiers were killed, the streets became empty and quiet. We heard shooting from further away.

It was almost dark when battle noises began to sound from the University of Warsaw. The Germans were attacking. A group of Polish soldiers ran down Oboźna Street, unseen by the German machine gunner at the police station.

Several civilians ran toward our gate. The gunner must have heard them, for the last woman did not make it. She fell to the street, shot through the hips. From our gate people threw a rope to her and pulled her in. On the third floor lived a lady doctor. She started taking care of the wounded. Fortunately for us, she was also caught at home, having been told to be at her station point at 4 PM.

Among the people who stopped at our house were two nuns from the St. Ursula convent. Mother invited them to come inside

223

our apartment. We sat in the little hall, which had no windows, making it safer than the two front rooms, which were in danger of ricocheting grenades or shooting from the street.

Our ground floor apartment had only two rooms, a hall, bath-room, and the kitchen with a little pantry. The hall led to the front door, outside of which a small entry led to the passage between the gate and the courtyard. On the opposite side was the staircase to the upper floors. The courtyard was surrounded by the house on three sides and an eight-foot brick wall on the fourth side. From the court-yard, one could enter another staircase and a gate serving the apart-ments on the Karaś Street side. Those apartments faced the theater.

It was already dark when a group of Polish soldiers ran in, rushed through the courtyard, and disappeared into the theater. Again, everything became quiet.

Mr. and Mrs. Stamm, who occupied the other front room, were too scared to even sit with us in the hall. They stayed in the cellar most of the time, George Stamm driving everyone crazy with his uncontrollable fears.

During the night, university buildings began to burn. A new wave of escapees sought refuge in our house. A little boy around seven years old and his mother were shot crossing the street, like the woman who had been wounded earlier. They were also shot through the buttocks. The doctor asked me and Ann to help take care of them. I sat on the edge of the bathtub, holding the boy, while the doctor washed his wounds. The boy closed his eyes and was very calm in my arms.

"I think he's fainted; wash him quickly," I whispered. He opened his eyes.

"No, I'm awake, but it's okay," he said. He was a brave little one.

In its three wings, our building had at least fifteen apartments. With all the refugees running in from the street, we must have had at least twice as many people as normal. All the tenants began to organize themselves. We had to feed everybody and divide them between apartments for daily necessities. Fortunately, our courtyard was walled-in and relatively safe, allowing many people to stay there during the warm August weather.

Another small grace was the existence of a little store in a corner of our house, which had typically meager supplies of rationed groceries. Still, there was something to eat. All supplies were divided among the tenants. There was a lack of fats or meat, and the tenants agreed to declare what they had and share. We formed a committee and voted in a house captain.

Needless to say, some tenants decided not to share everything. I had the good fortune to talk to an individual who claimed to have no meats or fats. But when the poor guy spoke to me, all I could smell was smoked sausage. I told the building captain. At first there was a lot of shouting and then a lot of laughing behind that individual's back. The general reaction was to shrug our shoulders and find humor in the situation. Real danger and tough times expose people's true natures.

On the fourth day of the uprising, our doctor told us she was running out of supplies for tending wounds. To make bandages, we had to find more cotton. Our apartment became the headquarters for this project. The two nuns, Mother, Ann, and I ripped thin, worn-out bed sheets into strips, boiled them in soapy water, rinsed them and hung them to dry. Next we ironed them with a very hot iron and rolled them by hand, hoping they would be sterile enough.

The first wounded woman died the next day. She was buried quietly in a corner of the courtyard, the only place where the soil was not covered by concrete and could be dug. The two dead soldiers' bodies stayed on the street across from our windows. Poles knew that German machine guns were set; the Germans probably did not know whether there were Polish troops in the theater, or they did not care. We kept the windows closed to keep out flies and the growing stench. The humid August air made the situation worse with each day.

The wounded boy was holding on. In another lucky coincidence, among the refugees was a mother separated from her baby and a baby with a mother who had no milk. The first mother was happy to nurse the baby, hoping that somebody was taking care of her baby, wherever it was.

At night we saw the glare from burning fires. First on Krakowskie Przedmieście, and then in the Warsaw University complex. The university fire had sent the last group of people that fled to the safety of our house. Finally, Sewerynów Street behind the theater started burning. Winds from Vistula carried cinders toward our house.

At night, we realized our roof had caught fire. The water pressure had gotten so low that we could get water only in the cellar and ground floor. We had to extinguish the roof fire or we would lose the safety of our building. People formed a water line from the basement to the roof, passing buckets hand to hand. I filled buckets in our apartment; somebody else did the same in the cellar.

Our "not so brave" tenant George Stamm came to the kitchen. All the men around me were trying to save our house, and that goldbrick was doing nothing! It enraged me. I gave him a bucket to carry; he tried to tell me that his liver was bothering him. I do not remember what I said, but I made him go upstairs. The men on the stairs helped him up higher and higher. We put out that fire, and George survived his miniscule firefighting effort. He did not have to ask what we thought of his lack of courage.

Fortunately there were many young men among our refugees. Some were caught on the streets by the uprising's premature start, as I had been caught at home. If the German police came to our house, I had an alibi, being a girl with my mother. Those young men would have been in real danger, so at night some started venturing out through the theater.

News began trickling back to us through that theater passage as well, as people brought Polish newspapers with the latest news from London, Berlin, and various parts of Warsaw. Some of what we read was not encouraging: "At the moment of the rising's outbreak, the German garrison in Warsaw numbered about 20,000 soldiers, policemen, and members of the SS."[1] Among the hurriedly called-in troops were police, the SS brigade under Dierlevanger, which consisted of criminals, a Cossack regiment of Vlasov troops, and other fighters.

We learned that "when the Third Reich Minister Himmler heard about the rising in Warsaw, he flew into a rage. He personally wrote to Dierlevanger that, by Hitler's order, Warsaw was to be razed to the ground, giving the German forces a license to kill anybody at their discretion. This order was willingly fulfilled."

The news traveled fast. The fate of people taken by the Germans was reported to London. London radio in turn kept Warsaw informed about what to expect. As a result, most people avoided being taken prisoner by the Germans, unless there was nowhere else to go, as was the situation later in the Old Town.

Luckily, we heard, the gas company was in Polish forces' hands. The water filters were also secured for a while, but the Germans were doing their best to cut off the city's water completely. Water pressure fell lower and lower.

_____

1 Quotes are taken from WWII historical data.

One of the newspapers had a story about a heroic young man named Bogdan who had been killed. Mother showed it to me, deep concern in her eyes. I read it and happily realized it was not my Bohdan. His name was spelled differently, and "Bogdan" was apparently a pseudonym. My Bohdan's pseudonym was Tarzan; besides, Bohdan was in the Mokotów district, and this young hero died in the center of the city. My panic changed to relief, and my reaction was strange: I started laughing. Mother made some remark, and all I could say was, "It's not him, it's not him!"

The days passed slowly. I do not remember what we ate, though I think Mother cooked and fed all those in our apartment. We also baked bread. I remember that I had several gallons of vodka, which I was preparing for sale on the black market. I asked our doctor if it would be helpful if I distributed it to everybody, with a shot per person in the evening. She gave me her blessing. Every evening, a line formed outside our kitchen. Some even got two shots.

Throughout those days, I remember staying very calm. Mother and the nuns sat in the hall most of the time; the young men in the courtyard also maintained a dignified calm. I was not afraid. As long as everything seemed all right, I didn't do anything. Whenever there was a problem, I immediately tried to help—organizing the fire line to the roof, helping prepare bandages, and pouring vodka to ensure a good night.

Ann and I slept on a mattress in the pantry. On August 8, I woke up crying. I did not remember my dreams, but I felt desperate and miserable. I could not understand what had happened. I looked at my left arm—and realized that my good-luck silver bracelet was broken, lying in a tiny pile next to me.

At that moment I knew what had happened: Bohdan has been

killed. This was the little bracelet that I gave him each time he went into danger. The last time I saw him, when I knew the uprising was imminent, I tried to give him my bracelet for good luck. He refused to take it, telling me to keep the good luck.

He always tried to make me safer.

Though I knew what must have happened when I saw the bracelet, my young optimistic nature eventually altered my reasoning. I told myself I was too worried and imagining the worst. Desperately, I tried to believe that Bohdan was still alive.

From the apartments on the upper floors, which faced Krakowskie Pradmieście and the machine gun position in the police station, our tenants could tell that the Polish forces had lost the furious three-day battle inside Holy Cross Church. The Germans must have held all the buildings on the main thoroughfare, for they were moving freely around the area. It was a matter of time before they came to check our house.

We prepared ourselves for their arrival. All the wounded and young men left the building through the theater to avoid the German inspection.

On August 12, the Germans came noisily, guns pointed. Since George and Maria Stamm spoke fluent German, we coached them to be our translators, but to translate and answer only specific questions without volunteering anything extra. The building's captain and the gatekeeper acted as official spokesmen. The Germans were ferocious, but stayed in the house only a short time. They did not even go toward the gate on the other side of the building, obviously afraid that Polish forces might be waiting for them.

The German inspection left no doubt in my mind: they would return soon. The next time, they might decide to take some of us with them, as we had heard they were doing in other parts of Warsaw. Hitler announced loud and clear on the radio that the citizens of Warsaw were not combatants but rebels, and should be killed like rebels.

Mother, Ann, and I agreed that Ann and I should leave as soon as possible. I split the money Bohdan had left me for emergencies into three equal parts, and we secured it on our bodies. Ann and I prepared one or two changes of clothes and packed everything into small satchels with toothbrushes and paste. We went through our preparations matter-of-factly, without talking, rationalizing, or speculating. I realized that I had no way of guessing what lay ahead. Afraid to let our emotions get out of hand, we left our home on August 17 to join the Polish forces with a short goodbye to Mother. I did not know that this was the last time I would see my family home.

I was eighteen and destined to take care of myself from that day on.

Ann and I knew that we were in danger, but we were only going a few city blocks away, to a part of Warsaw that was in Polish hands. We planned to come back soon. At the back gate of our house, we had to wait until a Polish soldier appeared in the entry to the theater. Then we ran across the street. The theater was held by Polish forces. They told us how to walk to the center of town. We were going only six or seven blocks, but we had to walk around the houses and streets held by the Germans, and we had to frequently cross streets under machine gun fire.

We passed from one building to another, using cellars where holes in the walls had been knocked out to connect the buildings. Since the Nowy Świat thoroughfare was in German hands, the Polish troops had dug a communication trench across the street and built barricades out of dugout rubble on both sides.

After a tense journey, we came to the barricade on the corner of Nowy Świat and Chmielna Streets. While waiting to pass, we enjoyed talking to members of the Polish platoon holding the position there. "This barricade is the only connection between our troops in 'Powiśle' (the Vistula River area) and the center of town," they told us.

"During the day the Krauts bring their tanks and knock holes in the barricade. At night we build it back up," a young soldier laughed.

It was a great pleasure to see our compatriots wearing white and red armbands with all kinds of outfits. Some soldiers had military helmets or caps decorated with white and red Polish insignia or the Polish eagle.

We were about to enter the Polish center of Warsaw.

The barricade on Chmielna St. Photo by Sylvester Braun, pseudonym "Kris" courtesy of Historical Museum of Warsaw.

The soldiers told us exactly where the Germans were shooting from, which section of barricade the Germans could hit, and how low we should bend to be safe. "Good luck and go," they told us.

Finally, we arrived in Center North, a large area of Warsaw held by Polish forces, andwere directed to area command. I reported that I had been separated from my unit and volunteered my services; Ann also enrolled. We were assigned to a unit being organized with quarters on Złota Street.

For several days we essentially did nothing. We helped in the office and provided entertainment in a military café, where I sang military songs while Ann accompanied me on the piano. Our favorite song was "The Red Poppies of Monte Casino / That Drank Polish Blood Instead of Water." That song reached us shortly before the uprising, accompanied by stories of General Anders' Polish troops fighting in Italy and taking extreme casualties before they captured the Monte Casino monastery.

With the closest German positions more than five or six blocks away, we felt safe. The only danger was unexpected explosions from mortars, artillery, or bombs dropped by planes. As we had a good deal of free time, we asked for permission to go see our mother. We were able to get to the barricade through Nowy Świat and then to Tamka, where my aunt lived, but we could not go any farther. Germans advancing from the Vistula River already held our house and the surrounding blocks. We came back without reaching our mother or seeing home. We hoped that Mother's frail body would save her from German attempts to kill her.

Captain Wojciech became our commanding officer. He was training boys—as much as one can train without the use of guns. Arms were scarce and used only on the front lines. Women served as couriers, guides, and nurses.

In Good Company

Our unit finally formed on August 23, twenty three days after the uprising began. We were thirty-two persons under Capt. Wojciech and Lt. Bogusław, and were assigned to Col. Wacław's group. We underwent minimal training as we prepared to go to the front lines. During this time, our quarters on Złota Street were hit with artillery and burned. To extinguish the fire, we had to form a human line to pass water buckets. We extinguished the fire, but had to move our quarters one block away to Bracka Street.

Amidst the chaos, I contracted dysentery. Fortunately, one of the boys remembered that his mother always used dried blueberries as a cure. He was able to go home, brought me a little jar of them, and in a short time I was better.

In the meantime, our troops in the Old Town were being decimated by the Germans. They were completely surrounded and the Germans were throwing everything at them: bombs, artillery, strafing planes, tanks, and machine guns. The situation was growing hopeless; to make matters worse, the Germans refused to recognize Polish troops as Allied combatants. Hitler called us criminals, bandits, and many other terms to justify the fact that the Germans were not taking prisoners. The news reached us that in many areas where the civilian population was unable to retreat with the Polish forces, the German troops were not distinguishing between military and civilians. Following Himmler's orders, they killed everybody they caught outright or sent them to concentration camps to die.

Polish troops started escaping the Old Town through the sewers. In the darkness, through the maze of crisscrossing tunnels, some found safe exit in the center of Warsaw, among our positions. On September 2, I saw many of them emerging from the sewers on Napoleon Plaza.

Unfortunately, some people became lost underground and emerged in the midst of the German positions, allowing the Germans to realize how Polish troops were escaping from the Old Town. In response, the Germans found a deadly weapon: they started throwing carbide into the sewers. Combined with the ever-present water, the carbide formed a deadly gas, killing everyone inside.

On September 4, I realized that somebody—an angel?—must be watching over me.

Ann and I were walking a short distance from the old quarters to the new ones. At first I was urging Ann to hurry. In the middle of the street, we met Capt. Wojciech. We talked a while, standing a short distance from our new quarters. Suddenly we heard the "winding up" sound of the incendiary rockets we called "krowa," or cows. We ran to the entrance of a house and hid behind a brick wall near the gate.

The first rocket hit a few houses away. We waited. The tension was incredible. What direction would the next blasts go?

A second rocket spilled burning inferno onto the street in front of us. We felt the wave of heat and we saw fingers of fire crawling through the opening in the gate.

The third rocket hit directly above us, striking our quarters. The remaining three rockets landed farther away.

Without speaking the words aloud, Ann and I realized that if we'd left sooner, we would have been upstairs amongst the blackened bodies in our unit's new quarters. On the other hand, if we had been any further from the sheltering gate, we would have been burned by the liquid inferno on the street.

It was hard to believe that our small group had survived. The sight on all sides of us was unbelievable; the incendiary rockets left black death strewn all around. Even the asphalt on the street was burned black. Upstairs, the flash-like fire consumed everything flammable, leaving a sea of black—including the singed, naked human bodies.

There was nothing left for us to do but leave. We stumbled away, trying to forget the sight and the smell.

The next day, my guardian angel aided me again. Ann and I were walking on Szpitalna Street, not far from the previous day's rocket attack. Suddenly, without any obvious reason, I grabbed Ann and pulled her into the nearest house. We were barely inside when a mortar exploded on the street, on the spot from which we'd just fled.

Each time, my premonition or instinct was extremely strong. Somebody was taking care of me. I decided to listen to my inner voice – whatever its source.

From the beginning of the uprising, Polish forces had held the beautiful, historic Old Town. Unfortunately, the whole district was surrounded by Germans and eventually only "4,500[1] of the defenders, mostly wounded and terribly weakened, got to the Town Center through the sewers." We were told by the troops from the sewers that many Poles were wounded or unable to walk. Nurses and doctors were taking care of them, and Prince Radziwiłł, whose palace was also in the Old Town, stayed to face the Germans.

On September 3, Old Town fell. Later we heard that when the Polish forces there capitulated, Prince Radziwiłł stayed with the people, hoping he might use his authority to save them. It was felt that the German *Vermacht* (army) would respect him; to become an officer in *Vermacht*, one had to be an Adler (of the noble class). By contrast, when Hitler created his trusted SS and Gestapo units, he specified that they be of the plebeian class; the immediate class friction this created was demonstrated when the *Vermacht* generals formed a conspiracy against Hitler.

However, at the time of the Old Town capitulation, there were no longer any army units surrounding Old Town or any other areas of Warsaw. Only Dierlevanger's cruel SS troops remained. Luckily for Prince Radziwiłł and the forces who surrendered, the Germans did recognize the internationally respected name of the prince and initially allowed him to represent the fighters of Old Town—until they were marched to the refugee camps outside Warsaw.

The following story, which I remember from those days, demonstrates the frictions between the *Vermacht* and the SS, and the ruthlessness of the SS troops.

In the early days of the uprising, in a central part of Warsaw, the Germans were preparing to storm a barricade in front of the Polish

---

1 Exact numbers are drawn from the historical data.

position. The Polish troops observed an unusual commotion among the German forces. It appeared that SS or police were pushing German army soldiers into action. While going to the attack, one of the German soldiers in the front line tied a white handkerchief to his uniform. The Poles decided to recognize it as a white flag, withheld their fire, and opened the gate by the barricade. Without a shot, the German soldiers ran in and the Poles were able to shoot at the surprised and exposed SS forces behind them.

After being taken prisoner, the German soldiers admitted that they were reluctant to fight during the Warsaw uprising. They were fully aware that their forces had been decimated in Soviet Russia and were retreating, and knew that Germany had no strategic reason to hold Warsaw. Further, they understood that the Soviets were as much the enemies of the Poles as they were of the Germans, and that the Poles were trying to win Warsaw prior to the arrival of the Soviets as our next occupant.

The *Vermacht* platoon prisoners were well treated by the Polish forces; even when the Poles capitulated, the German soldiers were not turned over to the German authorities. But after that incident, no more members of the German Army fought against Polish forces. All the other units of SS, police, Russian, and Cossack troops joined the Nazi forces in battle, but no *Vermacht*.

The Front Lines

Holy Cross Church and Krakowskie Przedmieście. Photo by Sylvester Braun, pseudonym "Kris" courtesy of Historical Museum of Warsaw.

The next day, our company was assigned to the front line, relieving another company from the priest's house behind Holy Cross Church. We were closing the circle. Holy Cross was next to the police station on the Krakowskie Przedmieście—across from our house, which we'd left nineteen days before.

Our company was truly going to war. We arrived in the priests' little house, where the outgoing officer briefed us about our position and what to expect. Under the adjoining church, we heard the sounds of excavation.

"Yes," the officer said. "The Germans are mining, approaching this position. On the other side," he pointed to Traugut Street, "the machine gun position is zeroed in on this little house." He turned to Cpt. Wojciech. "Whenever you send someone out or have someone come back, shoot at the machine gun position to cover your movements."

We listened calmly, aware of the difficulty and danger into which we were entering. The officer was ready to leave when suddenly he added, "There's not much more to worry about, except the planes, which have been on bombing runs for the last two days. It's a miracle this house is still standing."

In sum, then, we were the forward most Polish position, with machine guns to the left, Germans undermining us from beneath the church, and the whole street in front of us held by the Germans. The vast area to the right was a field of leveled rubble, the city blocks left in ruin by the bombing in 1939. Now that field was open to fire from the German positions on Nowy Świat Street.

Capt. Wojciech did not bother with pep talks. He knew that we were all novices who'd never even smelled fire, and we knew that there was a job to do. The Captain started assigning boys to various shooting and observation positions around the building.

Ann and I decided that if we were to eat anything, now was the time. In the pantry we found some young potatoes from the priests' garden and a few other items. We built a fire in the stove. The chimney was damaged and smoke filled the kitchen, but we managed to cook a meal.

As we prepared to distribute the fresh but meager portions of cooked potatoes, the captain asked me if I could try to lift the spirits of the boys on position against the machine guns on Trauguta Street. The boys were overwhelmed by the situation and just plain scared. Most were not even twenty years old. I walked to the room holding steaming plates of potatoes, pretending not to pay any attention to the Germans. In reality, I was very aware of places in room where I would have be in line with the possible machine gun fire.

I do not remember exactly how I did it, but by the time I left with the empty plates, the boys were making jokes about shooting "Krauts" and looking at them through the cracks in the walls. Somehow my mission was accomplished!

From underneath our little house the sounds of tunneling grew closer. The captain called me and gave me another task: I was to find the neighboring unit of Polish forces on the right side of our position. The captain did not know exactly where they were; he thought they should be somewhere on the field toward Świętokrzyska Street, operating from the cellars in the field of rubble.

"Kora," he said, "find them and let them know that we're about to be blown up. When this happens, they'll be open from the left flank. Watch out for the German positions on Nowy Świat. Lately, the Germans haven't been shooting much from there, but you never know."

"Yes sir."

We were both silent for a while. He knew that I understood the situation, and I knew that I didn't know what to expect. The captain seemed bothered by something, but finally concluded in a matter-of-fact voice: "When you're ready to run out of this house, we will give you fire cover. As soon as you hear us shooting, run!"

"Aye-aye, sir."

A statue of Jesus Christ outside Holy Cross Church, the scene of our front line engagement. Photo by Sylvester Braun, pseudonym "Kris" courtesy of Historical Museum of Warsaw.

I walked out through the window and stopped at the edge of the building, ready to run into the open area. The boys started shooting at the German machine gun position. I ran out; by the time the machine gun blasts started hitting near me, I was already covered by the next wall. I ran toward the field of rubble, where I expected to find our right flank positions. There was nothing there except rubble. Finally, I saw a metal grid on the ground. I tried to lift it, only to find it was locked from the inside. I called; nobody answered. Looking around desperately, I spotted planes coming in my direction. I hadn't seen them earlier because they were flying very low.

The first light bomber strafed the area and started shooting at me. Machine gun bullets hit the ground, approaching me in two lines. Instinctively, I started running toward the plane, keeping to the middle, the bullets on either side of me. The first plane passed over; the second sent a few short bursts in my direction. I kept running toward it. The first plane began dropping bombs behind me, in the vicinity of the priest's house. I ran up to a low wall nearby, looking for cover. I wanted to climb over, to be on the opposite side away from the bombs, but the next plane was shooting at me. I hit the ground, lay flat against the little wall and prayed.

The next bomb exploded not far away, sending shrapnel whistling above my head. I smelt ammonia, and something hit my back; I reached around to feel it. No pain, no blood. It was only a piece of brick. Several more bombs hit the area around our positions near the priest's house. Amongst the billowing clouds of dust, I could not tell if the priest's house was still standing. The planes flew away as quickly as they had come, leaving eight or nine craters in the field. A thick cloud of dust hung over the whole area. I didn't have to worry anymore about being visible from the Nowy Świat. I rose and ran toward the buildings to look for the command, still trying to deliver my message.

Many people were milling around, all covered with white plaster dust. I found our local military command, gave them my report, and was told where I might find the rest of my company. As I was left, a new group of people covered with dust and plaster walked in. Among them was a little boy who looked familiar, but his face was so dirty that I couldn't discern his features. I walked toward him. He also gave me a questioning look. Suddenly we recognized each other. It was Ann, who hadn't recognized me either, as I was equally dirty. Shortly after we left, the captain had sent Ann outside with another message.

Together, we located the rest of our company. They'd left the priest's house, which in that short time became useless as a military position. The bombs hit nearby and were well aimed, but they did not kill a single one of our soldiers. Captain Wojciech was exuberantly happy to see me and Ann alive, and eager to tell us that the Germans had done great damage to their own positions. He was laughing, telling us that the first bomb hit the corner of the house right where the Germans were tunneling in to detonate a bomb beneath us. The second bomb eliminated the German machine gun position on Traugut. None of our boys were injured. We were christened by the fire and in high spirits.

Our company was sent to the rear to rest. I remember lying down on a mattress and falling asleep, exhausted. Later, I heard voices telling me to get up and do something, but I was unable to react. Unable to wake me, they finally left me alone.

The next day when I woke, Ann told me they were trying to get me up to carry food to the front line positions, but I could not be awakened. Ann went instead.

The next day, we were assigned a new position in the gate of a partially ruined house on St. Cross Street (Świętokrzyska). This position was one block further from the German positions on Nowy Świat than the priest's house. We were to guard against possible attack from Nowy Świat and maintain a connection with the positions behind us.

The house above our position was badly damaged. The gate and the base of a stairway still stood, but the rest was in ruin, a mere skeleton. The next house behind us was also in ruins, but partially standing; on the higher floors, the Germans were somehow able to move around. We had no way of telling which of the empty windows would reveal a German helmet. Our boys watched carefully, occasionally shooting. There were also unexpected shots from the opposite direction.

Kazik Stebelski was one of the boys in our company. I knew

Kazik's family—they were cousins of Alinka. Kazik was around seventeen, a pleasant and polite boy with the most unusual violet eyes, as striking as his mother, whom I remembered well. That day, Kazik was standing not far from me, watching the upper windows. Suddenly a shot rang out and he collapsed softly, a little hole appearing in his head.

Shortly after Kazik's death, another boy got shot in the chest. He was lying on the ground, shaking from cold. The captain told him a nurse would come soon and asked me to stay with him. I covered him with something that I found and held his hands to keep him warm. I had never been close to a dying person before, but comforting him felt natural. I talked soothingly, promising the boy that he would be comfortable soon. He was calm, looking at me and listening, and I could not tell if he knew that he was dying. Soon he closed his eyes and fell asleep forever. I got up and looked at the captain. He knew. "God, please don't let this happen to Bohdan," I prayed.

Captain Wojciech then sent me to command with a written message. I came back through the ruins of the post office, ready to open the gate directly across the street from our position. Instead of running across the street, I kicked open the metal gate to find out if anybody was watching. The gate's hinges squeaked loudly; as if in response, machine gun bullets hit the metal gate in a buzzing roar of sound. I had my answer.

Evidently the Germans could see this side of the street through the ruins of the house above. I kicked the gate open again; again, bullets rang on the metal. After a few more kicks and machine gun bursts, the German gunner must have gotten tired; or maybe he thought the movement was the wind. I ran across to our position's gate. The machine gun sounded behind me. I was greeted with cheers from my company, who had been watching my cat-and-mouse play.

As the battle progressed, Captain Wojciech's wrist was wounded. He left for the rear to get his arm tended. Major Sep ("Hawk") was now our commanding officer.

A courier from another company reached our position. She came from the commanding officer in the rear and was going back to her company ahead and to the north of us. Major Sep asked me to go with her to find out their exact location. We ran in the direction of our earlier, abandoned position near Holy Cross Church. We planned to run through the big square area of rubble, which was pocked with multiple bomb craters from the previous days' attacks.

My fellow courier ran ahead, moving from crater to crater; the German machine guns trying to pick her up. I got through two craters behind her, but then realized that the gunner had given up trying to shoot her and was waiting for me. I stopped. The girl reached cover at the end of the open area. I untied the scarf from my neck and waved it in the air. Bullets sang out. Following would have meant meeting with the inevitable. I decided to run back. I made it through; when I was out of the bullets' reach, I looked up to see Major Sep watching me with a big smile of relief on his face. I apologized for chickening out and turning back. The Major assured me that I had done the right thing.

"A dead courier would not have been of much help to us. We need you alive," he said. But I was bothered by my failure to fulfill orders.

Several hours later, I had to face an even bigger challenge. In the army, we all knew panicking could mean death. A day or two earlier, when we came from the rear to this position, we could move safely as we were covered by the barricade across Mazowiecka Street. But now a German tank had put a hole in the barricade, spilling rocks below and making it impossible for us to move safely through the area. Through the hole, the Germans could now shoot exposed, running people from their position on the upper floors of the cross street (Mazowiecka).

Yet, we had no choice. Our only connection to our back lines was along the street and under this barricade.

Since we could not see the German position from which they were shooting, Major Sep decided to watch for the line of the trace bullets. He realized that the Germans must have been positioned low in the building which made them unable to hit anybody who was crawling. The hole in the barricade was high enough to cover anybody crawling the short distance to the edge of a crater created earlier by a German bombing.

Two of our boys started "losing their nerve." The major knew that the stomach aches and appendicitis they claimed were only fear. But he also realized that their fearful behavior had a demoralizing effect on the others. The major sent them to the rear, telling them explicitly to crawl from the edge of the hole in the barricade, around the mound of knocked-out rubble, to the crater. Shortly after they left, Major Sep asked me to take a message to command. Again, he emphasized the importance of crawling and the futility of running.

I walked along the street to the edge of the barricade. Now I could see the problem clearly. The fallen rocks made a little mound next to the hole. I had to crawl away from the barricade to the left, to the bomb crater. It seemed so much simpler to just run those few steps, but I knew I had to obey the major. Approaching the edge of the hole, I got down and started crawling. The Germans must have heard me, because bullets began to fly above me. I made myself as flat as a pancake. It felt like covering those ten feet took ten years. Finally I reached the edge of the bomb's crater and pulled myself over the edge. Out of danger, I let myself roll down inside.

A sick sensation hit me—I had landed on the still-warm bodies of my two frightened company members. They must have panicked and run instead of crawling.

The report from Major Sep's which I carried informed command that we had been forced to abandon our position. I was told not to walk back. We were able to communicate by sight without risking a courier's life. Later, another company—which had been fighting further out toward the main German forces, helping our company defend the hotly contested handful of city blocks—withdrew under cover of darkness. The remainder of our company followed.

I waited, sitting in the darkness. Again, I found myself in a large passage in a building, between the street and a wide open area. We were safe there; the German positions were on the other side of Mazowiecka, a whole block away.

In one corner, some nurses worked at the table under the dim light of a candle or carbide lamps. People sat on benches and spoke in low voices or dozed. Somebody made a place on the end of a bench for me to sit. To my left, a young soldier slept in a wicker armchair. His right arm stuck out toward me over the chair's armrest. I tried to tell him to move his arm inside the chair, but he wouldn't wake up. I took his arm gently and lifted it, trying to put it down on his lap. His balance altered, and he fell to the floor.

He was not asleep. He was dead.

On Tuesday, September 5, our company went to the front lines thirty-two strong. Four days later, on Saturday, September 9, Captain Wojciech's arm was in a sling and a young soldier, whose pseudonym was Tiger, was so wounded he could barely move. Captain Wojciech, Tiger, Ann, and I were the only members of our company still alive.

The Days Until The End

Our company decimated, Ann and I were again assigned temporary quarters. Since leaving home on August 17, we'd seldom slept in any one place for more than two or three nights. Usually we were told: "Find a place to sleep in this or that building or apartment, and report for duty in the morning." Our quarters were usually so close to the front line that the civilian population had already vacated them. On many occasions, I did not know who was sleeping next to me.

In spite of these close quarters, I never experienced any improper sexual advances. It only can be explained by the fact that we were all young men and women who respected each other. The opposite did take place, but not often. Some of the "old timers" had difficulty adjusting to having female soldiers around. They tended to belittle us or try to inflict their middle-aged testosterone on us.

One evening, I had to guide a small group of Old Town fighters to their new quarters. They were members of the few units which had successfully left Old Town through the sewers. While walking through the dark corridor, one "non-gentleman" grabbed me in an unquestionable way. Since I'd noticed him eyeing me earlier, I reacted instantly, smacking him good and hard across the face. The loud smack was followed by deadly silence. Nobody said a word. I delivered them to their destination and left. I was not surprised that the officer did not report my behavior, which was disrespectful conduct by a private. Nor did I lose any sleep over the incident. I understood that this individual had been through absolute hell during the battles in Old Town. What could one say?After September 9, our company ceased to exist. Ann and I were assigned temporary quarters to rest for a day or two after our ordeal. We had a room in a house that was still in good condition. There were several rooms in that ground floor apartment. One was used as a nurses' station; another was the sleeping quarters for two lieutenants, who were brothers.

In our room, Ann sat on the couch. We were talking and joking, as we frequently did to offset the reality of our situation. Without warning, Ann fell to her right, a smile still on her face. Not understanding why she would choose such an uncomfortable position, I admonished her: "If you want to lie down, get your head to the left or lie on a pillow." The funny smile stayed on her face, as it did when she was fooling around with me. I lifted her to a sitting position, but she went limp and fell down to my right. With a sinking feeling, I realized that she had fainted and ran to the nurses' room. We came back to find Ann awake and unaware of what all the fuss was about.

By this time, the water pressure was so low that we could not use the toilets in the house. We had to go to dug-out latrines in the middle of the courtyard. As always, when going to the latrine I made silly remarks: "If I get killed on the latrine, please make sure my obituary reads: 'Kora died on the field of glory or in the line of duty'!"

I stepped out of our room and followed behind Lieutenant Bob. He was walking toward the open house gate, a few steps ahead of me. We heard the whistle of a mortar; instinctively, he turned away from the open door and I squatted, still behind him. The mortar exploded in the courtyard before us. Bob took a hit on the back, but "it's not too bad," he said, and turned to walk back to the nurses' station. I had a burning, needle-like sensation in my left cheek.

When I came back from the latrine, Bob was lying on the table and the nurses were dressing wounds on his back. The wounds were small and weren't bleeding much, but Bob's breathing was becoming more labored, as if he had water in his mouth. The nurses looked at each other. He was dying. The mortar's shrapnel had punctured his lungs. I felt lucky to be safe, but guilty that Bob had to lose his life to save mine. If his body hadn't been there, it would have been me.

As one of the nurses used tweezers to remove the tiny shard of shrapnel from my cheek, I looked at Bob's body and wondered again what angel put me behind him.

Ann and I were quickly assigned to the communication company, where we operated the field telephone switchboard. It became our job for the remaining three weeks of battle. Our Signal Corps Company was located more centrally in our district, to facilitate the telephone lines going to the front in all directions.

Being further from the front lines put us among a higher number of civilians. The Polish military forces were trying to protect civilians by telling them to leave whenever Polish forces lost ground, but since there was no system or organization to take care of the civilian population, they had to take care of each other.

The sight of civilians made me think of my loved ones, of Bohdan and my mother. Subconsciously I knew that Bohdan had died the day I woke up crying, but I kept hoping, holding my love for him in my heart. I feared for my mother as well, but hoped that her old age would somehow save her from being sent to a concentration or labor camp.

Whenever our forces got access to food supplies, those supplies were divided between military and civilians. Early in August, the Polish forces got control of a large warehouse. They acquisitioned a lot of sugar and cheap red wine, which lasted us till almost the end of September, but our other supplies were meager. Even our military group ate pancakes made of flour mixed with sawdust and fried in *stearin*, or candle fat. A layer of sugar on top made it semi-palatable. In retrospect, I truly do not know how so many of us managed to survive on such a diet.

When the uprising broke out, Warsaw was overpopulated. The majority of the civilian population was caught basically unprepared. Most of them were like our small group in Mother's apartment: sitting, waiting, trying to survive. Those innocents who fell immediately into German hands were dealt with in a terrible fashion. I heard stories of cruelty and bestiality which were difficult to believe. Even though we helped the civilians move away from the immediate front line, "the rear" was frequently just a few blocks away from "the front" line.

Again, Ann and I were told to find ourselves places to sleep nearby. The area where we stayed had modern buildings built shortly before WWII. It was the middle of September. We were all aware that the uprising could not last much longer; but Ann and I knew that we had to somehow keep on surviving. It was the beginning of the end. We were numb, going through the motions of a daily routine, feeling little or nothing.

The last few days were not encouraging. One night the Americans tried to help, sending planes to drop supplies on Warsaw. But this action had less than desirable results; the supplies landed only partially in Polish hands. The airdrops were packaged with parts of arms, and consequently our troops received half of the mortars or bazookas. The Germans got the remaining parts. Or we got ammunition for guns that were dropped on German positions.

In preparation for that operation, Stalin, the great friend of Roosevelt and Churchill, refused to make Soviet bases available for the Allied planes to land and refuel. The American planes thus had to fly a direct route, which forced them to fly above areas still held by the Germans. This caused large, tragic losses of planes, lives, and the supplies we needed so badly. Surprisingly, this example of Soviet "friendship" and "loyalty" did not teach Roosevelt and Churchill a lesson—not yet.

We were fully aware of the tragedy of the Polish situation, which was difficult to describe. While we were fighting the Germans in Warsaw, in August Soviets troops had arrived in Poland and reached the eastern side of our city without any practical opposition from the German forces there. To the Russians, this proved that the Germans were now too weak to resist military force. However, those same Germans were not too weak to keep murdering the Polish population in Warsaw, as Hitler had ordered.

The Soviet troops stopped at the Vistula River on the other side of Warsaw. They could have easily attacked the German positions with artillery or planes, but they did nothing. The Soviets wanted more of us to die. Both our enemies were succeeding. During the uprising, Warsaw lost 200,000 persons, many of them intelligent young people like my friends. To occupy our country, Stalin's Communists needed the population to be less skillful and educated, and without natural leaders.

Meanwhile, Hitler hated the Poles for resisting his atrocities, and was determined to take us down with him.

We learned at this time about another horrifying example of Soviet Communism's perfidious cruelty; this time, certain Poles were forced to witness the act in question. In the Soviet Army, many Poles had been forcefully drafted from the eastern part of Poland, acquired by the Soviets in 1939, when Hitler and Stalin were yet bosom friends, Hitler granted that part of Poland to Stalin. Later, in the Yalta Agreement, Roosevelt let Stalin keep those lands.

It was painful to the Poles of the eastern territories to see Warsaw patriots being killed by the Germans while "their" Soviet army watched idly. They wanted to help their compatriots, and eventually the Soviet leaders allowed them to do so. All Polish volunteers were given permission to move across the Vistula River, theoretically to attack the Germans. But in the end, the operation was carried out as if the Soviets and the Germans were cooperating.

At night, the Polish volunteers loaded the boats provided by the Soviets and started crossing the Vistula. The Germans were waiting. When the boats reached the middle of the river, German machine gunners killed everybody, to the last boat and the last man. The Soviets watched from the riverside. They must have known that there were German positions down river. And the Polish volunteers did not know that they would get no fire support from their own troops.

No, the Soviets knew what they were doing, and it was painfully clear to us as well. We had no illusions about Germany and Russia's intentions, but what was extremely painful was the fact that the Soviets were American and British allies. We could not understand how Roosevelt or Churchill could be so gullible, so naïve. Didn't they know that neither Germans nor Russians ever kept their agreements or pacts?

Somewhere between September 15 and 20, Ann and I sat in the basement of a building, taking care of the field telephone switchboard. We had been fighting for nearly six weeks. On that night, we made sure the lines were operating between various stations. The artillery shells, bombs, and street fighting caused frequent breakdowns, after which our platoon boys, called "the wires," had to go reconnect the broken lines.

We had no idea what was going to happen. Our commanding officers had suddenly grown mute. We were given no news, good nor bad. Fortunately, sitting by the switchboard gave us an opportunity. When connecting the lines between several commanding officers, Ann and I had to listen to make sure the connection was successful. We learned to listen a little longer.

From one of these conversations we learned that, as insurgents, we were doomed should we decide to surrender. The London radio had reported that the Germans continued to refuse to recognize the Polish troops as Allied combatants.

I remember the day we talked about it. There were four or five of us standing outdoors in a fairly big garden-like space, surrounded by greenery and several recently dug graves. The September sun was warm; the sounds of battle were either far away, or it was one of the rare quiet moments in the midst of the battle for Warsaw.

Being the youngest, I mainly listened while Ann and the men spoke, speculating about whether the Germans would send us to the concentration camps or just kill us, as they had done to combatants in the parts of Warsaw that capitulated earlier. Such speculations made no sense to me.

"We cannot surrender," I finally declared. "We will have to fight to the end." My proclamation was matter-of-fact. Characteristically, I shrugged my shoulders and walked away, appearing unperturbed.

When I think about it from the distance of my old age, I wonder how I managed to be so logical and calm. Obviously, the reality of being shot and killed was very real to me. But I preferred being killed in a battle than being murdered by Nazis, and that probability seemed equally realistic. So I did not worry about it anymore and went about my daily routine. Why worry if we do not know what the worst thing that might happen to us might be? And dying is definitely not the worst thing.

The apartment that Ann and I found to sleep in was on the third or fourth floor of a modern apartment house. All the lower apartments, which were safer, were occupied by civilians, but we did not mind being up high. We had been in more dangerous places. The apartment had all its furniture, but like all vacant places in Warsaw, it had already been broken into and ransacked. There were no blankets, so we went around to other apartments, foraging for bedding. We were lucky. We found two down comforters, which we took to our new quarters.

We decided to enjoy our newfound luxury—going to sleep in a clean bed—by making ourselves clean as well. That, however, created a problem. We could heat water in the kitchen, for there were some pots and we still had gas, but first we had to get water. Water was available only in the cellar, where it was barely a trickle. The lines of people with buckets and other containers stretched out all day and all night. Those poor people needed water for drinking and cooking.

I decided to wait till dark and go to the water reservoir, built in preparation for air raids and located on the Polish side of a large park not far from our quarters. The Germans shot there sometimes, but I decided to bet on the darkness and my ability to move quietly. I found two buckets and Ann and I went to get our precious water.

We were giggling, for everything we did seemed to make such loud sounds. The water reservoir was away from the building, with greenery around it and German positions on the other side. We did not know how far away they were or whether the soldiers were watching. The night was dark and we walked quietly to the edge of the pool. The water level in the reservoir was so low that I had to lie on my stomach and almost fell in, reaching for water. Our buckets scraped the side of the reservoir, the water gurgling as it fell in. It was a miracle nobody heard us.

Finally, we returned to our apartment with full buckets. We used every drop of precious water, washing our heads and later our whole bodies in the same water.

It was late when we finally collapsed into our luxurious, clean bed; we fell instantly asleep—only to be awakened suddenly by the sound of an explosion and the violent shaking of the bed. We covered our heads with our comforters. Plaster started falling, and we felt the bigger pieces strike against our blankets.

The world fell quiet. We looked around. In the first light of the morning, we saw plaster all around us. As if on command, without saying anything, we stood up on the bed and lifted our comforters, letting the rubble fall down to the foot of the bed. Without talking, we lay down, covered ourselves, and went promptly back to sleep.

That time the German heavy artillery did hit our apartment building, but fortunately not directly above us. We decided the probability that the Germans would shoot again at the same house was nil. Undaunted, we decided to keep staying in our quarters. It was September 17th.

For the next two weeks, we tended our duties at the switchboard and waited for the end. Finally, on October 1, we learned that the

Germans had recognized us as combatants and that we, the military troops, would evacuate after the civilians, who would be taken first to labor camps. We would then leave Warsaw on October 5 to go to the Prisoner of War (POW) camps.

Our commanding officers busied themselves preparing lists of the dead and the living, their names and pseudonyms, military ID cards and pay in Polish occupational złotys. I was going to put my soldier's pay with the pile of money Bohdan had given me "for a rainy day," which I dutifully carried.

On October 2 or 3, Captain Wojciech came to the switchboard to ask whether I would like to be submitted for a Krzyż Walecznych award.

"Me, an award for bravery?"

"Yes, I think you deserve this cross."

"I haven't done anything that everybody else wouldn't."

He smiled. "However, some didn't do it, and some got killed doing the same things. I am asking you because, though we are preparing lists and trying to make things as formal and organized as possible, we do not know whether our documents will even survive." He paused, his words hanging, seemingly suspended in air. We stood, looking at each other, regretting the loss of life, the ruin of the city, and above all the reality that the Soviets, an enemy as bad as the Germans—if not worse—waited on the other side of the Vistula to follow us, hoping to benefit from our futile efforts and eventually kill more Polish patriots.

"I don't know," I said flatly. "Nothing makes sense. Forget it; don't bother with awards. My being in your company made no difference."

"Kora, I know how you feel, because I feel the same way. But please remember, you made a big difference. Only the thirty who could have told you this are not here, except for Tygrys and me." The captain spoke softly, referring to our company members, dead in action against the Germans.

"Thank you," I said. I wanted to say more, but I had a hard time holding back my tears. I tried to remember that I was a soldier talking to my commanding officer. The captain might have had similar thoughts, for he looked at me, forced an awkward smile, and said, "Kora, take good care of yourself."

"I'll try."

I did not talk to him ever again.

We were told that our Center City Army Units would be the last ones to march out of Warsaw. The civilian population was gathering to leave in groups prearranged by the Germans.

During all that time, I was without feelings or thoughts. I could not think practically and I did not care what I was doing, nor did I worry about preparation for the next days, weeks or months. Ann took the initiative for both of us. She knew that the war was not going to last much longer, but we had to get ready for the unknown journey and for the coming cold months. Until that day we wore what we had. When our clothing got dirty or torn we had to find something else. Now Ann made us scrounge for warmer garments. Knowing that I could sew very well, Ann came up with a great idea.

"Why don't you make us capes to wear on top of whatever we manage to find?"

A perfect solution. Boys from our communication company found two kinds of lining-type fabrics and a sewing machine, and I went to work. I decided to use the gray rayon as a top, and to line the capes with white and beige cotton. I made two grey capes and two backpacks. Nylon parachute cords served as straps to tie the capes together under our necks. More parachute cords served as straps for the backpacks.

Ann also insisted that we take our down comforters. We rolled them tight, like a soldier's blanket, on top of the backpacks.

Finally we all received military IDs with our names and rank and the military pay. Ann made sure that I did not misplace my money, which suddenly seemed as worthless to me as everything else did at that time. Thank God I listened to her.

On the fifth of October, we marched out of Warsaw.

As announced, our troops from the center of Warsaw were the last to leave. We lined up by our military groups on a big area I only vaguely remember. We began marching in the morning and kept walking. Germans lined both sides of our route.

The end. Leaving Warsaw October 5, 1944. Photos by Sylvester Braun, pseudonym "Kris" courtesy of Historical Museum of Warsaw.

We moved through Warsaw's streets toward the outskirts of the city. The sounds of roaring explosions and crackling fires demonstrated how systematically the Germans were following Hitler's orders not to leave anything standing in beautiful Warsaw, our city that Hitler hated as much as we loved it.

My mind drifted back a year earlier, to the ghetto. At least now there were no people inside those demolished buildings.

I do not remember resting anywhere or getting anything to eat or drink. My backpack felt very heavy and the parachute cords cut into my shoulders, making me lose my breath. For two months, we had been poorly nourished and allowed no movement outside short spurts of walking or running. Now, when we were all badly out of shape, we had to walk for 28 kilometers (18.5 miles) to Ożarów, the relocation camp for all Polish military personnel.

It was already after dark when the local Polish population filtered into the road, sharing the way with us. A man in a horse wagon rode up from behind. He let us put our backpacks on his wagon and kept moving beside us as slowly as we could walk. The Germans, standing with their machine guns on the both sides of the road, continued to look unfriendly but did not otherwise object.

Finally, late at night, we reached the army barracks in Ożarów. Warsaw, our beloved city was burning, in ruin behind us. In those ruins were buried our hopes. We rose, and our uprising was lost. I did not know which of my friends had died, and which had survived. I knew that Ann and I were still among the living, but somehow I knew that the big parts of me, the parts called Kora and Diana, had been left there, to lie in the ruins of Warsaw forever.

I could not think anymore. I did not feel anything. I was too exhausted.

Prisoners

On October 7, we awoke in the German military detention camp in Ożarów. My shoulders hurt from carrying my backpack the day before. I owned very little, but the poorly constructed straps on my backpack were a heavy burden for my tired body.

Marching out of Warsaw felt like a bad dream. I could not understand why, after we capitulated, the Germans had to blow up and burn one building after another, leaving some areas that were a little less devastated in complete ruin. In my eighteen-and-a-half-year-old mind, none of it made any sense.

In the morning, our commanding officer Major Sęp looked for Ann and me, wanting to talk. He told us that the Germans had announced to the Polish command that all sick personnel should report immediately for transfer to the Polish Red Cross in southern Poland. All military personnel would otherwise be transported to the POW camps in Germany. The major wondered whether we would like to take our chances and stay in Poland—with the caveat that we would automatically lose our military combat status. Major

Sęp pointed out that the POW camps in Germany until now were only for males; he worried about how the Germans would treat, or mistreat, female combatants.

At this point, as young, inexperienced and ignorant as we were, Ann and I knew some "facts" to be true. The Soviets were coming fast on the heels of the retreating Germans. The five-year German occupation was horrid, but Russian "liberation" would likely be worse – if that was even possible. While the Soviets were allied with the Americans and the British, Stalin had secured already a large chunk of eastern Poland in his cruel hands, and was going to cut off our access to Western Europe by occupying the East Germany.

There were other dangers too, more personal ones. Our noble family heritage made us "bourgeois pigs," enemies of the proletariat working Communist nation. Since the October Revolution in 1917, the Soviets annihilated the Russian aristocracy and nobility. We did not expect anything different once they settled in Poland. Also we had heard what was happening to young, pretty girls caught in the path of the incoming Soviet military hordes. There was also the terrifying possibility that the Soviet NKVD had data concerning my unit's involvement in counter-espionage, a threat which had become clear when we learned the Polish Communist underground organization was watching our apartment in Warsaw in the spring of '43. Considering all of the above I knew that I had to run away from the Soviets.

But... we still had hopes of finding our loved ones.

I was hoping to find Bohdan.

Deep down, Ann and I knew that we should escape before the Soviets came—but maybe not yet. The Soviet/German front was still miles away. Ann and I looked at each other, the question in both our eyes: "Why should we go to Germany right now?"

As complicated as the decision must have appeared, it took us less than five minutes to make up our minds. We told Major Sęp, "We'll take our chances; please report that we're sick." We decided to fake the type of illness that could not be easily diagnosed by a military doctor. Ann was skinny and pale; with a little well-placed makeup, she could qualify for TB. I was more of a problem. My strong build, fair complexion, and rosy cheeks didn't give me many alternatives other than three or four months of pregnancy.

Within a few minutes, the German soldiers marched our small group of young women outside. We "sick" people were loaded onto a truck and driven out of the military camp. We knew that at that point we were losing our military status. The trucks were covered and, "just in case we should change our minds," one or two soldiers sat with machine guns at the back of the truck.

After a short drive, we arrived in Pruszków, the civilian population relocation camp. Trucks entered the camp through a big gate surrounded by cyclone and barbed wire fences. German military personnel, arms at the ready, passed our truck in. Nothing looked friendly, but at that point, we didn't expect anything decent from the Germans.

We could see that we were in a very large railroad assembly and repair plant. There were railroad trucks going in all directions and into most of the buildings. As far as we could see, every building—or rather a huge hall—was fenced in with barbed wire and cyclone fences, as if to separate each area.

Our group of twelve young women was unloaded and directed to one of these railroad warehouses. We walked through a large gate into a massive building.

A young man bearing a Polish Red Cross insignia came to greet us. Ann and I immediately recognized him as Tony, whom we'd known in Bydgoszcz years before the war. He also recognized us, and told us that the German doctor would soon come.

Indeed, the doctor walked in shortly after, dressed in full German army uniform. His medical paraphernalia consisted only of a little note pad. He barked at the first girl: "Name? Problem?"

Tony translated. Any problem or illness was irrelevant to the doctor. "You can work," he replied repeatedly. Finally, he pointed at Ann.

"What is your problem?"

"I have TB," Ann said.

"For how long?"

"Two years," Ann lied.

"We can use you for a while longer."

I was next. "I am pregnant."

"How long?"

"Three or four months."

"You can work easily till seven months."

The doctor finished his examination-interrogation-questioning and turned to Tony. "I'll be here the day of the transport. If any of these twelve girls is missing, you will take her place." He started to leave, but turned back and added: "And I want them all in this room." He pointed his stubby finger at one of the small side alcoves and left.

Tony looked at us, the most sheepish look clear on his face, silently pleading with us not to even try to escape. One of the girls assured him that it would be stupid to risk our lives at the end of war. We asked Tony if there was a Red Cross doctor around. Every one of us must have had a scheme in her mind, but as we did not know each other, we did not reveal our plans... Ann and I were the only "unit" of two sisters.

Tony tried to be very friendly, telling us about our surroundings and what we might expect. He explained that, at the moment, the warehouse was empty because the transport to Germany had left early that morning. However, people would be brought in each day until the building will be full for the next transport—perhaps a week or so. Tony made sure to remind us that at that point the German doctor would come back. He suggested that we all stay in the little alcove, so as to be more comfortable and to keep our space separate from the masses that will arrive in the next few days.

Left alone, we looked around. We were being held in the railroad service yard. It was huge; it probably served the same purpose as a roundhouse, but it was long and straight, with only one line of railroad trucks passing through the middle. It could have easily held two locomotives on the tracks. On both sides of the center area were huge, square columns supporting a very high roof. Outside the columns, lower-ceilinged passageways held entrances to side alcoves originally used for spare parts and tools.

One of those little rooms now became our group's sleeping quarters. High windows provided us with light.

The passage between the columns and the alcoves led to a smaller hall in front of the building; there were about ten toilets on the left side and big windows on the right. Tony exited a room at the end of this smaller hall and told us that now we could use the toilets, but once the hall got full, it would be impossible to accommodate everybody; we should then use the open latrines outside in the yard.

We stood, listening to Tony, and looked at the opposite wall from the toilets. The large open windows beckoned. A few feet away was a tall barbed-wire fence; another fence was visible in the distance.

"Don't even try it," Tony said, reading our minds. "To the far right, there are German guards between the two fences. You'd be a sitting duck."

Tony directed our attention to the room from which he'd just emerged. He opened the door, walked inside and opened a little window in the door. He told us it was his quarters, from which he was running a kiosk and selling a variety of small items. Obviously, everything was in black market prices, but we were happy to be able to get some extra food and asked him to get us some sausage and fresh bread. When Tony came back with our "order," we devoured our first decent meal in more than two months.

Later, another Polish Red Cross worker came to see us.

"Doctor Kozika," I exclaimed, and told her my name. She had not seen me since the war started, and she remembered me as a girl five years younger. Dr. Kozika was a dentist and a friend of our mother, with whom Mother frequently played bridge. She told us that Mother had passed through this camp and been transported further into Poland as part of a transport of old and sick people. I did not have to ask my next question.

"I cannot help you now," Dr. Kozika continued. "Please do not try anything, till you get checked for the transport."

At her words, a light flashed in my mind: *"once we get checked in, there may be a chance to escape".*

Transports full of Warsaw's civilians started arriving by the hundreds. I have completely blocked from my memory the particulars of those several days we stayed in the warehouse, waiting for transport. I only remember that we were glad to stay in that little alcove. The huge main area was crammed with people from one end to the other. I do not remember how or what we were given to eat, where we washed or how we spent the days. It is one of the periods in my life that I call "suspended animation".

However, I do remember one remarkable meeting. With the hall almost full, we were forced to use the outdoor latrines—just as Tony had predicted. We stood, waiting in line, when suddenly a woman's voice called, "Anka, Zosia!"

It was a mother and one of the younger dancers from Mrs. Wanda's school, also waiting in line for the latrine!

Within seconds of greeting one another, we started reminiscing about our last show, particularly a dance entitled "Wanderers." Mother and daughter told us how every part of their exodus from Warsaw reminded them of "Wanderers."

"Mrs. Wanda created an incredibly visionary dance, one that foresaw our tribulations," the mother said.

I vividly remembered "Wanderers". I did not take part in it; it was more of a dramatic play than a dance. A large number of students moved dramatically across the stage to the somber music of Beethoven. The wanderers walked in various groupings and exhibited varying degrees of desperation and exhaustion. One by one, they then fell down, unable to continue.

As the last wave of wanderers passed through the stage—the third, maybe the fourth time—Mrs. Wanda joined the few remaining survivors. Mrs. Wanda played the role of an individual who, unable to cope with the situation, lost her mind.

For a moment, the four of us stood, moved by the memory of a dance so drastic, dramatic, and unforgettable. Emotions and thoughts tore through me.

"I can't afford to lose my mind or get desperate", I thought.

A few minutes later we parted, never to see each other again.

Days passed. The warehouse bulged with humanity. Finally, Tony came and told us that our transport would leave the next day.

"Please, stay in this alcove till I come with the doctor," he said.

Several feelings and desires were driving me. I wanted desperately to find Bohdan and to see my mother. The transports themselves presented many potent dangers: the people being transported were locked in cattle wagons and often denied food or water; trains were being bombed; even if one reached the labor camps, horrid conditions prevailed there. But I saw no reason to succumb to despair or confusion if I did not have to, preferring as always to do things my way.

The next day, when Tony and the doctor came, our meager belongings were packed and ready for the transport. The doctor counted us up, all twelve, checked our names against his list, and released Tony. The Germans made certain that the only way we could go out was through the huge gate in front into the cattle cars, which waited to take us to the slave labor camp in Germany.

Soldiers, machine guns at the ready, lined the back of the hall. There was only the one huge door, through which people were leaving. The masses started moving. I stalled a little; I was not in a hurry.

Half of the hall emptied. All the side alcoves behind ours were turned out by soldiers with guns, following a short distance behind the last stragglers.

We could not linger any longer. Ann and I had to start moving.

At that moment, I noticed that there was only one soldier walking in the narrow passage behind us, between the row of large columns and the alcoves. When that soldier moved to the center of the building, the passage was left empty. I grabbed Ann and pulled her past the column into the passage. The soldier was far enough behind us now; I saw that the row of columns were making a solid cover for the length of the passage area.

In a straight line, we ran to the room with the toilets, then onward to Tony's kiosk. The door was not locked; we slipped in and closed it behind us. Inside was Tony's young helper, who tried to object. But I did not give her much chance. I locked the door and pushed Ann and the young girl into the next little room.

"Keep her mouth shut," I told Ann.

I heard soldiers running, opening and shutting the doors of the toilets. They must have either seen us running or realized that two individuals in very distinctive gray capes were missing. I took off my cape and coat and shut the door to the little room, leaving Ann and the girl inside.

Soldiers banged on the kiosk's door. I took a deep breath. A package of cigarettes in hand, I slowly opened the little window in the door. With an unquestionably innocent, surprised face I greeted the soldiers.

"Zigaretten?" I asked, smiling, and shoved the pack of cigarettes at them.

I could only guess that they were asking in their animated talk whether I had seen two people. (I guessed the number by looking at their pointing fingers.) I tried to accommodate them, raising my shoulders in an expression of utter bewilderment. With the air of one trying to be helpful, I pointed at the only possible line of escape, past them, through the open windows. The soldiers followed my suggestion.

I closed the little window in the door and sat down. My legs were trembling.

When Tony came he was not too happy to see his new "guests," but he was obviously not going to do anything drastic.

Transport Back Into Poland

We stayed in the little compartment for several days, having asked Tony to tell Dr. Kozika that we were his guests. She came eventually, and we paid for a big dinner for the head German doctor, at which Dr. Kozika managed to get him drunk and gave him two release papers to sign.

Several days later, Dr. Kozika walked us from our room to another big warehouse where the "really" sick people waited for transport to Poland.

The warehouse had bales of straw for bedding, unlike our previous "accommodations," which had only a concrete floor; the outside area was also larger, allowing us to sit away from the stench of sick and incontinent people and the insects that plagued them. We were faking our illnesses, but as the people surrounding us were very pregnant and/or ill many were unable to take care of themselves. Consequently we were all plagued by lice and other pests.

The September weather a month earlier, during the Warsaw uprising, had been beautiful and sunny. I had gotten a suntan, which lingered, making my normally rosy cheeks even rosier than usual. It made me even more conspicuous, so I decided to make myself appear more pregnant. I studied the walk of expectant mothers and learned to lean heavily back while holding my heavy "belly," which was stuffed with towels and extra clothing. I also developed a dramatic gesture, repeatedly wiping my forehead with the top of my hand. With those little theatrics I blended in with the crowd.

Finally, the day came for the transport. From the warehouse to the train was a distance of several hundred yards. The slow-moving column was eight to ten people wide. Ann and I assisted a very old man, whom we held up between us, and kept our faces down. Dr. Kozika stood on the right side of the column next to a German officer, the head doctor who'd signed our release.

We were still several rows away when the doctor pointed his thick finger at me. An animated Dr. Kozika told him that not only was I very pregnant, but "Do you see her red cheeks? She may have a heart attack!"

I pulled out my release paper and showed it to the officer. Reluctantly, he waved us through. Perhaps he preferred not to see a signature he could not remember scrawling, because he was in a drunken stupor at the time?

After we passed them, I had a hard time not sprinting to the waiting cattle cars. Suddenly, nothing stood between us and freedom. Reaching the train, we jumped into the next empty car. It was a high-sided open-roofed railroad cattle car with a little guardsman's box in front. Ann and I placed our belongings behind that guard's box, where they would be safe from the winds and locomotive smoke.

Other people began climbing in and distributing themselves about the floor of the car. Dr. Kozika came to bid us goodbye and tell us about her efforts to convince the doctor of my inevitable heart attack. She was very happy for Ann me, and asked us to remember her to our mother.

The train started moving. An older German soldier came to occupy the guardsman box in the front of our car. He was from Silesia. By communicating in his broken Polish and Ann's broken German, we learned that he was as happy as we were that the war was almost over.

"Is it okay for us to sit on top of your box?" I asked, eager to feel free.

"Sure!" He replied.

Without drawing unnecessary attention, I was able to drop all the towels from my pants under the concealment of the loose cape hanging from my shoulders. Perfectly slim and not even a little bit pregnant, I packed my faux-pregnancy padding with the rest of my belongings in my backpack. Then Ann and I climbed onto the guardsman's box and looked forward, enjoying our move into the unknown.

As the train clattered along, we chatted with our German guardsman, who told us that we would be released to the Polish Red Cross in Nowy Sącz, a small town in the Carpathian Mountains. The guard even shared some of his schnapps with us.

The train moved relatively slowly; the warm air felt good in our faces. We were pushing south, toward my beloved mountains. Ann and I watched the scenery with great pleasure, taking in a typically Polish landscape: fields empty after the harvest; other fields full of people digging out potatoes. After a time, the landscape changed. Farther south, the land became less flat, with rising hills and more and more forests.

Suddenly, at a road crossing, we saw something we could not believe. Several men in Polish pre-war military uniforms waited, arms across their shoulders or in their belts. We waved at them; they waved back. I looked down at our old guardsman, afraid of his reaction. He saw the men, smiled, and shrugged his shoulders with a silent expression, as if to say, "I see nothing."

I suspect that even if he had been younger and more patriotic, he would not have bothered to confront the Polish partisans. They were the masters of that area. They knew the forests and hills.

Before that day, I had never thought it could feel so good to ride on the top of a cattle car.

Homeless Gypsies

We sat on the roof of the guardsman's cabin for several hours. The train moved at a constant speed, stopping only infrequently at railroad sidings. In the foothills of the Carpathian Mountains, we slowed, moving up the grade. Later in the afternoon, now at a much higher elevation, we became chilly and jumped down to the floor of the car to get our gray capes.

Our agility must have been striking to the sick people sitting on the floor. We jumped down and climbed back onto the roof of the guardsman's cabin with the ease of healthy, fit individuals. However, nobody asked us what illness had saved us from being sent to the forced labor camps, and we instinctively chose not to speak about it. While there must have been others like us who managed to bribe their way to freedom, the vast majority of the people on that train were old, sick, and unfit to work, persons useless to the German labor camps. It made me feel a little guilty

By evening, we reached Nowy Sącz, a town high in the Carpathian Mountains. We, the human freight, were transferred to the hands of the Polish Red Cross by the Germans who left. We were directed to a big building next to the railroad station. As the door on our car rolled open, Ann and I jumped eagerly to the ground and entered. Inside, Red Cross workers waited at several tables to process us.

We approached an older gentleman to be registered.

"Zofia and Anna Srzednicki," I introduced us.

The sound of our name provoked a sudden response; the man looked at us, a question in his eyes. "Pomian Srzednicka," I added, as there was also a Kossak Srzednicki family in Poland.

The gentleman looked at Ann, recognition lighting his face. "You look like Tadeusz Srzednicki from Dębogóra; are you his daughters?" he asked.

I could hardly believe my ears. "Yes, he was our father. Did you know him" we exclaimed.

Finding someone who knew our parents sent a rush of happiness flooding through me. In this moment of recognition, my sister and I stopped being a piece of Germany's discarded cargo; we were humans, a family once more.

"I knew your parents very well," the gentleman continued, "and I felt very privileged to be a frequent guest at your father's famous hunts." He began filling out our registration papers and asked where we intended to go from Nowy Sącz. I told him that our sister Alina was in the nearby village of Raba Wyżna; we wanted to go there as soon as possible.

"No problem. A half-hour train ride and you will be there." He finished writing and gave us a warm smile. "Everybody will spend a night in a temporary Red Cross shelter, but I hope you won't mind spending the evening with my family? It's the least I can do to reciprocate for the many wonderful old days I spent in your parent's house."

We were elated; it was more than we could dream of. The gentleman interrupted his registration duties to walk us to his home. His wife also remembered our parents and was happy to offer us her hospitality. We were so very happy to be there; it all seemed unreal. We were in a normal country home with people who had cherished the friendship of our father—so much so that they treated us like special guests. Suddenly, we became celebrities instead of hunted animals. That evening we experienced the first normal meal and night since the days before the Warsaw uprising three months ago. Three months that felt so much longer.

During dinner, conversation bounced between our recent ordeal in Warsaw, our hosts' recollections of our father and mother, and their cherished memories of good times spent with our parents during the long ago days before the war. Our host felt he could trust us with a piece of very special news.

"I wish," he said, "that your transport had been here two days earlier. You would already be in London. A little plane from Britain dropped some people in the mountains and left with two empty seats."

"Too bad," I said.

While we'd missed the plane this time, Ann and I were becoming ever more certain that our destiny lay somewhere in the West. At the moment, however, our objectives were clear: find out which of our loved ones had survived and where they were.

The next day, we took a train to nearby Raba Wyżna to see Alinka and her children. Ann and I walked through the fields to the Makowski family farm, where Alinka and the children lived. The Makowskis were happy to see me alive, but Alinka and the children were not there. For unknown reasons, the Germans had evicted the Zduń-Głowinski family from their Raba estate. They were forced to move out of their home with all their relatives and workers to a small "homestead" in Sieniawa, the next village, where they had an additional few acres of land.

Ann and I walked the three miles to Sieniawa, and I asked the first person I met on the road: "Where is Mrs. Zaremba living?"

Without hesitation we were directed to a little house nearby. Alinka and the children were overjoyed to see us alive. Mother, Alinka told us, had been released from the Pruszków camp; she was staying in the little estate of our cousin Tadea, in Rzeki near Radomsko, where I'd spent my vacation a year ago. Aunt Hala, our mother's sister, was also nearby in a little town called Rabka, where Anek and Oluta's parents were living. We did not know where Aunt Hala had been earlier in the war, but having surfaced she was occasionally able to help Alinka and the children.

The news that two young women in gray capes with backpacks had arrived at Mrs. Zaremba's quickly reached the main house of the Głowiński family. A few minutes later, several young people descended upon Alinka's little house: my dear friends with whom I had spent two past summers. Thrilled to see each other, we exchanged what information we had about common friends. Głowińskis: John, Antoni, and their sister Rose were staying in Sieniawa, but not officially. Both young men were hiding from the Germans; every time the Germans came to inspect something, John and Antoni had to jump out the windows and run into the forest.

That evening, we gathered for supper in the manor house. At least sixteen of us sat around the big table, with Grandma Zduń presiding at the head. The main house in Sieniawa was now dominated by Grandma Zduń, who ruled in the same manner she'd ruled Raba Wyżna. She was the ultimate matriarch; she reveled in keeping her brood properly disciplined. Alinka and I could never discern the true nature of her attitude toward me. Was Grandma really afraid that John or Anton would fall in love with me and the estate would end up without a hefty dowry?

It seemed foolish in the face of the war. But Grandma Zduń's mentality was still that of the pre-war days. She must have believed that once the war ended, her family would again have their estate; that they would see their "old" life restored to them. And perhaps this would have been halfway possibly if the Soviets had not occupied Poland—who can say? In reality, occupation awaited.

At dinner, everybody except Grandma Zduń peppered me and Ann with questions about the latest news from Warsaw. Some bad news had already reached them. I learned that several of my dear friends from the past summers had been killed: my sympatia Felix, my friend Andrew, Felix's brother John, and John Erenberg were all gone.

In talking to us, the group was too excited to let Grandma Zduń assume her preferred air of importance. We could not stop talking, and Grandma was getting annoyed. We were young; we had barely survived our recent hell; and we were stirring up Grandma's normally peaceful atmosphere and disrupting her dominance. Finally, Grandma Zduń raised her voice to silence us. Looking at me and Ann, she asked pointedly: "And what are your plans now?"

Dead silence fell in the room. The question sounded ridiculous to all of us, who had been living from day to day, trying to avoid prison or death. We could not have made any plans in that tumultuous political situation—other than trying to stay alive.

Yet something made me respond in a most unusual way. I looked at Grandma Zduń, unperturbed. With a polite smile, I answered, "We are going to California."

Everybody digested my words in utter silence, which was

shortly broken by poorly conceived chuckles. Ann looked at me in disbelief, but rising to the occasion she chimed in, "Oh yes, it seems like a good idea."

"My sisters are crazy," Alinka muttered to herself.

To this day, I cannot decide what put those words in my mouth. I had never talked about California before—or even thought about it. I only knew that California was on the other side of the American continent, an ocean—a world—away.

The next four weeks kept me and Ann constantly in motion, like homeless gypsies. The Germans relentlessly hunted refugees from Warsaw, labeling them terrorists, criminals, or partisans. We were visible even among other Poles, with our long strange capes covering the mixed-up clothing underneath.

Two days after our dinner with Grandma Zduń, Alinka and the children took a train with us to Rabka to see Aunt Hala. Aunt Hala had offered to take care of Maciuś and Basia, and we urged Alinka to join us and go to Krakow. Chuckling, we told Aunt Hala that Alinka needed her younger sisters to protect her; she would have been too frightened to travel alone. After two or three days with Aunt Hala, we left.

In Krakow, we stayed sleeping on the floor in Alinka's husband's relatives' house for only a day or two. Czeslaw Zaremba, my voice teacher from Warsaw, was in the city with his wife. They had also walked out of Warsaw with their lives only.

Every household in Krakow seemed to be overflowing with relatives or friends from Warsaw; the city quickly grew overcrowded. We did not know anyone who could offer us a place under their roof.

Fortunately, there were apartments where the owners had extra space for a bed or two and wanted to make a few złotys. We followed signs on buildings that read: "Bed for a night, 3 złotys," or more. One woman renting her apartment expected us to squeeze into one bed rather than two. But most of the renters were kind, and allowed us to leave our backpacks so we did not have to carry them around all day, while wondering around the city, hoping to find a familiar face.

Using Alinka's information, Ann and I decided to travel to Rzeki to find our mother. There was no way we could notify her or my cousin that we were coming, for there were no working telephones in their country home. But I had been at Tadea's estate a year ago and had no problem finding the way.

We arrived in Radomsko by rail and walked several miles to the remnants of the estate where our cousin Tadea lived with her husband, Alexander Chrzanowski. We were on the road, cutting through the fields, when a man with a horse cart approached from behind. He was one of Tadea's workers; we recognized each other from the past summer. Ann and I climbed onto the wagon and rode with him the rest of the way. He told us that our mother had arrived several weeks earlier. Two other ladies from Warsaw were also staying in the house.

As we approached the estate, he did not turn towards the service entrance as he should have with the wagon. Instead, he proceeded toward the beautiful alley leading to the manor house's front door. When I questioned him, he said that when people in the manor house will see him approach this way, they will know the special guests are coming.

We had barely reached the final circle when several people ran out onto the front porch, hands clasped in anticipation. Again, we were greeted with joy and tears.

"I told your mother that you were too crazy to get killed," Tadea repeated happily.

Mother emerged, and we all cried tears of relief. Her hand was bandaged; explaining her wounds, she told us about the horrible treatment she'd endured after leaving our house in Warsaw. The German officers who came to tell people to prepare for evacuation acted in a civilized manner, but following them were soldiers who looked like Mongols from the Vlasov army, wild individuals from the Soviet forces. One of them told Mother to take off her signet ring. She could not, because her fingers were very swollen. The Mongol took it off—along with the skin of her hand.

The atmosphere in the house was peculiar, burdened by the uncertainty of the present situation. The Russian front was nearing. The news in the German papers was inconsistent and confusing. The Germans could never admit that they had been defeated and were running for their lives. We were all aware of intensifying danger. The bad news from already occupied parts of Poland did reach Tadea and Alexander: Communists were arresting and killing Polish intelligentsia and the upper classes; Soviet hordes were raping women to death. Members of the Polish underground, the AK, were being arrested and tortured under interrogation by the KGB. Everybody was storing every tidbit of information, searching in memories of similar situations in past history trying to make sense, where none existed. We all had to plan against the utterly unknown.

Tadusia, as we called my cousin Tadea, diplomatically indicated to me that the two "resident" ladies from Warsaw were wearing their welcome very thin. We got a sample of their shallowness at supper that evening. There were only a few of us around the table: Tadea, her husband Alexander, mother, Ann, me, and the two ladies from Warsaw, a mother and a daughter. The daughter must have been in her early thirties.

The moment conversation started, they began interjecting themselves, seemingly unaware that they were projecting themselves in a very negative light. Ann and I quickly formed an opinion about these ladies' role in the uprising: they were too scared and self-centered to do anything except feel sorry for themselves and worry about their worldly possessions. When Ann and I tried to share the story of our ordeals, the two women continued speaking blithely about their burned apartment. When Ann told Mother, "We saw our friend, Jasio Stebelski, shot in the head," one of the ladies replied, "We had such beautiful Oriental rugs." Everyone at our table ignored the implication that rugs and life were somehow comparable. We knew that they'd hopelessly lost perspective. Still, it was hard to remain polite.

"In three days of action, our company lost twenty-eight people.

Only the captain and the two of us survived," I said pointedly.

Finally, the five members of our family excused ourselves and went to another room for a private family conversation. We had to discuss the uncertainty of the near future. With the Russians approaching, we were concerned about Tadea and her husband. They were no longer rich, but they were landowners and members of the upper class—a dirty word for the Communists. The villagers liked them, but one can never be sure who will try to get rich fast by denouncing the "bourgeoisie."

With this in mind, Tadea and Alexander were ready to leave before the Communists' arrival. They were already packed; their top employee knew which carriage and horses they wanted to take. They would slip away somewhere where they could lose themselves in the crowds. Meanwhile, Mother's age and poor health would keep her safe, we hoped. Ann and I told our family members that we would go back to Krakow and get lost in the big city. We did not mention our plan to go west, to America. It was so hard to say goodbye to Mother, knowing that we had to lie.

We had no idea how we would leave or when, but we knew that it would be when the chaos of the front drew close. We also realized—heartbreakingly—that whatever our plan for the future, we could not do it with Mother.

After a day or two, we left Tadea's estate early in the morning and walked to the Radomsko railroad station. I don't remember why they couldn't supply us with transportation, but we did not want to wait till the afternoon or the next day.

Ann and I walked through the forest in silence. Welling up from deep in my heart, the realization that I would never see my mother again overwhelmed me. Tears flowed down my face. I looked at Ann and saw her crying as well. We started talking, trying to rationalize, to tell ourselves that one occupation by the Germans was bad enough. We should not, could not, wait for another occupation by the Eastern hordes.

Still, we felt guilty.

During the remaining kilometers I thought about my poor mother suffering but still taking care of our apartment in Warsaw; about giving her painful injections while unable to console her; about the warm words I'd held in my heart—words I now wished I had found the strength to say.

In Radomsko, we boarded a crowded train. A lady standing next to us asked if we were from Warsaw. She told us about an orphaned girl from Warsaw who was now living with distant relatives in Radom. The 16-year-old girl was from Warsaw's Mokotów District.

"During the uprising," the lady continued, "this young girl left her home, where she lived with her parents, sister and sister's baby. A short time later, when she came back, the house had been demolished by bombs. The whole family perished."

The lady remembered only the girl's first name: Sophie. When she described her further, however, we knew it had to be the one and only Zosia Perczyńska, one of the dancers from Mrs. Wanda's school. The lady gave us her address. On the spot we changed our plans and got off the train in Radom. For years Zosia, whom we called "Zosiunia" to differentiate her from me, had admired Ann; they became very close friends. Now we found her house.

When we arrived, poor Zosia melted into tears. We stood by the front door, crying, embracing and crying some more. After a time, Zosia pointed me up the narrow staircase to her room. As we walked, Zosia told us fragments of her disastrous recent past. Then her next words struck me like a knife.

"Diana, do you know that Bohdan was killed?"

My heart sank. My world ended. The reality of Bohdan's death, of his being gone forever, tore my heart. My premonition of his death back in Warsaw hadn't been a mistake. That night, when Bohdan came in my dream to say goodbye, I tried to believe that it was only a nightmare. Deep down, I knew the cruel truth. But I had to hope; I needed to hope. Now, there was no more hope.

I did not cry for long. Instead, I sat up, deadly calm.

"Please tell me everything you know about him," I asked.

Zosia lived with her parents in Mokotów, not far from the infamous SS barracks which Bohdan's company had planned to attack. One day, while walking on the street, Zosia saw a fresh grave with flowers and the simple sign: "Bohdan Fidziński, pseudonym Tarzan."

His company had attacked the German SS barracks, she told me. Bohdan was shot through the legs and left lying on the field. The Germans shot at the Red Cross patrols that tried to pick up the wounded; they even shot at the priest trying to carry the holy sacrament to the dying.

Bohdan stayed on the field until nightfall. Under the cover of darkness, two of his buddies went to bring him back. He was still alive, but gangrene was setting in; the doctors in the field hospital could not save him with their primitive supplies. He died on August 8, the night I woke up crying desperately, my little bracelet lying broken next to me.

Bohdan. My great love, the beautiful young man with whom I shared a perfect love, was dead. My life, I knew in that moment, would never be the same again. As a child I heard this saying many times: "in a lifetime, there is only one true love". Even if that wasn't true, I knew nobody would ever take Bohdan's place. I was numb, empty inside.

And yet. We had to keep going—without knowing why or where.

We took a train back to Krakow, to wait for a moment when the Germans would be escaping and wouldn't care what anybody else was doing.

Historical Krakow is built around the old town, a big plaza with a market square in the center. Whenever one goes to town, the journey usually starts or ends at the marketplace. The day after returning from Radom, Ann and I were meandering around the square, approaching the famous Mariacki (Saint Mary's) church. We could hear organ music. Walking into the darkened church, powerful chords hit us. We looked for the service that would demand such music, but there were only a few people around.

A man saw our questioning looks.

"This is a pianist from Warsaw who comes to play here," he told us.

Ann and I sat in an empty pew to listen. The classical piece ended, and there was sudden, total silence. *Please keep playing*, I prayed.

In that moment, the low rhythmic chords of Chopin's "Funeral March" began reverberating through the church, striking our bodies and hearts. The slow melody, like the uneven steps of mourners, moved in lower tones, struggled higher, and then moved higher again in strong octaves.

The music matched all our memories from the last two months in Warsaw. Many individuals had died, but there were no funeral marches. Neither did the mourners have time to mourn.

I sat there and felt the pain, unable to think, tears washing down my face. Ann also cried in silence. I don't know if I prayed, but I know I was remembering those who - like Bohdan - were buried in shallow graves dug by their comrades, or left on the ground where they fell.

The powerful last chords again descended into the gentle melody of the slow opening, like the Alpha and the Omega, like life and death.

Shadowy listeners slipped out of the church. Like automatons, we did the same. We were still alive; we had to eat something.

If I was able to leave some of my pain with Saint Mary, why did my heart still felt so heavy?

Surviving The Last
Days in Kraków

In the past, I knew that I had no answers for many questions. Now, nobody else seemed to know anything either.

Even the Germans, the so-called "master race," were acting confused. They had been beaten by the Soviet army as it moved west into central Poland. In their dealings with the Polish population, the Germans were still acting as if they were in command of the situation, but their actions were becoming even more erratic and unpredictable, nastier and louder. In public, the Germans shouted orders and banged their boots on the pavement with yet more fervor – if possible. They were getting desperate; something was amiss. We had to be extremely careful not to test them. During the war we had learned that, like the Soviets, the German forces were likely to exert senseless cruelty on innocent people when frustrated with their own situation.

At the time, it was an open secret that the whole old town of Krakow, including ancient Kings' Wawel Castle, was mined, ready to be exploded by Hitler's Governor Frank. Hitler seemed to hate Krakow less than Warsaw, for the modern town was not mined. Only the historical and cultural part was meant to be eliminated. Unlike razed from the face of the Earth Warsaw.

I could not believe the barbaric actions I saw much later were possible. During those last days in Warsaw, the Germans went wild, even in the Łazienki Palace, the beautiful eighteenth-century residence of the last Polish King, Stanislaw Poniatowski. Acting on Hitler's orders, the Germans crashed Carrara marble statues with sledgehammers and burned whatever they did not manage to smash. In a rush to escape the approaching Soviet army, they did not manage to destroy the walls of the palace, but they cut priceless paintings from their frames and took them back to Germany.

Years later, I was privileged enough to speak with a Polish restorer who was on the palace grounds immediately after the Germans left. He showed me photographs of the devastation, pictures one would never wish to see.

In November 1944, surviving each day in Krakow was not easy Ann and I slept in overnight houses, using the money issued by our military command in Warsaw, plus the pile of złotys Bohdan left me for "the black hour." But everything was extremely expensive, especially food, and we had no idea how long we would have to depend on that money.

Again, Krakow was full of escapees from the Warsaw area, and we did not know anybody who would give us shelter. To make matters worse, German arrests of young Warsaw refugees were intensifying. They did not want us, the revolutionary element, to contaminate the peaceful Krakow. The Polish underground did operate in Krakow, but on a much smaller scale than in the always more vibrant capital. Traditionally, Krakow was known in Poland as an "emeritus" town, one with a more docile general population.

One evening while riding a streetcar, Ann and I saw Richard, an old acquaintance from Warsaw. Two or three years earlier, we'd met when he replaced our pianist for a day in Mrs. Wanda's dancing classes. Richard was a terrific piano player, but on that occasion his playing did not gel with Mrs. Wanda's directions.

Though we had never spoken with him before, in the streetcar we recognized each other instantly. Richard was a man of small stature, about 5'6". But whatever he lacked in height, he made up for in his manner of speech. That evening, in that sleepy town, he was a welcome source of excitement; it was refreshing to talk to a man who'd been through the same ordeal as us. In a short exchange, we learned that Richard had already managed to find an official position that secured him a new Kenkarte, issued in Krakow. This Krakow ID made him safe from the German arrests. Richard was working as an officer of the Anti-Air Raid Fire Department, with the impressive German name of the LHD (Luft Hilfsdienst), and a rank of First Lieutenant.

Richard offered to help us find similar positions in one of the related organizations then operating in Krakow. Within a day or two, he learned that we could join the anti-air raid nurses' team, which would give us a place to sleep and eat as well as a safe Krakow ID. I jumped at the opportunity.

Ann was not interested. I vaguely remember that she had by then found quarters with a friend of friends to whom, for whatever reason, she never introduced me. This was typical behavior on Ann's part; I was so accustomed to it that it did not seem to bother me—much. With an always-sweet smile, she hinted to me and Richard that she was "barely" able to get a place, and including me would be impossible ... but she remained a regular at our restaurant dinners.

Those dinners came about because one of the fireman working for Richard was also working evenings as a waiter in a very good restaurant. He invited Richard for dinner and introduced him to the owner. When the owner heard Richard play piano, he offered him occasional free meals in exchange for entertainment. Upon learning that I had a good singing voice, Richard offered to talk to the restaurant owner to see if Ann and I could be included in the entertainment-for-food package. We got a deal.

To avoid overstaying our welcome, we went to the restaurant only once or twice a week. The owner always greeted us effusively. Richard's piano playing was entertaining and technically very good. Having no access to another piano, we "rehearsed" my singing and Richard's accompaniment *en route* to dinner. Richard could play anything by ear and could adjust the key without difficulty to accompany my mezzo soprano range. We knew many popular hits of that era: say, "La Habanera," a popularized version of a song from the opera, *Carmen*, and "Vioaleta" from *La Traviata*. Both songs suited my vocal timbre and were very popular with the restaurant owner and his clientele. Thanks to Radio Free Europe, we'd also learned a new Polish soldiers' song, "The Red Poppies from Monte Casino." It was the song Ann and I had performed at the beginning of Warsaw uprising while staying on Złota Street. The ballad imagined bloody battles in an Italian monastery-turned-fortress, and narrated the death of Polish soldiers, whose blood was as red as the poppies. In Krakow, my performances of the ballad touched the audience's patriotic heartstrings.

Richard and I had fun performing. We enjoyed the public's appreciation and made the restaurant owner happy; the tasty, warm dinner at a table with a white tablecloth was a balm to our hungry stomachs and worn-out psyches. Our less than perfect dress did not seem to matter. If anything it added to the character of our act, and the people who frequented the restaurant appreciated us even more.

In the meantime, I was washing myself in the overnight houses where I slept; in order to wash my hair, however, I had to go to the hairdresser. On one such visit, as the man started setting my just-washed hair, the Gestapo walked in. They knew where to catch what they could have called "homeless Warsaw refugees."

They barked: "*Kennkarten*" and everybody reached for their ID. Mine, issued in Warsaw, was exactly what they sought. I did not yet have employment as a nurse, which meant I hadn't been given a proper Kennkarte.

"*Kommen Sie mit*," they ordered. Pretending not to understand, I looked at the owner of the beauty salon, who spoke German.

"They want you to go with them," he translated.

My reaction was spontaneous and purely intuitive. "Tell them I cannot," I said, looking very calmly at the Gestapo man and waiting for the translation to sink in. He gave me a questioning look. "I have very wet hair," I said. "It is freezing outside, and I won't do your country any good in your labor camp with pneumonia."

It was hard to believe, but it worked. Everybody seemed to see the reason behind my statement; the Gestapo man looked at the owner and asked how long it would take to have my hair dried. The hairdresser, visibly baffled, gave a response specific to the minute: it was going to take him ten minutes to set my hair, forty-five minutes to dry it, and ten more minutes to comb it out.

"She will be ready in sixty-five minutes," he concluded.

The Gestapo man must have liked his exactness, but he did not miss the opportunity to assure the hairdresser of the obvious: if he let me disappear, they would take him in my stead. The Gestapo then left, announcing that they would come back in an hour and five minutes.

After they were gone, I reassured the owner that I'd stay but asked to use his telephone. He acquiesced instantly, unwilling to question a person who'd already performed one miracle. I called Richard. Fortunately, he was at the fire station. I gave him the details of my situation.

"We'll be there," he said.

The hairdresser set my hair, dried it, and combed it out. Precisely one hour and five minutes later, the Gestapo foursome drove up. They were still on the street when a fire engine, sirens blaring full blast, squealed to a halt in front of the store. Richard walked in behind the Gestapo. In his characteristic dramatic, assertive manner, and in perfect German, he told the Gestapo that I was very important to the fire department; my papers were being processed. If I hadn't been so scared, I would have started laughing. Richard was so theatrical, somehow convincing and full of BS all at once, and I loved him for it.

The Gestapo swallowed his story. Richard walked up to me and said, "Leave through the back door." Ostentatiously saluting the Germans, he left. The Gestapo followed. I did not waste any time; I left through the back door and ran. When the fire truck left, as the Gestapo reached the street, the cool air must have made them realize that it was all a joke. They went back to the hair salon, but I had already vanished.

By the time this incident occurred, Ann was involved in her own group of friends. I was not included. But that particular evening, Ann was invited with Richard and me for supper at Richard's Aunt

Tosia's (Kozikowa). The dear old lady lived in a house seemingly untouched by the war. I do not remember the particulars of the apartment's décor, but I remember the warm, peaceful atmosphere and her gentle, hospitable manners. Her brother, Julius Czechowicz, was an artist who occupied one room in her apartment.

We were sitting peacefully and talking when Julius asked me bashfully: "Would you mind if I draw your profile?"

"Please go ahead, it's my pleasure," I said.

We continued talking, deliberately not including Mr. Julius in our conversation, as he was very bashful. He sketched my head in pencil, showing us the drawing when it was finished. "I'm very sorry I cannot give it to you yet; I have to preserve it," he said.

I assured him that it would be safer with Aunt Tosia—at least for a while. Years later, when Richard visited Poland, she gave him my portrait, and he passed it on to me. It hangs today in our hall in California.

Several days later, I did get my anticipated employment with the Luft Hilfsdienst nurses' group. That nursing, taking care of old, sick, lice-infested women, was the hardest work I have ever done. My poor patients were miserable, robbed of their dignity and unable to care for themselves. With the other young girls, I did my best, but the work was difficult, smelly, hard, and unpleasant.

Fortunately, it did not last long. We could hear explosions from the rapidly approaching front. The Russians were coming. We had to find a way to leave.

While only a few weeks ago the Germans were still eager to arrest Poles and ship them to labor or concentration camps, now it became impossible to even try to get exit permits for the trains going west.

Leaving my country was a logical but very difficult decision. Without Ann or I to take care of her, Mother would be for all intents and purposes alone: Alinka was more likely to need help than to be able to help Mother. Permanently parting with Ivo Gall was another painful reality. I hoped had survived and would open his theater somewhere in Poland—though certainly not in our beloved, ruined Warsaw. I could have worked with him and been fairly safe, as the Soviets were known for taking good care of artists and theater people.

On the other hand, if I left Poland and Polish theater, I knew that I would never be able to speak Shakespearean English. Enacting anything else seemed to me like the performances of the Bohemian lower class, in which I had little interest. And as much as I loved theater, I could not see myself ever performing without Bohdan.

In addition, if I stayed in Poland, I would have to survive the turmoil of the passing front and the beginnings of Soviet occupation. I wasn't afraid; I'd learned in Warsaw not to fear, but my inner voice told me I had to escape. When the predictability of Soviet cruelty was considered, I knew I would probably not be of any help to my mother; indeed, I might become a liability. I had no idea how I would escape, but my faithful inner voice was urging me strongly: *GO AWAY!*

Ann found an escape route for herself. The friends she'd recently associated with had managed to get tickets to Prague and were going to take her along. They hid her in the train's bathroom and stashed their suitcases in front of the door. With the train full to maximum capacity, even orderly German conductors could not squeeze through the crowds to check whether anybody was hiding in the bathroom.

Before departing, Ann left me a contact address in Prague, given to her by one of her friends. I still did not know what I would do, but Richard came to the rescue. He'd learned that fire engines would be used to evacuate some of the Germans in his LHD department. Richard made himself available as a driver, and suggested that the Germans should have a nurse with battlefield experience evacuate with them. They were grateful for this arrangement, and Richard recruited me as that nurse. Little did they know that the only battlefield nursing I'd ever done was holding the hands of dying Polish soldiers.

Glad and nervous, I packed my few belongings and went to the LHD Fire Station to travel into the unknown.

January 1945:
Escaping Communism

I left my poor country on January 10, 1945.

Richard drove the LHD fire truck; I sat next to him in the co-driver's seat. In the back was a group of German officials and their wives. We led a convoy of three fire engines. The roads were crowded, mostly with German cars, but occasionally a horse cart got in the way, slowing traffic and making us nervous. The Russian front was approaching Katowice, where we could be cut off; we were hoping to get past it as soon as possible.

Looking at the map we saw that the advancing Russians and our road were about to intersect. Richard and I knew we would be in real trouble if the Russians caught us with the Germans in a German fire engine.

Explosions from the approaching Soviet front grew louder, making us tense and uncomfortable. Everybody in the car was extremely quiet. We kept driving and breathed a sigh of relief when we passed Katowice and the sounds of explosions began to fade behind us.

By evening, we'd reached the town of Opeln, or Opole in Polish.

Since we were evacuating the fire department officials, we stopped at the Opeln Fire Department. It felt peculiar to be a quest of the German officials.

After we'd been assigned cots for the night and were waiting for a meal, Richard and I found we were in the middle of a paradoxical situation.

Richard and I sat on one side of the big dining room, away from the rest of the group, and—as always—hovered instinctively near the piano. The Opeln Fire Department Captain, a jovial Silesian, approached us and started talking.

This was the first time I'd met a Silesian. Silesia is a large district in southwestern Poland. A part of Silesia further south belonged to Czechoslovakia; the western part belonged to Germany. Over the centuries, our countries fought for every inch of Silesia's land, which was rich in coal and minerals, and the boarders shifted frequently. The population, mostly miners, for centuries shared common customs and traditions and spoke Polish and German or a mixture of both, with the addition of Czech in the southern area.

When Hitler came to power, he did initiate a fierce propaganda campaign that stoked xenophobic hatred between national groups. For centuries border areas belonging to one country or the other, their national status dependent on the winners of wars, were known for local animosities and strife, but Hitler's polemics elevated this tension to extremes of hatreds. However, some older individuals pretended to hate, but did not—we saw an example of this that night.

When the captain came to talk to us, Richard told him that we were Polish and that I did not speak German. To my surprise, the captain addressed me in a Polish Silesian dialect, and we were able to communicate. He was a jovial and friendly older fellow, but I found myself wondering cynically whether he would have spoken Polish if the war hadn't been coming to an end—or if the other Germans had been within earshot.

Richard asked the captain whether he would like it if Richard played piano. The old captain flung open the piano and enthusiastically invited Richard to sit down. Soon he gave me a questioning look and asked if I could sing. Not knowing how the rest of the Germans would react, I told him that I could not sing in German. He looked back at the German couples, smiled, and surprised me with a most unexpected statement.

"Our proud German women are good wives, but one Polish lady will always stand out in a crowd of a hundred German women. Look," he motioned to the room behind, "look how these men are staring at you. Please do us all a favor and sing us a song."

Just in case, Richard and I decided that a French song would be more palatable than Polish. As I sang, the captain's remarks were verified. Everybody applauded heartily and cried out for more. I was learning new peculiarities about the German nature.

The next day, we drove to Breslau/Wroclaw,[1] further west in German Silesia. The roads were covered with snow, the weather bitterly cold. Again we stopped at the local fire department. Since there were no extra empty garages where we could park, our fire trucks had to be left outside. As a knowledgeable driver, Richard had drained water from the carburetor and thus had no problem starting the engine the next morning. The other two drivers were not so responsible. One carburetor was completely busted; the other, though drivable, was damaged.

---

1 All border towns have different names in Polish and German.

In the meantime, since we were now on German soil, we were told that we could exchange Polish złotys for German marks. Richard and I accompanied the Germans to the local bank. I was happy to have a large pile of złotys. In Breslau, the bank teller exchanged all our zlotys for German marks and did not question the amount. I was able to get one mark for every two złotys, and those marks had real value in Germany, where prices were government-controlled, by contrast to the high inflation in Poland.

We left Breslau more crowded, having had to leave the fire truck with the broken engine behind. We also had to drive more slowly to keep pace with the other damaged truck. Richard and I did not care whether we moved quickly or slowly, for we were already a safe distance from the front.

Finally, we arrived in Dresden. The German evacuees and the fire engines found their destinations. The local officials realized that Richard and I, being Polish, had no business staying free in Germany, and we were put in the nearest foreigners' labor camp, which was on the outskirts of the city. After we were registered, we were told that for the time being there was no work for us. As the war dragged to its end, the German nation found itself unable to manufacture anything.

The camp was full of persons of all nationalities. The most privileged were the Latvians, who had easy jobs and cleaner, better quarters. In contrast, easterners from the Soviet Bloc were definitely scratching themselves a lot.

We were issued barely palatable daily rations of food. In the morning we received a slice of dark bread, its bulk increased by wood shavings mixed with flower, a tiny square of margarine, and a slice of sausage, which might have contained some meat, though we doubted it. In the evening, we could get a bowl of soup made of overripe woody kohlrabi, which made many people sick. I chose not to eat it. In order to digest the stuff, one had to burn more calories than the soup contained. One small piece of bread thus had to last us from morning till night.

After a few days, Richard noticed something that upset him greatly. In our part of the camp, the shower rooms, which never had any water, were in the process of having new pipes installed. Richard was afraid that the pipes were not meant to carry water. Were the Germans installing gas pipes in the showers?

Richard's suspicions didn't affect me. I saw the work that caused Richard's suspicions to be far from completion—much farther away than the end of the war. But I had no objection to his plan to maneuver our way out of the "Easterners" part of camp.

Prior to going to the camp's *arbeitsamt*, the labor department office where we registered initially a scheme was crystallizing in my mind, and I decided it wouldn't hurt if I prettied myself up. I applied the mascara and lipstick I still carried with me from Warsaw (along with my toothbrush, which somehow I never lost). I also had my hair set as well as I could. We decided that I would talk, while Richard would translate. After all, it was a man in charge of the labor office whom I needed to convince.

"I always understood Germans to be clean people," I began. "I am beside myself in this camp with lice and fleas and God knows what else crawling around."

Richard kept translating. From the expression on the official's face, we could tell he was intrigued. Perhaps no other foreigner had ever talked to him in this way. Since his facial expression did not seem hostile, especially when he was looking at me, I decided to press my luck. "May I request that you assign work for me, and give me living quarters in which I will be able to stay clean?"

The official looked at me without saying anything.

"I am sure you understand. German people do like cleanliness, after all." I wanted to make sure that the guy's German ego was stroked.

"What kind of work can you do?" He asked with a hint of a smile.

"Any work," I answered with total conviction.

"With those hands?" the man asked, pointing at my delicate, manicured hands. Now he was smiling openly. I smiled too, lifting my shoulders apologetically.

Whatever I said, and whatever Richard translated, worked. The German official actually apologized to us for the filthy conditions and lack of work and assigned us to new bunks in the Latvian working peoples' quarters.

At this point, our conversation took a surprising turn. Richard mentioned that we had always heard Dresden to be the most beautiful city—not only in Saxony, but in the whole of Germany. The German official got the right idea. He told us that he would give us day passes, but warned us that he would get in trouble if we tried to escape. Richard translated his words to me, and we burst out laughing, assuring the official that we were escaping from the Soviets and preferred to stay as far away from them as possible. As foreigners without ration cards, we could not survive anywhere. This practical argument convinced the man, who must have felt magnanimous and decided to be nice. Richard and I received a pass for a day to tour the town of Dresden. The man even told us what streetcar to take to the center of town.

As we left the office, Richard whispered that he had told the German I was his fiancée. "Why?" I asked.

"Because he was considering giving you employment and quarters in his apartment," Richard said, laughing.

"Oops, thanks for your quick thinking. Do get on one knee and propose," I teased. "I don't think I'll say yes, but you should try it anyway."

We were still hungry and hoped to buy something in town, but as we'd told the official, we had no ration cards. Nevertheless, being a tourist was appealing even with an empty stomach.

Our Dresden escapades became a daily routine. Early in the morning we would go to the German labor office, telling "our friend" enthusiastically about all the beautiful things we had seen the day before. Soon we did not even have to ask; our passes were already waiting. Since only Richard was talking, I made sure to give the German charming smiles—but not too charming.

Our camp was on the outskirts of Dresden. Each day, then, we took a streetcar to the center of town and wandered. We saw every animal in the zoo and walked into every museum or church that was open. We rested in beautiful *cafés* drinking ersatz coffee like everybody else in Germany; we even managed to get some lousy cakes if the waitress was nice or felt sorry for us.

Dresden, the capital of Saxony, was a beautiful town. It was a special pleasure to walk for hours and play tourist. At my side, Richard complained bitterly. He'd never liked to walk much.

After a month, we realized that being in the Dresden labor camp was not bad luck at all. As a matter of fact, we should have thanked our lucky stars for putting us there. If we had been allowed to live in Dresden's hotels, this story would never have been written. My mother always said: "There is nothing so bad that it could not turn out well (*Nie ma tego złego, co by na dobre nie wyszło*)". How incredibly true.

The first air raid alarm sounded at 10 PM. Everybody ran out of the bunkers. Beautiful green flares on little parachutes floated above our heads. In the distance, we saw many red flares; almost immediately we heard distant explosions, which shook the ground beneath our feet. These were not the small bombs we had experienced before. This was something else.

We ran to the nearest bunker. I stood next to a small cold stove rather than huddling by the walls. The earth shook.

When the sirens sounded the end of the raid, we walked outside. The Allied planes had departed; the air was calm. In the distance we heard occasional explosions and saw huge fires and clouds of smoke in the direction of the river Elbe. We went back to our bunks to sleep.

The next air raid sirens sounded at exactly 2 AM. Again, we raced to the bunker. This time the explosions were louder and closer together. It sounded like a rumbling earthquake. After that air raid, the fires grew; more smoke reached us, filling the night air. We snatched a few more hours of sleep, but the sirens woke us again at 6 AM.

We heard traffic and voices on the streets next to the camp. People were fleeing the city. We stayed put and waited for orders. The rule of the game was not to give the Germans a chance to panic and shoot us if we did anything they found wrong.

When the last air raid alarm sounded at 10 AM, everybody started running to the bunker. I followed—but then something stopped me. The same intuitive voice that had saved my life before was now leading me away from the bunker.

By this time, I'd learned to follow my instincts. I jumped into an open ditch; Richard followed, complaining that my actions were ridiculous and left us completely exposed. Indeed, small incendiary bombs were falling all around us. We squatted against the dirt walls of the ditch and prayed. Finally everything went quiet.

As we struggled out of the ditch, we saw that our bunker had been hit. Several people were wounded; one young woman was dead. She had been standing next to a little cold stove.

"Thank you, my Guardian Angel," I whispered.

"How did you know?" Richard asked, his face pale.

We realized that being in the labor camp had saved our lives. Only the locations originally marked by the green flares survived. The rest of Dresden took a pounding from every kind of bomb in the Allied Forces' arsenal. As we learned later, Hitler was given an ultimatum: surrender or Dresden would be bombed. Hitler refused, believing that the Allies would not dare to bomb such a historic city. The Allies proved him wrong.

For us, the devastation felt peculiarly good. "This is a revenge for what the Germans did to Warsaw," we whispered to one another. We loved it, the great joy of justice being done. "This is God's wrath for Warsaw!"

Eventually an announcement sounded, directing everybody to leave the camp. We marched out of Dresden in an "organized manner" that can only be described as complete chaos. Masses of people flowed out of the burning city. Many were wounded or burned. We felt no empathy. Half a year earlier, this master race had systematically razed Warsaw to the ground, burning and bombing one house after another as they obediently followed Hitler's orders to annihilate our city. Now it was their turn.

Everybody from our labor camp was told to form a column as we marched. Armed soldiers escorted us. Soon we were joined by other groups of foreigners, and we learned that the green flares had fallen above every one of the foreigners' camps. My group wound up walking directly behind a group of men and women from a French POW camp. After a while, the French started to sing a waltzing tune: I enjoyed walking to the rhythm, but the Germans did not appreciate the singing and shouted, "Halt!"

The French column stopped. The Germans shouted, "March!" The French resumed walking and singing. The Germans grew frustrated, for the French group, with perfect innocents did not seem to understand that they were supposed to stop singing, not to stop marching. The Germans began frantically looking for someone who could translate French.

Several people in our labor camp spoke German, but nobody except me spoke French. Finally, Richard decided to offer some help; he told the German soldiers that he could translate to me, and I could translate to the French. After this exchange we began walking with the French POWs. They had one fellow who spoke German, but during the singing he was much farther front, translating for another French group. His name was Alex du Pain. Richard was able to communicate with him, and I had fun talking to everybody else. The men knew at this point that they could assert themselves; the Germans were fast becoming helpless. They taught me their song, "Sur La Route Qui Va" (On the Road that is Going). To this day, that song summons pleasant memories for me.

We walked to a town in the hills north of Dresden, where we stayed for several days in temporary quarters. The Germans struggled to decide what to do next, not only with us foreigners, but with their own population, en mass evacuating Dresden.

Other foreigners who had seen the bombardments from the hills above the city told us that the precision of the bombing was unbelievable. The first wave outlined the river and railroad lines with firebombs. The enormous explosions we'd heard were caused by the detonation of war materials amassed on rail and river. The second raid used heavy bombs, causing whole city blocks to fall like a house of cards. The morning raids dropped clusters of small incendiary bombs, causing the chaos we observed from the labor camp.

German narratives of the bombing were different. The Germans were beside themselves, distraught and angry with the Allies for bombing Dresden, which was a cultural and historical landmark. The fact that the city was full of gas, oil, ammunition and military supplies made no difference to them. The Allies, in their view, were uncultured barbarians.

A few days later, Richard and I decided to take advantage of the chaos. We would try to get travel permits as far southwest toward the Alps as possible. We hoped to get close to the mountains, where the borders would be harder for the Germans to guard, and sneak through, possibly to Switzerland.

We went to the Gestapo field office and told the German officers that in the Dresden labor camp, the labor office had been preparing papers for us to work in a restaurant in Berchtesgaden. We were able to prove that Richard was going to work as a driver, as he had while coming to Dresden, and that I was going to work as a waitress. The Gestapo gave us railroad passes and even ration cards for the duration of our travel, but reminded us severely that we would be hanged if we were lying. Afraid I would burst out laughing, Richard did not translate these words until we were safely out of sight.

"We would never lie to them, would we?" I said wryly.

To leave, Richard and I had to walk to the other side of Dresden. The whole town lay in ruins. People roamed through the rubble in all directions. Some appeared to be searching for something; some carried bundles or struggled to move wagons or strollers which they could not wheel, for there was rubble everywhere. As we neared the zoo, we saw the bodies of wild animals that had been shot in the street. Vultures, freed from their cages, circled above the town. Whole blocks of houses lay collapsed on the streets, as if a giant vacuum had pulled out the walls, causing the floors and roofs to drop straight down. Dresden, that town of German supermen, was completely disorganized, the stench of rotting bodies permeating the air. It was eerie, as if some supreme justice had prevailed.

Eventually we came to the functioning railroad station on the south side of Dresden. The train going south was full of people. Darkness fell; Richard spoke to a man sitting next to him. The man, an obvious deserter from the German army, was going to the last town before the Czech border. We got out with him, and he told us how to cross the border into Czechoslovakia. As a gesture of thanks, Richard gave the man his heavy sheepskin coat.

Richard and I started walking, our faces set in determination. It was a dark night. We followed the railroad lines going south. When we felt the rumble of approaching trains through the tracks, we dropped to the ditch below and waited for the train to pass by. When the early light of down started breaking, we approached a railroad station where we could read the Czech name of the town.

I went inside and bought two tickets to Prague. Nobody asked me for permits or papers. Without any questions, I was able to pay for our tickets with my German marks.

One step at a time, I told myself. We had escaped Germany, but we were still in a German-controlled state. If I felt anything on that hazy morning, it was curiosity about what Czechoslovakia would be like. And perhaps excitement. In a way, we were one trip closer to the Allies.

Prague, City of International Espionage

Richard and I arrived at the Prague railroad station late in the morning. We had no idea what to expect in Czechoslovakia. In 1938, the Czechs allowed the Germans to take over their country without a single shot being fired. We realized that, as a small country, they had no chance in a fight against Austria and Germany, their bigger, stronger neighbors. At the time, however, the Poles accused the Czechs of cowardice and opportunism, while the Czechs mocked the Poles for fighting any enemy and disregarding potential losses.

During my vacations in the Carpathian Mountains' Raba Wyżna, I learned that relations between Poles and Slovaks were amiable, and the border smuggling trade was flourishing. Relations with Czechs were not so warm. A historical resentment existed also between Slovaks and Czechs. To our knowledge, Slovaks were kinder and easier to get along with; with time, the more industrially prosperous Czechs had become materialistic and difficult. In 1622, we learned in history class, the Czechs murdered their entire aristocracy and nobility, becoming a nation of plebeians without clear cultural leaders.

Now, on Czech soil for the first time, Richard and I felt apprehensive, wondering how the Czech people would treat Poles like us. With the end of the war, we hoped their opportunistic tendencies would lead them to favor anybody but the Germans. I decided to trust the Czechs. I spoke to them in Polish, they answered in Czech, and we were able to understand one another. Both languages are Slavic and have the same linguistic roots; the Slovak language is even closer to Polish.

The first item on our agenda was to find Ann; we hoped that after two months in Prague, she would be established and able to guide us. We bought a map and took a streetcar in the direction of the address Ann had given me back in Krakow, arriving at a multi-story apartment building. Richard went alone to the address on the third floor. Uncomfortably speaking broken Czech, he asked the woman in residence if she spoke German. She did, and he explained to her with his fluent German that he understood she might be able to direct him to Ann. He was met with complete denial. The lady did not know Ann, nor had she ever heard of her.

I waited for Richard two floors below. He came and told me that the address was wrong. "*Psia krew, cholera*," I swore in exasperation (dog's blood, cholera). "What are we going to do now? Finding Ann in a big city like this will be impossible!"

"Are you Ann's sister?" came a voice from above. "You sound just like her."

I looked up and saw the lady leaning over the balustrade. Thank heaven she heard me and realized that Ann and I had identical sounding voices! We went back upstairs. The lady teased Richard for acting and sounding too much like a German official. She said that she'd learned to watch out for people like that, as they were usually Gestapo. She told us that Gene Schmidt had placed Ann in Šroubek Hotel, where he also stayed.

On the street, Richard asked, "Who is Gene Schmidt?"

All I knew was that Gene Schmidt was a Volksdeutch who frequented the Fregata restaurant in Warsaw, where Ann had worked as a waitress. From Ann's descriptions, he was a nice older guy, always helpful to waitresses, giving them big tips. I might have seen him once or twice, but I had a low opinion of him. According to Ann, "He appeared to be harmless to Poles and with the German name of Schmidt he declared himself to be of German nationality." That was what "Volksdeutch" meant.

To me, he was a cheap opportunist who benefited himself by collaborating with Poland's occupiers. Back in Krakow, Ann had only mentioned his name to me in conjunction with her attempt to escape Krakow by train.

As promised, we found Ann at the Šroubek, the biggest hotel in Prague, located on *Vaclavske Namesty* (Plaza of St. Vaclav). Ann suggested that we register there as well, which we did, trying to blend in with the surroundings.

Ann told us that Gene Schmidt had arranged for her to stay at the Šroubek; there was also a young man named Tolek involved, with whom Ann had some questionable (to me) relationship. At the time of our arrival, Tolek was away on a trip. "What is Ann's connection to these men?" I wondered. I never got a clear answer. Nor was it the time to probe. Ann had been in Prague since early January and was already well-settled.

Thanks to the Czechs' total collaboration with the Germans, life in Czechoslovakia was relatively normal and easy. We exchanged our currency at the official rate. The exchange of marks into Czech crowns was even better for us than our prior exchange of złotys for German marks. In fact, these two favorable exchanges gave me enough money to pay for hotel rooms and eat restaurant food for a time. The only question remaining was this: how long would it take us to reach the American front?

Eating all our meals in restaurants allowed us to hear other diners' language and accents; within one or two evenings, we met two other Poles. Hubert and Albert were colorful individuals who introduced themselves as representatives of the Polish Brigade of the St. Cross Mountains, a group of Polish partisans who managed to leave Poland as a unit on horseback with the German army's permission. The St. Cross Mountains Brigade was comprised of members of Polish military, all drawn from the far right political party NSZ (*Narodowe Siły Zbrojne*) or National Armed Forces. Since their opposition to the Communist left was well known, they managed to get permission from the local German Vermacht (Army) commander to evacuate. While Hubert and Albert were in Prague taking care of their business, whatever it was, the brigade and their horses were supposed to be stationed somewhere in the country not far away.

Such movements would once have been questionable to the Germans, but in the chaos of the war's end, Germany must have decided to trust any anti-Communist sentiments—especially since the whole brigade was also well-armed. The Germans likely preferred not having to deal with this well-trained partisan unit.

Hubert and Albert became our companions. We enjoyed hearing the stories they were willing to share, though we knew that not everything we heard was exactly true.

In the next few days, we met another peculiar duo. Stanley and

Joe traveled with two big suitcases and changed hotels frequently. We learned that Stanley's father was in England, and that Stanley had attended school there. Soon we learned from Stanley not to question Joe about his family. His pain was too fresh and unbearable. Joe had seen his wife and children murdered by the Soviets; he had a hard time talking about it and was unable to hide his grief and hostility. I never learned how he managed to escape the Soviets himself, and did not ask.

Our Polish group of friends had a peculiar dynamic. Since the four men changed hotels frequently, like Stanley and Joe, or moved in and out of Prague, like Hubert and Albert, we met most often in Ann's large hotel room. On a very few occasions Gene Schmidt appeared, as did Tolek, who held a subservient position to Gene with regards to Ann. Gene, Tolek and Ann had traveled together from Krakow to Prague. Tolek kept his belongings in Ann's room, but according to Ann he was frequently out of town. Whenever he joined our gatherings, the atmosphere was tight and constrained. Nobody seemed to trust him.

In truth, considering the political situation, none of us was completely frank with another. The constant reality of the German Gestapo, who at any moment could have us arrested and interrogated, hung over our heads. The less we could tell them in that case, the better for everyone involved.

At eighteen, I was five years younger than Ann and Richard; everybody else was even older. As at so many prior times in my life, I felt that I was once again in the shadow of the "sophisticated" Ann, who enjoyed playing her manipulative games with the men. She flirted with handsome Hubert, and he reciprocated, not being sure what Tolek's role was. Albert, the quieter of the two, appeared to be making sure that Hubert did not blurt out something we would all regret later. Similarly, quiet Joe watched over Stanley, the obvious mover who made most of the decisions for the two of them.

Hubert did not appear to be concerned with whether or not Tolek was Ann's boyfriend; he was too much of a lady's man to worry about such trivial matters, and seemed more concerned with Tolek's political associations. Tolek could have been working for the Gestapo, the Communists or—most probably—for both.

Richard and I must have also seemed like a strange couple. If it hadn't been for Richard, I wouldn't have had an easy escape from Krakow; similarly, Richard claimed that if it hadn't been for me, he would have been wounded or killed in Dresden. Though Richard and I were unquestionably loyal to each other, somehow Richard and Ann started treating me like an *enfant terrible*, a troublesome youngster, and the rest of the older men followed this pattern to varying degrees. On occasion, everyone protected me or treated me like a younger sister. That role gave me an opportunity to observe the group's games and machinations. I saw much more than they would have liked.

When we had nothing constructive to do, which was most of the time, our group enjoyed playing tourists in Prague. Prague is fondly called by the Czechs *Zlata*, or golden. It deserved its name, for it is one of the prettiest Eastern European cities. Our ability to speak Czech was fast improving, and the Czechs were happy to share information about their historical treasures with us. We were having fun.

One rainy afternoon in Ann's big hotel room, Stanley and Joe started discussing political news, which made everybody automatically lower their voices.

"I still can't get over Yalta,"[1] Joe said.

"What about Yalta?" Richard asked.

"Didn't you hear? Roosevelt and Churchill sold Poland to Stalin," Joe said.

"Yes, they had the 'Big Three' meeting on the Crimean Peninsula, and Stalin got their agreement for the Curzon Line," Stanley said. "What's worse, Churchill and Roosevelt don't seem to realize that they'll have no control over what will happen to Poland."

"We could never stand the bastards!" Albert snapped. "Before we left Poland, the NSZ had verified information that the Russians had established a puppet regime in Lublin, which they promised Roosevelt and Churchill not to do, and were doing horrid things there. People were being arrested and interrogated, Beria style."

There was a shocked silence. "Who is Beria?" I asked.

"The biggest son-of-a-bitch chief of Soviet *bespieka*, security," Hubert said.

Again, silence descended over the room as everybody was left to his or her own thoughts. Once more, I was the one to break the somber mood:

"I know the facts of this war fairly well, but I do not understand the political machinations of our friends, the British and the Americans," I said. "Are they too cynical, too uninformed, or too stupid?"

Didn't they remember that Stalin was Hitler's bosom buddy as recently as September 1939? I wanted to add. They could not deny the facts they'd learned from General Anders and all those who managed to escape Russia about what Stalin had done to them—not to mention the International Red Cross records detailing the 1940 Katyń massacre of Polish soldiers.

---

1 The Big Three Yalta Agreement took place on February 5, 1945.

"I thought that our government in London was inefficient," Stanley interjected, "but I am starting to believe that they are simply helpless dealing with our allies."

"Yes," Joe agreed. "Our big allies sang praises for our fighting Polish troops when they needed them, at Tobruk, London, Monte Cassino. Now it seems the Poles can get lost. The Allies want to finish the war and are afraid Stalin will double cross them."

My frustration was getting to me. "I don't want to think about it," I cried. "I'm glad we escaped before the Soviets came, and I hope we will find new, free lives in America. I hope I'm not a traitor, but if I made it out of Warsaw alive, maybe I was meant to go away!"

Everybody was looking at me. I had to stop talking. I got up and turned, trying to compose myself. This was no place to start crying.

I had heard about espionage in general for years, especially in conjunction with my Aunt Władka's political activities during World War I. In Warsaw, I did some spying myself, but it was on such a small scale that it was not worthy of the name "espionage."

Now, at the end of March 1945, we were in the midst of it. With Vienna's imminent fall into Soviet hands, everybody who was somebody was coming to Prague. And not just Prague. It seemed that they were all staying in the Šroubek Hotel. Prague had the distinction of becoming Eastern Europe's new temporary espionage center.

We had fun examining the various tables in the dining room, trying to pinpoint the nationalities at play. Since many of those present spoke German, albeit with differing accents, we paid more attention to their way of eating, mode of dress, and manners. There were British, Swiss, Norwegians, many persons of Spanish decent we could not differentiate, and—amongst them—Germans pretending to be anything but Germans. Those were the poorly disguised intelligence agents who had also escaped from Vienna.

While we were wondering who was who, it was obvious that they were also wondering who *we* were. Nobody would have believed that we were nobodies waiting for the war's divided fronts to draw closer. When the chaos grew bigger, we hoped to escape to American lines without being arrested—or killed by mistake.

By the first of April, Easter was fast approaching. Shortly before, Ann told me about an interesting new friend who had offered her his apartment to bake goodies for Easter. Since Ann did not know how to bake, she accepted the invitation on my behalf.

Ann's new friend, a German test pilot, Wolfgang Merzenich, confided to her that he hated Hitler and the whole Nazi system. However, as one of the very few test pilots still alive, he was too valuable to the Nazis for anybody to check his political sentiments. It sounded like a risky disclosure to a Polish woman he barely knew, but Mr. Merzenich claimed that the Germans needed his piloting skills whether he was a Nazi sympathizer or not.

Ann and I went to his apartment a day or two before Easter. Mr. Merzenich came home just as I was leaving with my fresh baked goods. After I left, he told Ann that he planned to be gone for a time; the next day, he was going to fly to Berchtesgaden to check on Hitler's escape plane.

Back at our hotel, Ann shared the exciting news. At the first chance to speak alone with Stanley, I offered him some baked goods—and the news about the owner of the apartment. For some time now, I'd been certain that Stanley's big suitcases must contain a radio. If my suspicion was correct, the fact that Hitler's escape plane was in Berchtesgaden might be very useful information indeed.

A few days later, Wolfgang returned to Prague and met with Ann again. Ann related his story to me. It seemed Wolfgang could not test Hitler's escape plane. The day he arrived in Berchtesgaden, the Americans bombed the field where Hitler's plane was hidden. What a coincidence! I told Stanley, and we both smiled.

Spies, Familial
and Otherwise

On April 7, 1945, Vienna fell into Soviet hands. I did not know it at the time, but the Soviet arrival saved my Aunt Władka's life.

Back in Warsaw, we had heard gossip that the Gestapo was looking for Aunt Władka. What we did not know was that during 1942 and 1943, she traveled four times to Vienna as a so-called "deep reconnaissance" courier for AK. She also traveled to Heidelberg, maintaining highly dangerous and risky contact with the Polish Intelligence network in Germany, and sent materials obtained from them to London. The British were desperately seeking the place from which the Germans launched their deadly rockets, the V1 and V2 bombs, and Polish espionage had made a decisive discovery. Among others, my aunt's Polish network from twenty years ago played a big role in this breakthrough.

On April 8, 1943, after transmitting materials pertaining to the V2 bomb factory in Peenemunde, Aunt Władka was arrested by the Gestapo. While she was being held in German prison under the name on her false papers, the Germans were searching Warsaw for the infamous Władysława Macieszyna, Polish senator and WWI spy.

Unable to get any information from Aunt Władka, the Germans tortured her during interrogation. My aunt bit through her veins, trying to commit suicide, but the Germans managed to save her. Next she went on hunger strike. Fortunately the medical doctor assigned to keep her alive became her friend and suggested she simulate insanity, which he would medically verify. It worked. The Gestapo stopped their useless torture.

However, Germany's investigation of the Polish intelligence network lasted for a long time; the case against my aunt only ended on February 22, 1945. Aunt Władka was sentenced to death by guillotine, which was confirmed by Berlin on March 14. Execution was delayed, however, supposedly because there was no guillotine in Vienna. Meanwhile, Aunt Władka fell sick with symptoms of typhus.

These are the official words of her case. Back in Poland, Aunt Władka told the rest of her story. It was the prison doctor, her friend, who helped her simulate typhus to delay the execution. Then the executioner had to be brought from Germany to perform the vile deed, but that particular information was transmitted to the Polish underground and the executioner, together with the train upon which he rode, was sent to oblivion.[1]

---

1 After returning home, Aunt Wladka lived for a long time in difficult conditions. She died in Warsaw on June 21, 1967, and was buried in Powązki Cemetery. Among other commendations, she was awarded the Cross Virtuti Military, 5th class, and the Cross of Independence with Swords. In 1926 she married Adolf Maciesza. (The name can be interchanged with Macieszyna, which is the female form of that name). On March 26, 2010, in the President's Palace, Władysława Jadwiga Maciesza was posthumously awarded the "Commando Cross with the Star," the highest Civilian Polish Award, by the President Lech Kaczyński.

My aunt Władka Macieszyna was released from the prison hospital on April 7, 1945, when the Soviets entered Vienna. Thus ended her problems with the Germans.

But our problems in Prague were only beginning.

With the influx of refugees from Vienna, we realized that we were walking a thin line between being able to enjoy ourselves and barely surviving day to day. Once Richard came back from town laughing and told us how unskilled one of his shadows had been. Earlier, he had left the hotel to run errands in town. After he walked out of the hotel, he suddenly turned back, realizing he had forgotten something. He almost bumped into an agent who was following him too closely.

Realizing this was the same man he'd seen shadowing him several times before, Richard decided to play a game. He waited out of sight, and then walked out again at the same fast pace. The agent emerged from the shadows and started to follow. Watching his own reflection in the store windows, Richard turned into a side street and stopped in front of a store. When the agent emerged from around the corner, eagerly scanning the street, Richard walked up and informed him in his perfect German that, in case he would like to know, he mentioned all the places he was going to visit and even added an anticipated time schedule. While the flabbergasted agent stood, his jaw hanging open, Richard turned and jumped into the last wagon of a passing streetcar, leaving his poor shadow without the ability to follow. Later, Richard finished his errands, came back to the hotel, and found his shadow anxiously waiting in the foyer. Richard acknowledged him with a nod and a smile.

We all laughed at Richard's story. But we also knew that once people started watching us, they wouldn't stop sniffing around.

Only a few days later, we were having supper with Hubert and Albert in a pleasant restaurant, enjoying our food and the live musical entertainment. Toward the end of our meal, a group of uniformed Germans walked in and started to noisily check everybody's papers. As the Germans steadily lost ground in the war, they had rapidly become unpredictable and danger had mounted. Now we were in trouble.

We looked around for the back door, but had no chance to disappear unnoticed before the Germans reached our table. We were all arrested and taken to the Gestapo station. The Gestapo took our *Kennkarten* and put us in a dark room to wait. Realizing that the Gestapo was listening, we talked appropriately with each other.

Finally, a Gestapo man walked in and asked Hubert to follow him, alone. We waited, tense and quiet. Losing our lives at the very end of the war didn't make any sense. I was very tense and consequently very quiet and alert. My whole being was ready for whatever came next. *If the result of the present situation was good*, I thought, *there will be nothing to worry about. But if it was bad... will there be two ways out?*

There always may be a way out, I reminded myself. I had to be ready for it.

As if in line with my thoughts, Hubert came back from the interrogation with our IDs and told us that the Gestapo was letting us go. On the street, he told us that he'd given the interrogators lots of B.S., and warned us that they would probably keep watching, hoping to pick us up again later. For safety, he suggested we all should change hotels. First thing the next morning, we followed Hubert's advice—except for Ann, who seemed to be secured at the Šroubek.

Though we were all staying at different hotels, we continued to gather in Ann's room before going out for dinner. We hoped that the Gestapo were scraping for agents or had decided that we were unimportant small fish.

The opposite possibility was very real, however. If the Gestapo did not know who we were, they could have relieved themselves of uncertainty by arresting each of us again—or even shooting us, which would put an immediate end to their problem.

One day, in the hotel foyer, a young man in a Hitler Jugend uniform heard us speaking Polish and introduced himself. He also spoke Polish quite well and was eager to convince us that he really was a Pole. We wholeheartedly played this fool's game and spoke with him, but we never gave him our room numbers or names.

Several days later, we were again in Ann's room when I heard something outside the door. Pointing, I motioned everybody in the room to keep talking, but more quietly. All the hotel rooms had double doors; I opened the inside door as everybody lowered their voices and waited. Hearing clothing rubbing against the wood, I pushed the outside door with all my might. What a coincidence! I hit the young Hitler Jugend's head so hard that he fell down. Acting very concerned, I started to help him up, but stepped on his Hitler Jugend's cape, knocking his shoulders back down to the floor.

Embarrassed, he kept explaining that he was "about to knock on the door!"

"But of course!" I exclaimed sweetly. We did not ask him, *since you didn't know where we were staying, whose door did you expect to knock on with your head?*

We never saw the boy again. He was easy to deal with. But who would be next?

In those long, tense days, we grew impatient, waiting for any chance to move closer to the American front. The Russians were in Austria, but the Americans were still in Germany on the other side of the Czechoslovakian border. We were running out of money. Desperation was setting in.

It must have been the second half of April, a quiet, still evening, when Richard and I were confronted with expected but still unpleasant news. We had come to our hotel for the night; the attendant, while giving us our keys, casually said, "While you were gone, several gentlemen came, asking for both of you. They said they would come back tomorrow morning."

We thanked him, equally casual. We understood very well who those gentlemen were and gave the attendant several Kronen[2] as a token of our appreciation.

We decided to leave our hotel at daybreak.

---

2 Czech Crowns, the currency used in Czechoslovakia.

May 1945:
The Last Days of War

"What you don't know can't hurt you" was a frequently cited principle during the war. Therefore, when Richard and I left our hotel in Prague very early in the morning, we did not tell anybody that we were leaving or where we were going.

I felt guilty for not even talking to Ann, but thought she would be safer not knowing, or we will be safer if her friends Tolek and Schmidt did not learn it. Richard and I boarded the train to Pilsen, where we planned to catch a connecting train to Eger, the westernmost town in Czechoslovakia, on the border with Germany. All I knew about Pilsen was that the very famous Pilsen beer was brewed there.

We arrived at the Pilsen railroad station late in the afternoon. Our connecting train to Eger was scheduled to leave around 5 AM the next morning. The station was full of people, and it did not take me long to decide that I could get a good night's sleep in any hotel until at least 4 AM. After our stay in Prague, I'd become a tourist who treasured her comforts.

"I'm going to a hotel," I told Richard, giving him no chance to question my decision. As I'd suspected, he promptly objected.

"Why don't we just stay here for these few hours?"

"If you'd rather stay, go ahead. Do you also want to watch my bags?"

Richard made confused, frustrated gestures, unable to come to a decision.

"I'm tired and I want to sleep in a bed," I said.

"I don't feel like carrying my suitcase," Richard said, unconvinced.

"Neither do I. Let's leave the bags in storage." I pointed to a little stand nearby. Not having to schlep his suitcase made Richard to decide to go with me. We checked our bags and went to town. We had to walk for quite a while; Richard started complaining, but I was unmoved. Finally, we found a nice looking hotel and booked two rooms.

After our last night in Prague, when we were preparing to leave and worrying about whether or not the Gestapo would come early enough to catch us, I was dead tired. I fell asleep before my head hit the pillow and was deep in slumber when I woke to the loud banging on my door, to air raid sirens screaming outside and the sound of people running through the corridors and down the stairs. Richard was already dressed, upset that I could sleep through all the noise.

I dressed quickly and we ran to the shelter in the cellar, which was already full of people. Soon we heard loud explosions and felt the ground shake. People around us quaked in fear. Richard and I looked at each other, mutual understanding in our eyes. After being in Warsaw and Dresden, a few bombs no longer scared us.

The bombardment did not last long, and soon the sirens announced the end of the raid. I intended to go back to my room to sleep, and asked Richard to wake me at 4 AM. However, more noise on the streets made us decide to investigate.

A crowd of people straggled past our hotel, covered from head to toe with a heavy layer of white chalk and dust. The railroad station, we learned, had been totally demolished. Those people had managed to survive because they were outside the railroad station.

My guardian angel. Again. Richard looked at me and shook his head.

"Witch," he murmured to himself. "You saved my life again".

"At least we can sleep as long as we want." I started wondering to myself who my guardian angel was and why he or she was telling me how to avoid danger.

In the midmorning, we went back to the station. I was determined to see if we could salvage our luggage.

The station was cordoned off by German soldiers. Other uniformed Germans patrolled loosely inside. The center of the station, several stories high the night before, now laid flat, a gaping hole open to the skies. With only a few bombs, our Allies had eliminated German East–West railroad transport through Czechoslovakia.

German trucks were parked at one side of the railroad station; soldiers and scores of other uniformed people were carrying dead bodies dug out of the rubble. We decided to go to the other side of the station where there was almost no action and only a few German soldiers watching. This was the side from which we'd left the night before. To my surprise and joy, I saw that the storage area where we'd left our suitcases seemed to be standing, intact. I decided I could sneak in without being noticed and shared my plan with Richard.

"You're crazy," he whispered. "They'll arrest you."

"Then you stay here and watch," I responded.

Calmly, without looking around, I walked straight to the storage area. I couldn't believe my eyes. Right on top of the pile of all kinds of luggage were our two suitcases.

One of the patrolling Germans noticed me and started shouting. I pretended not to hear, moving closer to our suitcases. I was next to the storage area when the shouting German came too close for me to ignore. I turned, looking at him with a smile. In response to his tirade, I raised my shoulders in an exaggerated shrugging motion, indicating that all his screaming was in vain; I did not understand a single word.

To show him my right to my belongings, I handed him my storage receipts and pointed to the two bags on top of the pile. That must have appealed to his *"ordung muss sein"* (order must be) mentality, for he did not object when I indicated that the luggage I was picking up had the same numbers as the slips in his hands. Resignedly, he handed me my slips.

"Danke," I said, giving him a smile to ensure that he would not change his mind.

Trying to conceal my satisfaction I carried our bags toward Richard who stood loyally outside the cordoned-off area, like the good guy should.

"At least we have a change of underwear," I quipped. "So. What would you like to do now?"

"How could you think that you'd get away with that? Are you really a witch?" Richard laughed, trying to justify his earlier objections.

"I thought it was worth trying. And with that many dead bodies around, I figured they wouldn't need mine."

Richard was getting impatient. "Let's get out of here," he whispered. He picked up his suitcase and started walking.

"And when it comes to me being a witch–" I continued, chuckling. "Maybe I am, but at least let me be a benevolent witch."

There was nobody around us to hear, but Richard admonished me nonetheless. "Don't laugh, at least not for another ten minutes, till we're out of this deadly place." He looked at me, smiling in spite of himself, happy that we were alive and in possession of our few belongings.

At the nearby official checkpoint, we inquired about the next functioning railroad station. It was comical to see how the Germans tended to cooperate whenever their efficiency was in question. They directed us explicitly to the next undamaged station. With our meager possessions, we went west, continuing our journey toward the American front. After a long walk to the railroad station and an even longer wait, we boarded the train to Eger.

In Eger, our luck ended. The Americans were already in Germany, on the other side of the Czech border. We had hoped that we would be able to stay in town and wait for them, but after going from one official to another, we realized that we had better leave. Eger was almost at the front line, and the German orders not to allow anybody to stay were strict. Moreover, fears of an American army within shooting range made the soldiers desperate and unpredictable, their fingers unsteady on the trigger.

The next morning, then, we started walking back east in the direction of a resort town called Marienbad, roughly twenty-five kilometers (more than fifteen miles) away. We hoped to find a place to stay in a village *en route*.

We had been walking for quite some time when Richard started to feel sick. He was coming down with fever and felt very weak. Though he struggled to walk and carry his bag, we had no alternative: there were no villages nearby; we had to keep walking.

As we staggered forward, a plane flew above us and I saw something fall out of it. Thinking it was a bomb, I immediately hit the ditch. Richard burst into laughter. "Since when are you afraid of a gas tank falling on your head?" He gestured at the empty gas tank as it floated slowly to the ground. "Look," he added, pointing at a man running from a nearby house with two containers. "This farmer is going to collect the last drops."

This incident lifted Richard's spirits, but despite his rush of energy, I saw the poor man get sicker and sicker as we slowly approached Marienbad.

It was already night by the time we arrived. By hook or by crook or a good tip, I got two rooms in a hotel, but for one night only. Marienbad was a hospital town; technically no foreigners were allowed to stay in the hotels. When I inquired as to which authority might give me permission, the clerk scratched his head and replied, "Maybe the *burgermeister*?"

The next day, we decided to go to the town's mayor, the "*burgermeister*," to ask for permission to stay. By this time, Richard had a visibly high fever and could barely move. He sat quietly, leaving me to deal with the Mayor. The Mayor was Czech, but he acted like a bold German official, and he was unwilling to let us stay. He would not even talk to me in Czech; instead, he spoke officially in German to his secretary and let her translate. Despite his rudeness, I kept arguing; I was determined and desperate and not willing to take no for an answer.

"This is a hospital town," the Mayor said stubbornly.

"Then give us a hospital bed for Richard. Look at him; he's as sick as a dog."

"Hospitals are only for Germans."

"Then let us work at the hospital," I said desperately.

"NO!"

"Where should we go?" Mind whirling, I decided to remind him that there were not many days left for him to hesitate. "The Russians are about to enter Prague and the Americans are next to Eger. Besides—" I repeated the following sentence many times, willing it to work, "I know that *you*—" speaking so as to emphasize his importance, "can give us permission to stay."

As desperate as I felt in the face of Richard's illness, the situation is comical in retrospect. If that mayor did not let us stay in the town, where could we have gone? With the imminence of the war's approaching end, we could help whichever forces came first to hang the nasty man. He may have realized this himself, for he finally caved and signed the permits for the hotel rooms.

We went back to the same hotel where we'd stayed the previous night; with a small tip, we got two beautiful rooms. The Czech hotel employees were seemingly happy to make a good impression on us Polish Allies. They helped me call a doctor, who diagnosed Richard's malady as measles and ordered that he be kept in a darkened room. So far, so good, but ... we had no food ration cards and for some reason there were no restaurants open. Desperate to find something for both of us to eat, I went to town.

Marienbad was very pretty, full of green avenues and parks. As I moved down the main avenue, I heard Polish being spoken behind me. Two ladies were walking to work. I told them about our dilemma. They happily assured me that they had a solution. They were working in the children's kitchen. "Our everyday job is to cook plenty of farina for the children. Come to our kitchen, and we'll have it ready for you."

I followed them to the children's center, where I planned to meet one of them at noon. Promptly at 12 PM, one of the women came out with a container full of hot farina cooked with milk. "Don't worry," she said in response to my thanks. "We'll add an appropriate amount of water, so the amount of food will remain the same. Come back tomorrow, and don't forget the container."

I rushed back to the hotel to feed Richard the nourishing, warm food.

Several days later, I was walking along the beautiful wide avenue toward the children's center. From afar, I saw two tall figures with big suitcases walking toward me. When Stanley and Joe saw me, they reacted as if they'd met an angel. They had just arrived by train from Prague, and had already learned they could not stay in Marienbad. Their heavy suitcases were making them weary.

I listened to them for a while without speaking. Perhaps I was paying them back for the times in Prague when they treated me like a youngster who could not be taken seriously. Now, their eyes were glued anxiously to me.

"Richard is sick with the measles, which is very contagious," I said finally. "But I have a big room. I can share with you if you like."

With those words I became a real angel to them. While we walked back to the hotel, I told them all the up-to-date news I knew.

"Marienbad is a hospital town," I said. "There are no defenses, no troops visible anywhere." The only uniformed soldier I had seen was a boy, no older than sixteen or seventeen, throwing his gun into the bushes and running away.

After we spoke, I left Stanley and Joe in my room and rushed off to give Richard his farina. It was May 8, 1945, the day of Stanley's patron saint.

In my hotel room, Stanley got on his shortwave radio and reached the commanding officer of the nearby American division. In response to Stanley's news that Marienbad was an open town, the American captain on the radio said, "If there are no German troops or any defensive lines, then come to our positions to meet us."

That evening, Stanley and Joe went for a walk on the same road Richard and I had arrived by a week earlier. In the middle of the night, they returned.

"The Americans will come in the morning," they told me, and we all fell happily asleep.

May 9, 1945:
The End of World War II

By the time we woke, the Americans were in Marienbad.

It was hard to believe that the war was over. The doctor's orders held that Richard should stay in bed for another day or two, but the good news cured his measles; he dressed and went with us to greet our American friends.

It was such a pleasure to watch the American soldiers. Their bouncy, soft walk did not make any noise on the pavement—so different from the German's, whose loud, crushing boot steps we had heard for the last five years. While the Germans looked nasty and mean, these American soldiers had the kindest smiling faces. We smiled back and greeted every one of them, telling them that we were Polish. Stanley asked for the captain he'd spoken with the previous night. The captain immediately directed us to get some food and invited all four of us for a military dinner later that day. We were moved by the fact that he thought immediately of our hunger. He was right; all four of us had barely had enough to eat for days.

When we entered the mess hall that afternoon, the forgotten smell of delicious food hit our nostrils. Trays in hand, we joined the lines of soldiers being served fried chicken, mashed potatoes, peas, rolls, butter—even a dessert. It was an unforgettable feast. The soldiers were told who we were and appeared to enjoy having us among them. I was teased and asked whether I minded being the only girl. Exuberant and happy, I was talking to soldiers of Polish or French descent with whom it was easy to communicate. Whenever we could not understand the words, we understood the warm smiles and love on one another's faces.

We learned that the war with Germany had ended the day before, on May 8. "Then why didn't you come here twenty-four hours earlier?" we had Stanley ask the captain. "Because you did not radio us earlier," the captain replied, making everybody laugh.

The whole atmosphere was full of joy, friendship, and safety. I was savoring a piece of pie when Richard interrupted my euphoria: "Zio, come to the piano. This is the least we can do for them." Richard told me that the captain was overjoyed when Richard asked if he could use the grand piano, which stood on a little stage.

Richard was always an exceptionally good piano player. That day – if it was possible – he played better than ever. His fingers stroked the keys passionately, with the perfect beat and expression. Visible enjoyment lit the listening soldiers' faces.

After playing for a while, Richard looked at me, winked, and introduced one of my songs. I began to sing. The boys loved it and cheered. I sang my heart out, thanking them for bringing us freedom, for being brave, for fighting, for being my idols. Finally, warmed-up and happy, I knew I would be able to "blow" – as Richard used to say – all the high notes with my strong, clear voice.

To the boys' great joy, I launched into the popular Jeanette Mac-

Donald song, "Rose-Marie." I sang it in French, but the boys loved it anyway.

Soon after, the time came to say good night and go to our hotels, where we would sleep our first night in peacetime. Stanley and Joe easily secured rooms for themselves.

Earlier that day, we had learned from the American captain that, according to the agreement between the Allies and the Soviets, post-WWII Czechoslovakia would be occupied by the Soviets. If we wanted to get into the American zone, we needed to find a car. The captain would give us papers for its requisition. He urged us to leave as soon as possible, and we were eager to comply. The thought of waiting for the Soviets made us nervous. We had come so far, but the damn Soviets were still breathing down our necks.

The next day, though, we still felt jubilant. The American soldiers were relaxing, able to feel safe and rested as they celebrated the end of the war with us. The two Polish ladies who kept feeding us farina came to my hotel room. It seemed that we were the only Allied foreigners in Marienbad sharing our victory with the Americans. Several American soldiers brought in bottles of wine confiscated from the hotel to share.

It must have been early in the afternoon, for I vividly remember the room being full of sunshine. We sat or stood, making toasts to our American saviors. Stanley and Richard decided to go look for a car. Some of the Polish and French-speaking American soldiers also left to take care of their duties.

The two Polish ladies stayed with Joe and me, drinking wine with two American soldiers. One of them lay down on a sofa and fell asleep. The other sat next to his friend and kept drinking. The effects began to show, but we had no way to stop him. He was already visibly drunk when he picked up his rifle, aimed it at me and

Joe, and said something, which we interpreted as him thinking that we were German.

Joe and I sat across the coffee table, not more than eight feet from the drunken soldier and even closer to the end of his rifle.

"No, no, we are Polish, Polonia, Poland," we tried to convince him. Our words made no impression. The drunken soldier mumbled something, veering the rifle in our direction. I tried to get up to show him my ID, but he menacingly steadied his rifle on me. Joe pulled me back, hissing, "Don't move!"

I stared at the end of the barrel, trying to shift away ever so slightly. The situation was getting more dangerous by the second. I could never stomach looking into the hole of a gun barrel. The silence in the room felt deafening.

Suddenly, a gunshot rang in the air; a mirror to my right fell, broken, from the wall, drawing the attention of the drunken soldier. The soldier that had been asleep on the couch had grabbed the rifle from his drunken friend and pointed it at the ceiling. While staring intently at the rifle I did not notice the sleeping soldier awaken and seize control of the situation.

The sober soldier apologized profusely, took his drunken friend, and left. Almost immediately, Stanley and Richard returned with good news: they'd found a Mercedes that ran well. We shared the story of the last few minutes. Trying to make light of the moment, I got giddy, babbling, "We would have been incredibly embarrassed to be killed by a drunken American soldier after having survived the whole war!"

I lifted my glass of wine to Joe to celebrate our staying alive.

Though we did not tell any of the Americans about our ordeal, the next day in the mess hall the guilty, now sober soldier came to me with one of his Polish-speaking buddies to apologize. Seeing one of his eyes was black and blue, my own eyes opened wide in shock. "That was a punishment from the other soldiers for confusing a Polish lady with a German spy," his Polish-American friend explained.

The captain had already prepared the papers we needed to leave Marienbad and drive to the American Zone in Germany. We said our goodbyes while eating a last supper with our saviors. The next day, the four of us left in the Mercedes. It took only a short time to get to Eger, from which we continued our drive to Bamberg. We arrived in the American Occupation Zone, secure in the knowledge that the Soviets would no longer be able to breathe down our necks.

In Bamberg, we stopped at the MP station, where Stanley inquired about quarters. Waiting outside, I was happy to talk to the American MP, who understood either Polish or French. One of my first questions was, "When will the Americans take a stand against the Russians?" Not a good question, as the Russians were the United States' allies. The MP wanted to arrest me on the spot. Fortunately, Stanley came out and was able to talk fast and convincingly to get me out of trouble.

At the time, I didn't know why my question got me in trouble, but I knew that the Americans had a lot to learn about Communists in general and the Soviets in particular. There was no question in my mind that they would have to pay heavily for the mistake of making agreements with Stalin, agreements they were eventually unable to control.

In the end, I loved the Americans anyway, even the soldier who tried to shoot me. I felt secure away from the Soviets, on the American-administered land of now-harmless Germany. The only challenge left was to get to the other side of that small fishpond called the Atlantic Ocean.

PART III:

... AND THE REST OF MY LIFE

The War Has Ended - What Next?

Shortly after the incident in which the American MP attempted to arrest me, we met Captain Wiśniewski, an American liaison officer overseeing the Polish refugees. After providing us with something to eat, he put us up for the night in a house occupied by two Polish Jews, Adam and Joe. It was a welcome alternative to refugee camp. For the first time in five years, we felt safe; we enjoyed the nourishing American canned food and our ability to talk openly, revealing stories kept secret before.

A few days later, Capt. Wiśniewski helped Stanley and Joe plan their trip up north to the British Occupation Zone, where they hoped to contact Stanley's father, a Polish diplomat from the prewar days who had been in London since 1939. Richard offered to drive them, as he was not about to let either man take "his" Mercedes away.

We said goodbye to Stanley and Joe for the last time, and I never saw either of them again. Richard thought that he would return to the American Occupation Zone, but once in the north he decided to stay with the Polish corpus of General Maczek.

With their departure, I found myself alone in my new surroundings. The war was over, and the Americans were telling us that emigration would eventually start, but when? Nobody knew. In the meantime, we had to enjoy a life of eating, sleeping—and nobody trying to kill us.

There were other facts I tried not to think about: my nation was in ruins; my family home was gone; our estate was nonexistent. In Poland, my mother was enduring a second occupation by the Soviets. The Nazis had been replaced by the Communists.

Capt. Wiśniewski had supplied Adam and Joe with everything we needed at home and assisted them in establishing a Polish registration and information office. I helped the two men assemble lists of refugees to aid people searching for their next-of-kin or friends. The Americans and the UNRRA (United Nations Relief and Rehabilitation Administration) were doing an extraordinary job trying to provide housing and food for all the refugees, who had a new official label: the Displaced Persons or DPs.

I was a DP. Realizing how fortunate I was to be staying in a normal, comfortable house and not in the crowded refugee camp, I began to wonder: "Am I trespassing? Why has Capt. Wiśniewski placed me here? Why not in the camp?" The Captain had no reason to worry about me, but like a good guardian angel, he did.

At one point, I did say to Adam and Joe, "The captain has enough to worry about. Why did he put me in your house instead of the camp? And why are you two tolerating it?" Their response was simple: "How long would you survive in the crowded halls of the refugee camp? Don't you see that you don't belong there?"

What these men saw when they looked at me was a pretty, very young and very alone girl who was not completely naive or helpless, but was still a teenager. Most of the people in the camps were older, especially the women.[1] Though I had been roughened and toughened by two hard months of military life during the Warsaw uprising, my manners and language—as Adam and Joe pointed out—did make me a "strange animal" amongst the refugee population, many of whom had endured years in the hard labor camps.

Adam helped me to look even stranger. I was still wearing the few pieces of clothing I'd had on when I walked out of Warsaw. When Adam learned that I could sew, he found a sewing machine and some white material. I made two white summer dresses. These bright, well-fitting frocks, combined with my cheerful eagerness and optimistic personality, placed me in dramatic contrast to the grey look of most refugees. I was told repeatedly that I was a breath of fresh air, a creature from a different world.

Within a few weeks, Capt. Wiśniewski was transferred out and replaced by Colonel Wężyk, an American Liaison Officer. The Colonel was also of Polish decent. An "older" man of at least fifty, he was a pleasant, fatherly type. It soon became obvious that I was his favorite young friend, and that my security was often on his mind. He came frequently to our office, which was growing and developing into a full information center for Polish refugees.

One day, Col. Wężyk announced that he was going to the Murnau German Prisoners of War Officers' Camp to recruit Poles for Polish Liaison Officer positions. Without hesitation, I told him about my brother-in-law, John Zaremba, who had spent five years

---

1 During the war, the Germans took some very young men to do forced labor. However, they must have considered young girls poor material, for they left them in Poland until they were at least twenty years old. Consequently, after the war most Polish refugee women were in their late twenties or older. Many were married and/or had children who were born in the German labor camps.

in that POW camp and had studied English during his incarceration.

Even as I talked to Col. Wężyk about John, I wondered if John deserved my consideration. If nothing else, I hoped that six years of POW camp might have improved his character. Nonetheless, Alinka was my highest priority, and I felt that getting John out of POW camp would help her and her children.

Col. Wężyk arrived from Murnau with several Polish officers, John and Capt. Bronisław Poloński among them. John was delighted to be out of camp and to have a chance to earn good American dollars. Bronisław spoke to me fervently about the gratitude John owed me; if I had not given John's name to Col. Wężyk, Bronisław said, he would have not made it.

John and Bronisław were sent to the new field Polish Liaison office in Coburg to work in a large Polish refugee camp. Soon after Col. Wężyk's office was moved to Munich; out of consideration for me, he arranged for my move to Coburg, where I would stay in the Liaison Officers' quarters. My goodbye to Adam and Joe was tearful. I thanked them for their hospitality and care and left for the two-hour drive north.

Despite my sorrow, I felt comfortable moving to Coburg and secure with Bronisław. That John's position was dependent on Col. Wężyk also made me optimistic. I knew that John could be unfair to me, but I also knew that he would never cross his superior.

In Coburg, Bronisław and John greeted me warmly. We lived in one of the liaison officers' little houses, near a very big refugee camp located in the old German army barracks. With hopes of emigrating to America, I started fast, intensive studies of English. With prior knowledge of Latin and French, I pursued my work with gusto.

Coburg DP Camp

The nearby DP camp in Coburg held over ten thousand Poles, but only a few hundred individuals from the Polish intelligentsia or upper class. Despite their small numbers, these people were very active and worked to help the UNRRA officers run the camp efficiently. One of the first people I met was a professor of music and a brilliant classical pianist who had managed to acquire a piano, which he kept in his room. I became one of his few students, and practiced on another piano in one of the camp's small halls.

The day I met the professor, I asked whether he gave concerts in the camp. To him, and the other people who had recently been in labor camps, it seemed an absurd question. I did not argue, but to me it was a necessary activity. People needed art and entertainment. Concerts were the only logical solution. I went to an UNRRA officer with whom I could communicate in French. To my surprise, he and the other UNRRA officers were delighted by the prospect. They were supposed to provide entertainment for the camp's residents, but did not know where to start.

From that moment on, I could do no wrong. UNRRA even brought a German piano tuner from Coburg to re-tune the piano in the hall for our concerts. Now we were getting organized. My Warsaw masters would have been proud. Our concerts were incredibly appreciated by music and art-starved audiences. The professor included a lady pianist who played more popular music and a female singer. A man who used to work in a burlesque-type theater became our Master of Ceremonies. I recited various poems or prose, sometimes in the form of a declamation to the accompaniment of the pianist.

When speaking from that tiny stage, I realized that the faith Ivo Gall had in me was not groundless. My performances moved people from one deep emotion to another, and they told me that I lifted their spirits. It almost felt like having a "normal life," one uninterrupted by war.

As time passed, the abandoned hall began to serve as a recreation hall. After the first concert, we continued with regular performances and added other events, all with the UNRRA officers' enthusiastic support. I was happy to be useful and to bring beauty and entertainment to the camp's grey existence. Having discovered my organizational abilities, I realized with a sense of bemusement that I'd become a recreational hall director.

And there was a side benefit to the success of my performances. One day a surprise visitor was waiting for me. I went to our house to find two uniformed individuals sitting on the couch: a young man I'd never seen before, and another who bent over, hiding his face in his lap. As I moved closer "he" raised his head. It was Ann.

We embraced, happy to see each other again in different circumstances and in another country. Since our parting in Prague, neither of us had worried much about the other's life. Being by this time veterans of war and upheaval, we knew that dying during those few weeks after Prague—though still possible—was not very probable.

The other young man was Chester Gdyk, Ann's new boyfriend. They were members of the Polish Guard and Labor Companies, attached to the United States Army forces stationed in Munich.

Shortly thereafter, another significant reunion took place. The Saint Cross Mountain Brigade arrived in Coburg with their horses. This was the same brigade that had managed to leave Poland for Czechoslovakia. My two friends from Prague, Hubert and Albert, were not with them, but Major Sęp (Hawk), one of my commanding officers during the Warsaw uprising, accompanied the brigade. We greeted each other as only two soldiers who have survived a common battlefield can do.

The injustice and tragedies inflicted on Poland and her people were only partially visible to us. We knew about the Potsdam and Yalta agreements, in which Roosevelt and Churchill "sold" our country to Stalin, but we did not know that Roosevelt was doing yet greater damage by closing his eyes to Stalin's *de facto* occupation of Poland and other Eastern European countries. The United States and Great Britain were encouraging people to repatriate, publicizing rosy pictures of Soviet promises for a free Poland. In the post-war years that followed, there would be great turmoil due to international maneuvers of this type; Poles were pushed and pulled in many directions, caught between the USA and the Soviets.

In short time, the camp in Coburg became a major Polish repatriation center. It was conveniently situated near the border of East Germany in the Russian Occupation Zone. Despite the bad news filtering out of Poland, the inertia of refugee camp life wore down many individuals. Nostalgia and love of family left behind in Poland painted hopeful images in their minds, enticing them home.

Those of us who believed history would repeat itself and had seen the Soviets as an occupying force in Poland before had no illusions. We were determined to stay in the West and wait for emigration. We were also outspoken about historical hostilities and the machinations of Russians in general and Soviets in particular.

Simultaneously, an exodus in the opposite direction began: Germans moving to Western Germany. I learned that it was possible to fool the Soviets into letting Poles come back amongst the many Germans repatriating west from areas newly annexed to Poland. I met a young man from the Saint Cross Mountain Brigade who was "repatriating" in order to smuggle his family back. As he spoke, I realized that this could be our chance to bring over Mother, Alinka, and the children. At home, I announced to John and Bronisław: "I am going back to Poland and I will bring back Alinka, her children and Mother."

Bronisław got excited; John looked confused. Without waiting for their questions, I told them about my discussions with the young man and a Polish woman I'd contacted in the meantime. Janka was married to a German and living in town. She was also preparing to repatriate as a Pole on the next transport; then, as a German, she intended to return to Coburg with a missing member of her family.

As I spoke, John became pompous and began to bluster about his honor and duty. He told me he could not allow me to risk his wife and children's lives. Bronisław and I laughed and reminded him that I did not need his permission and that somebody had to go to Poland to get them now—or possibly never.

"Besides, I am afraid you would not bring Mother back," I said, looking at him and thinking how incredibly unfair he had always been to my mother. John knew what I was thinking. "Of course I will bring her back," he assured me.

"Promise?" I said.

"Yes." I looked at Bronisław, thinking, *You have witnessed this.*

John realized I wasn't bluffing. In a way, I left him no alternative. Flustered, he announced that he would go himself. "The next transport is in ten days. Will you be ready?" I asked, trying to make sure. Bronisław also questioned John and discussed the necessary next steps, as if to make sure John would not change his mind.

Bronisław and I were convinced that if I did not push the issue, John would do nothing, especially since he was enjoying his status as a single man with good pay and no family obligations. Now John went to Munich to clear his plans with his superiors. While in Munich, he met with Ann, who gave him a valuable ten golden dollars coin to help pay for possible expenses connected with bringing Mother. He also assured her that he would bring Mother along with Alinka and the children.

Within a few weeks, John and my Polish/German friend were back. They brought Alinka, Barbara, and Mathew—but no Mother. I was devastated and furious. John even had the guts to admit that he'd told Mother Ann and I would come back to Poland for her. He knew how determined we were to stay in the West, but had lied cruelly nonetheless.

Ann could not believe it. "How dishonest could he be?" She ranted. "Can we ever forgive him for leaving Mother alone?"

It was the same old John—but worse. And the window of possibility to repatriate amongst the rush of Germans was now closed. The ten gold dollars Ann had given John to pay for expenses? John temporarily forgot about that little coin. Much later, he gave Ann a paltry ten occupational scripts.

I couldn't blame Alinka for not standing up for Mother, as I knew that my dear sister had no backbone. And despite my sorrow, I was happy to have Alinka and her children around. They started to adjust to their new life in Germany, and I naively enjoyed the company, this sweet piece of my old family.

Shortly after, the new chief of the Liaison Officers arrived from Munich. I learned that Col. Wężyk had left Munich permanently; he sent his greetings and apologies that he had been unable to say goodbye to me personally. It made me truly sad. I had lost my friendly guardian angel.

At about this time, a group of Polish educators in the Coburg camp began organizing a lyceum. In the Polish educational system, this was the term for the last two years of high school. But unlike high schools, lyceums were specialized, focusing on the humanities, math, or science programs in preparation for higher study. In Warsaw, after my experiences in the Jewish ghetto forced me to give up school and start working, I missed these years. Now I decided to join the lyceum and get my high school diploma.

At home, the atmosphere grew difficult. I was helping Alinka and the children adjust to a new country, new conditions, and a reunion with John. To them, I was part of a well-known life—especially since Barbara and Mathew did not know their father at all. But in response to our closeness, John became quarrelsome and difficult, and started pushing me to move to the camp. Bronisław tried to intervene, stressing the importance of keeping our family together, but to no avail. John was determined to separate me from Alinka and her children. Why? Because he wanted to!

With Col. Wężyk's departure, my protection was gone. I had to move to the DP camp. There were friendly UNRRA officers, the recreation department, concerts, the Lyceum, other students and professors and *yet ...* I was painfully alone in the crowd.

After I moved to the camp, I started noticing peculiar physical symptoms, ones I had never before experienced. During my infrequent excursions to town, walking became tiring. I'd always been able to play piano for hours; now lessons or practice also became tiring. To resume my schoolwork was particularly painful. I was unable to concentrate and learn as I had done so easily in Warsaw. My ankles swelled and I often felt as if I had a fever.

I went to the Polish doctor in the camp, but he paid my symptoms no heed. "After the war, everybody has some ailments," he told me, and dismissed my case. Fortunately, I then found my way to the office of Professor Seitz, a German medical professor with a special office in the camp.

I'd barely mentioned my swollen legs, tiredness, and light fever to Dr. Seitz when he ordered and secured laboratory blood tests. After he received the results, he examined me for a long time with his old X-ray machine. My blood tests showed that my system was desperately undernourished; he feared that if I caught tuberculosis, which was then rampant in the camp, it would be extremely dangerous. In my age and with my weakened condition, it could turn into what was called in those pre-penicillin days "consumption."

Dr. Seitz started feeding me every other day with a big intravenous shot of what he and I called "the cocktails." The nourishment worked and I started feeling better, though too slowly for my liking. For several months I still lacked energy and could barely move without getting tired and drowsy. It was hard to accept the fact, that maybe, just maybe, I was not completely indestructible.

Outside of my camp activities, I was now visiting Alinka and the children infrequently and avoiding John as much as possible. Soon the Polish Liaison Officers were transferred out of Coburg; the office in Coburg closed. Alinka and the children left with John and Bronisław to another Polish DP camp in Wildflecken.

In Coburg, pressure to repatriate was mounting. Little daily pleasures began to disappear; recreational hall activities were cut. Several of my UNRRA officer friends were transferred to other camps further from the Russian border. Our Lyceum was rushing to graduate us by June.

I thought I escaped Communism when I left Poland. But as I learned later, the Soviet Communists had secured their influence. Among the intelligentsia, there was no question about the choices at hand. "It is insanity to risk your freedom and life to go back to Poland and live under Communist suppression, unless your family situation absolutely demands it," we agreed. On the other hand, we highly respected those who decided to go back to Poland, and our partings were teary.

Several of my school buddies hesitated, wondering what to do after graduation. I was a definite influence on those who decided to stay in the West. Slowly, I learned that I was in the middle of the camp's political gossip and intrigue. Immediately after graduation from *lyceum* and my teachers and the remaining students' departure, I was transferred to Wildflecken. My "eviction" was orchestrated by the captain of camp police, who I later learned was on the Soviet payroll. He and other Soviet operatives worked to squash my anti-repatriation voice. It was not the last time Communists would try to make my life difficult.

Wieldflecken

I packed my few belongings and prepared for the drive to Wild-flecken. I'd be traveling for several hours in one of the UNRRA car-pool cars. I tried to look ahead to the new and unknown; with my optimistic nature, I felt excited for my reunion with Alinka, Barbara, and Mathew. Being around John was a different story.

As we drove, I wondered why John had so frequently tried to separate Alinka from her supportive family. Was it a way to satisfy his hungry ego? Was he afraid that I, as Alinka's sister, would make it harder for him to dominate and control her? With the benefit of hindsight, I realize that Alinka was confused and struggling to ad-just to different surroundings and life with her husband after five years apart. But in my young eyes, she was a "full" adult in her mid-thirties, a woman who should have been able to give me at least some advice or support.

In Wildflecken, I found I no longer enjoyed looking pretty or being witty. Whenever I acted like my normal self, animated and laughing, somebody would get the wrong idea. This camp was exactly what Capt. Wiśniewski and Col. Wężyk, my guardian angels, had sought to keep me away from in Bamberg.

Ann was still in Murnau, serving in the Polish Life Guard Company with her boyfriend, Chester. I decided to visit them. We spent several days together, and while at the nearby Polish DP camp's festive celebrations, somebody had recognized me. To my great surprise, I was ushered to the stage. I recited some short pieces and was then asked to sing. Ann accompanied me on the piano. I remember singing "The Red Poppies in Monte Casino," that tune I had performed throughout the long years of the war.

That was the last time I performed for an audience.

It felt good to be warmly appreciated, but as I sang, I noticed that something was happening to my voice. The higher notes did not flow with the same ease. Maybe it was only temporary? Eventually, I learned that this was a result of my being forced to sing Helen's difficult last song by the Nazi guard in the Warsaw Ghetto.

My visit came to an end, and Ann and Chester suggested that I come and stay with the labor companies, assuring me that I could get some kind of employment. I thanked them and promised to think about it, but I knew that I wouldn't. It was nice to visit, but I couldn't imagine moving into that hornet's nest of eager males. As much as I needed friendship, love, and warmth, all I could see around me was a chance for sex.

Wildflecken camp life became a dull space of aimless vegetation. Once again, I felt like a "strange animal"; I had nothing in common with most of the people around me and no activities to fill my time. Characteristically and consistently, John made my visits with Alinka and the children unpleasant and difficult--this despite the fact that

Basia and Mathew craved my company. Or perhaps it was because of that.

There was only one person in Wildflecken whom I knew from the not-so distant past: Hubert, my old friend, who in Prague managed to talk us out of Gestapo imprisonment and who was now known as Karol Dembiński. He was the camp's police captain, and his close friend and associate was Lt. Marian Rudnicki. Hubert, now Karol, would not talk about his separation from the Brigade, and I never learned why he changed his name. The only thing I knew was that he and his buddy had had to leave Prague after our arrest, fleeing as quickly as Richard and I.

I was glad to know someone in that huge camp of strangers. My stories of my expulsion from Coburg and the corruption of the Coburg Police Captain found a sympathetic audience in Karol and Marian, who was his frequent companion.

One evening, Karol and Marian were at one of the many parties in camp, where the moonshine flowed freely. Alinka and John were there, and John managed to get into a stupid drunken argument with Karol and Marian. At the conclusion of this argument, John told Karol and Marian to inform me that he now forbade me contact with his wife and children. Marian and Karol were dumbfounded. Other people who were present tried to talk sense into John. There was no connection between me and the two men, and their argument had nothing to do with me. But John wanted me out of his family's life. Period!

If I had felt alone before, now I was truly desolate. I tried not to give up and tried to talk to Alinka alone. Even then, she was afraid to speak with me, though she knew John's edict was wrong. Looking for support from her was a waste of my time, I realized sadly. Alinka's character reminded me of mashed potatoes. I must have been very desperate to be naïve enough to expect her to stand up to John on my behalf.

"Why hasn't she learned from the past?" I asked myself. "At the beginning of the war, she allowed John to throw Mother out of the apartment, also without reason, even though John was going voluntarily to the POW camp and leaving Alinka helpless, alone, and pregnant with a baby!"

With this history in mind, why would she support me now? And why was she so afraid of her husband? I had never understood her before. Now, rejected by my brother-in-law and forbidden contact with my sister, I found Alinka's passivity the straw that metaphorically broke my back.

Karol and Marian felt bad for me and in a way felt guilty, despite the fact that they had nothing to do with John's idiotic behavior. Upset by this turn of events, we started spending more time in one another's company.

Another incident sent my fate still further into a spiral. I was in Karol and Marian's quarters during the afternoon, and we decided to make coffee. We did not have pots or pans, so we used a one-gallon can to boil water on an iron stove. When the water started to boil, I put in the coffee grounds and tried to lift the can, holding the smooth sides with two hot pads. The can started to slip, and I leaned it back on the stove. The can tipped toward me, spilling its boiling contents onto my leg. My right leg from knee to ankle became one huge blister.

Karol and Marian called the doctor and secured medicine and dressings. Since I had to stay in bed for several days, they found a room for me in the police headquarters, where they were able to supply me with meals and whatever else I needed.

Soon Marian became a primary figure in efforts to take care of me. Though I was not interested in him, there was nothing in his behavior to which I could object. He was an unusual man. He did not push himself on me, but I was confounded by his actions regardless. I did not want to be obligated to him, and I did not appreciate all the things he was doing for me. I fought to avoid being trapped.

But after my leg healed and I was able to move back to my quarters, I found that all those around us regarded me as Marian's girlfriend. My fears had come true: I was trapped. Worse yet, Marian started pushing for marriage. I did not want it, but I didn't know what to do or how to say no.

Looking back at my life, I can say how I felt at any given time but this. This was one of those moments when I had nothing to look forward to and nobody I could confide in. In my whole life I have never felt so alone, miserable and lost.

Married

On October 20, 1946, we returned from our civil ceremony in the German Standesamt, where Stanislaus Hyżewicz had served as our witness. Marian was not within hearing distance when Stanislaus expressed his wishes of happiness to me. I remember my response, because the words registered like a slap to Stanislaus' face.

"Happy? Maybe, but I doubt it," I said.

It had been less than six months since Dr. Seitz nursed my undernourished body back to the point where I could study. Subsequent events with the police captain did not help my weakened emotional and physical state. I tried to deal with everything myself, not understanding that I needed time to regain my strength. Moreover, while two years had passed since the Warsaw uprising, I had never had the right conditions to be able to grieve and regain my emotional well-being.

I will never understand why I married Marian. I believe that I have a clear grasp of my nature and my character. I was a relatively clearheaded girl, and I did not need to lie to anybody—not even myself. I had the courage to look danger in the eye and the optimism to believe that virtue conquers evil. I always appeared to be stronger than I felt on the inside. I knew my weaknesses, and I did not crumble easily. But at that time I think my whole life was falling apart.

Marian and I had known one another for only a short time. He appeared to be an honest, moral person, and I had no reason to distrust him. At that time I did not know much about his past, but I did learn that he had also been a victim of war's incredible cruelty. Could that have been my reason for saying yes?

Now I was a married woman, as always, there was only one thing for me to do: my best. As much as I was confused about getting married, once I became a wife I was determined to be a good one.

Stanisław was more than Marian's friend. He was recruiting Marian for an espionage organization. At first, I knew only that they were both very conservative anti-Communists. But I would soon learn more.

At this time, the Americans and the British still considered the Soviets allies. There were signs of strain in the relationship between East and West, but officially the Soviets were Western friends. At the same time, the Polish government in exile in London had begun gathering data about Communist infiltration of Western countries and other subversive actions. A Polish spying organization, called the Polish Anti-Communist Information Office (PAIO), was formed. PAIO badly needed a mole in the Frankfurt Polish Military Mission, which had recently been established in Western Germany. Stanislaus, a member of PAIO, knew exactly the man for the job: Marian.

I could not object. World War II had officially ended in Europe a year and a half ago, but I realized that the Soviets were a bigger threat to the free world than the Germans. It was only a matter of time before the Americans would see that danger, too. I understood that it was our duty to learn more about the Communists in any way we could, but I worried about the possible consequences. Were the Polish spies playing Don Quixote's games, tilting at imaginary windmills?

We all believed in the right cause. What we did not expect was that we would pay for it with wasted years of our lives.

In our married life, I was slowly learning what made Marian "tick": during the war, he had been imprisoned by Soviet Communists, interrogated, tortured, and sent to a concentration camp in Siberia near the Ural Mountains. Marian's body survived the ordeal, but his spirit was broken. His hostility and the desire for revenge, I would learn, ate at his soul.

Despite his battles with inner darkness, the Polish Military Mission in Frankfurt hired Marian as a driver and carpool supervisor. Everything worked out well for almost a year. PAIO received valuable information, and we found that the carpool was working well—too well.

It's the same perfectly predictable spy story: a political officer in the Polish Mission must have realized who Marian was and ordered his kidnapping, which Marian, with help from some members of PAIO, narrowly escaped. He was then ordered to travel to Dortmund, close to the border between the American and British Zones and a short distance from the Russian Zone. From Dortmund, there was an easy freeway drive directly east to Magdeburg and Berlin. This was the route many people "wanted" by the Soviets were using to disappear from the Western Zones, never to return.

Marian outfoxed the plans against him and returned safely. He left the Polish Mission the next day. The spy story ended, and I started to breathe freely. Marian was happy to have done an important job for Poland's allies, and we thought that now we might plan to build our lives around emigration to the United States.

What we did not know was that the Communists whom we had fooled would not forget us so easily. They had already started to build an invisible web around us.

1946: Emigration to America

NCWC[1] started organizing their offices in Germany and Austria around 1946. Father Stephan Bernaś was a director for Germany and Austria, and had his headquarters in Frankfurt/Main Hoechst. His deputy was Fr. Edward Bates.

The two Fathers were Americans of Polish decent, and both became my dear friends and benefactors, especially Father Bernaś, who aided me for the following eight years. During the time of Marian's involvement with the Polish Military Mission, we were already in contact with the fathers; they, like the Polish Bishop's Curia in Germany—but nobody else—were aware of the PAIO and Marian's work as a spy.

Alinka had found employment as a secretary with Fr. Bernaś; abruptly, John and Alinka decided to contact Marian and me. When

---

1 War Relief Services – National Catholic Welfare Conference, or WRS-NCWC, was one of the voluntary organizations organizing post-war refugee immigration for the DP Commission, as initiated by the US Congress.

I asked Alinka about the sudden change, Alinka offered her typical, "Zosia, let's not talk about it." The answer, I learned, was that their estrangement from us had been viewed as "peculiar" by Father Bernaś and by the priests in the Polish Bishop's Curia. John was afraid that the distance they had maintained from us might give him and their family a bad reputation.

Emigration to the United States had not started yet, and Fr. Bernaś advised John and Alinka to wait for the process to open. Alinka was willing, but stubborn John decided to take the first opportunity to get out of Germany. The family emigrated to Quebec, Montreal in the beginning of 1948. The textile factory owner who sponsored them and a number of young girls kept the group in oppressive working and living conditions for the contracted year. Eventually, after an intervention from the NCWC-NY office, they managed to leave Quebec and to move to Toronto, Ontario.

Shortly after Alinka's family left, the DP Act came into effect, starting immigration proceedings to the USA for World War II refugees.

When the Fathers started looking for Alinka's replacement, Ann and Chester were the logical choice. They spoke English fairly well and were educated, which was uncommon among the majority of refugees. That NCWC eventually employed all three sisters in my family was not due to nepotism, but was dictated by the scarcity of Polish and English-speaking refugees living in the Frankfurt area.

In the summer of 1948, Father Bernaś asked me to work for him. I would assist with the new DP Act immigration program. I set up the filing system for all fifty U.S. Archdioceses and hundreds of smaller dioceses across the country, and developed a separate filing system for eight NCWC field offices in Germany and Austria. No challenge was insurmountable, and I had fun eliminating problems.

This is when I realized once more that God had given me un-canny organizational abilities. Working for Father Bernaś was one of the most satisfactory experiences of my life. We all respected and adored the Father, who was a wise, charitable kind friend. I would not have survived the following eight years without him. Was it providence that we met, God sending me another Guardian Angel?

"When you emigrate to the USA, stay away from national ghet-tos," Father Bernaś told us. "It will slow your adjustment to the new country. And stay out of the eastern United States. There, the Amer-ican people may not be ready to welcome foreigners with different accents and mannerisms."

He told me to look for anonymous sponsorships from Califor-nia's San Francisco area. I found sponsorship for Ann and Chester from Notre Dame School in Belmont, California, and located anoth-er sponsor for myself and Marian. Ann and Chester's proceedings went smoothly, and at the end of 1948, Ann and Chester were ready to leave for the USA.

Soon after Marian's and my emigration papers were started, however, they stopped abruptly. The Counter Intelligence Center (CIC) rejected our application "for reasons which cannot be di-vulged under the law."

We were not surprised; it was less than a year since Marian had worked as a mole in the Polish Communist consulate. We were certain the clarification would be swift ... Not so fast! Our emigra-tion got stuck. We were very small fish in a huge political game. The following eight years were a gut-wrenching, miserable fight for my family's life. At first it appeared that the fight was with the CIC, but in reality it was a battle against Communist attempts to infiltrate American security.

In the United States, many magazines had begun to write about the Democratic Party's overlong stay in power. Franklin D. Roosevelt and Harry S. Truman had held the presidency for twenty years, despite hints of governmental corruption, bribes, and the possible infiltration of the U.S. government by Communist spies.

Father Bernaś and the other NCWC officials, especially one PAIO official who was a liaison between the PAIO and the CIC, attempted to intervene in our case. They were told that Marian was a double agent. When one by one of the CIC accusations were proven incorrect, the CIC officers promised to clear the case, but one by one they vanished, and our case remained closed. Fr. Bernaś and the others who worked to help us could not believe what was happening.

It became clear that the CIC officials had other obligations, which may not have been in the interests of the anti-Communist movement. Those CIC agents were themselves what they accused Marian of being: double agents.

Two years later, when we heard Sen. Joseph McCarthy's warnings about Communism infiltrating U.S. offices, we knew that he was fighting too big an enemy. Stalin must have been laughing. Even McCarthy was eventually defeated. In 1950, most Americans did not realize the skill and determination of the Communists and their ability to plan political actions many years in advance. The Western allies thought that they won World War II. In actuality, they allowed the Soviets to entrench themselves around the world.

Eventually the Soviet secrets and hostilities started to crack open. As Father Bernaś claimed, it was only a matter of time before the US government had to acknowledge that the Soviets were not American friends.

When President Truman decided not to run for a second term in 1952 and General Eisenhower, the Republican candidate, promised to "clean up the mess in Washington," I saw a glimmer of hope. A new idea formed in my mind: "Ike will win the presidency, and I'll write to him about everything I know!" I had many well-documented facts about the CIC and Communist infiltration. But, I thought, I'll write not to Ike himself, but to his wife, Mamie Eisenhower. That way, my letter will be more likely to reach presidential hands. I planned to send a similar letter to Mr. Brownell, the Attorney General. In the evenings I pored through my files of records and letters, sorting my documents and writing drafts.

I was in my fourth month of pregnancy when Marian and I went for a camping trip in the nearby Taunus Mountains during a warm, late spring weekend in 1949. During that trip, I had a vivid, memorable dream: in a little kitchen, two of my children sat at a table eating lunch. The older boy was seven or eight; the younger girl was four or five. The kitchen was modern, clean, and full of sunshine.

In the morning, I awoke with a vivid memory of the dream. When I spoke of it, there was no question in my mind: what I had seen would happen. My older child would be a boy. I didn't have to worry about finding a name for a girl—at least, not this time.

That Sunday morning we decided to name our son Christopher, after the patron saint of travelers. "If the CIC has to deal with a saint, they won't be able to win," I decided. Such small ideas of help were needed if I was to feel optimistic about the outcome of our emigration battle. The baby's middle name would be Stephan, like my dear friend Father Bernaś. And on October 13, 1949, Christopher Stephan was born.

Two and a half years of harsh work conditions, of strained

daily life, increased difficulty with Marian, and our unending battle for emigration later, my second child was born on April 11, 1952. The delivery nurse remembered me and asked, "Who will it be this time?"

"Mary Ann," I said.

"And let me guess: this time you don't have a name for the boy?" The nurse said, laughing. She – and I - was right.

When I wrote to California asking if Ann and Chester would like to be Mary's godparents, I received a surprising answer from Chester. Ann had left him; they had gotten divorced, and Chester did not have a forwarding address for Ann.

Letters to Washington, Journey to America

In November 1952, on Election Day, Ike became the president of the United States.

I waited through the inauguration, thinking that I would allow things at the White House to settle down. Finally, on March 2, 1953, I wrote letters addressed to Mamie Eisenhower and Mr. Brownell, the Attorney General. A year later, in early 1954, I had a much-awaited visitor.

A handsome young man came to our door while the children were taking their afternoon nap. In his hand, he held a familiar document: my typewritten letter to Mrs. Eisenhower. "Mrs. Rudnicki?" He said with a warm smile. "I have here a letter you wrote to our first lady."

The CIC representative's presence in our apartment convinced me that he had no connection to the Communist infiltrators of the last administration. Within a few weeks, we received a call directing us to the emigration processing center in Frankfurt.

Our emigration process became active. NCWC immediately

renewed the job and home guarantee in California. Next came the medical examination. To my shock and horror, my x-rays showed active TB, though the disease was already in the process of healing. Though I was deferred for a year to clear my medical problem, I was in high spirits. If I was able to overcome the CIC rejection, I thought, I would be able to clear my medical deferment.

Whenever I went to the consular medical offices for x-rays or consultations, I had to take Chris and Mary. I remember arguing with the friendly American doctors, pleading with them to shorten my deferment. The atmosphere in the medical department was formal but nice; the doctors argued kindly with me. In retrospect, I'm now convinced that they liked our visits and were ready to break any rules they could. And indeed, they finally told me that they were going to sign off on my emigration early—they joked that they would do so only to end my pestering visits.

For the third time, our emigration papers became active. In all those hard, long eight years during which I worked so desperately to win our emigration, my hope alone kept me going. My daily work was far from easy. Cold winters, expensive groceries and coal, and having to do all household tasks, including washing everything by hand and sewing my children's clothing, kept me almost too busy. But somehow I always found time to be with my children, whom I cherished.

Despite this hard work, I did not expect an encounter that occurred years later. When Chris was a teenager, he was asked by a counselor: "What was your life like as a little child?"

"It was great fun," Chris replied spontaneously.

When I heard about this exchange, I was so happy I wanted to cry. I could not have asked for higher praise from my children.

When we came for our interview with Mrs. Cobates, the United States Consul, she was visibly overwhelmed by the thick folder representing our case.

"Ma'am, may I please tell you what you'll find in that pile of papers?" I asked. "I've lived it for the last eight years; I know it all."

Mrs. Cobates stared at me, then at the pile of papers, and smiled. "Go ahead," she said. She listened, interrupting me only a few times. When she signed our visas, I saw open emotion on her face; she was visibly moved. It was August 3, 1956. Our fight for emigration was over. I had won the toughest battlefield of my war.

On September 26, the day I'd waited for so long came. We took a train to Hamburg, spent a night there, and in the morning boarded an American plane to Washington, D.C. with ninety-four other Eastern European immigrants from Germany. We took off from Hamburg, and few hours later landed in Island for the first refueling.

There, the plane navigator learned that I was an English-speaking emigrant and came by, sitting on my armrest to talk. "Don't judge California by the people you'll meet in New York," he told me. "New Yorkers aren't very nice, not like Californians." Of course, he was from California.

Our next stop was in Gander. It was already early in the morning. "Are we on the American continent?" I asked the attendants.

"Yes, you are in America," they replied.

"Will you please allow me to put my feet on the ground?" I pleaded. They were happy to accommodate me. Excited, I ran down the staircase. I was ready to kiss the ground, but it was wet and cold, so I only looked at the land and the sky and said, "Thank you for letting me come. I'll make a good citizen. I promise."

On September 28, 1956, in the early afternoon, we approached New

York for landing. We saw the skyscrapers, but the most important to me was the Statue of Liberty. Mentally, I shook the lady's hand, grateful to her for letting us come. Every September 28 since, I celebrate the lucky years of being here.

At the airport, while representatives of WRS/NCWC took care of our plane's passengers, I spotted my sister Alinka behind the barriers. She'd come from Toronto to meet us. I ran to her; we embraced and kissed, tears running down our cheeks. Soon, with typical concern, she scolded me for running to her without asking permission to go to the area in which she stood. Dear Alinka. She never changed. I only smiled.

Chris and Mary in front of the
United Nations Building in New York

We spent a few days in New York, and the WRS-NCWC office put us on *Good Morning America*. I enjoyed being interviewed. No, I did not talk about Communists!

Next, we flew to Chicago to visit with my dear Guardian Angel,

Father Stephan Bernaś. After two or three days, we flew on to Los Angeles to reunite with Ann and meet her new husband, Hall. On October 13, Chris' seventh birthday, Ann and Hal had a very special surprise for us. They took us to the newly opened Disneyland, that "Never Never Land" which at the time I had not even heard about.

Finally, we flew to San Francisco to settle and start our American life in Redwood City.

American Immigrants

In Redwood City, Chester, Ann's first husband, introduced us to a community of recent Polish immigrants. They welcomed us into their houses and lives. Marian got a job with the VW dealer in Burlingame, we rented a duplex, and Chris enrolled at nearby Hover School. Next to him sat his new bilingual friend and sometime-interpreter Losia.

In those years, we were enthusiastically learning to adapt to our new life. Some of our adventures were mundane, some funny. American luxuries, such as hot water, a washing machine, easy shopping, cooking, and cleaning, made my life much easier, and left me with lots of extra time and energy. When Chris became a Cub Scout, I became a Den Mother. I—the new immigrant!—led the boys into many first-time experiences, such as swimming at a pool at the local high school, a picnic and hot dogs in nearby Huddard County Park, and playing hide and go seek in the dark ... after I notified parents that we would be returning late.

Soon, Ann and Hal moved from Huntington Park to San Francisco. Hal was a special person, and the children and I loved him. He was an avid outdoorsman and greatly enjoyed camping. Our family joined him for a trip during our first summer in California; camping quickly became our favorite activity, too, especially in the beautiful California mountains.

But there were hard, sad days as well. I had hoped that once we started a new life among new friends, Marian would abandon the undesirable characteristics I'd observed during our hard eight years in Germany. Alas, he started drinking again, and behaved in an increasingly brawly, abusive manner. With Chris and Mary getting older, it was becoming impossible for me to conceal their father's bad behavior.

I knew I had to end it. After a drunken brawl, which the children unfortunately witnessed, I said to them: "I am sorry, but I have to get a divorce."

"You promise and promise and never keep your word!" Mary cried in response. I couldn't believe my ears; I'd been telling myself: *you must stay in your marriage for the children's sake.* But one sentence straightened up my thinking fast.

Since Marian frequently threatened me with serious harm, I knew I had to proceed with caution. Occasionally I played tennis with the wife of a District Attorney, who put me in touch with her husband. He told me that there was a 50-50 chance that an abusive husband would make good on his threats. He advised me to get a gun and helped me to sail safely through separation and later divorce, although his department never managed to squeeze any child support money out of Marian. I managed anyway.

My good friend Danuta's son was a student at St. Raymond's, a parochial school in Menlo Park. She told me that their school was planning to hire two Physical Education (PE) teachers, one for the girls and the other for the boys. "Why don't you apply?" she suggested.

"I don't know how to teach PE," I objected.

"Sure you do. With your coordination and dancing experience, you'll make a great teacher."

Her words stuck. I started thinking about my years assisting Mrs. Wanda and how I would adapt my dance instruction techniques to PE classes.

I got that job for myself and recruited Duane, a young man who taught Red Cross swimming classes to Chris and Mary during the summer. Once a week the nuns led their classes, from first to eighth grade, for 45-minute sessions. I moved my 40-plus girls in each grade vigorously, letting them discover the possibilities of movement in their bodies, hands, arms, and legs. The girls were eager students and loved every minute of it. Soon I heard from the nuns and teachers how much quieter and more attentive the children were after their PE periods.

Within a month Nativity, another parochial school, asked us to teach there, too. Nativity was led by the most adorable and enthusiastic sister, Mary Filipa, who frequently joined my class. I will never forget her.

The rainy season arrived, forcing us to teach indoors. Fortunately, Sister Mary Filipa discovered some old tumbling mats in the old big hall. In 1960, tumbling and gymnastics was a virtually unknown sport, but it happened that tumbling was Duane's favorite. For gymnastics, we combined our classes, which were received enthusiastically by the students. Our efforts soon led to an additional afterschool gymnastics program.

Chris and Mary were as enthusiastic about learning gymnastics as all the other children. The sport became an important outlet for them during our separation from Marian, and they found a kind and supportive friend in Duane.

I found teaching children easy and pleasurable. What else? Besides being direct and logical, young kids are open, honest, and eager to learn and to please. To a great extent, it was children who taught me how to teach and become a "professional" PE and gymnastics teacher.

I never forgot my good Guardian Angels who took care of me during World War II and the long, hard years in Germany. Now in America, I found I met the nicest people whenever I needed them most. Was I a very lucky person, or were the Americans just deeply kind?

In 1960, I remember, we moved to a tiny house with three rooms in a modest neighborhood by the Las Lomita school district in Menlo Park. My children made new friends quickly, and I was lucky enough to meet Sydney, who lived with her three daughters and husband Bill a few houses down the street. Sid was the best friend I could have asked for. Easygoing, intelligent, happy, and always taking up interesting projects, she led Mary's Brownies troop. Above all, Sid thought constantly of others, and I was frequently an object of her concern and assistance.

At this time, I was able to manage financially, but we had a serious problem upon which I couldn't justify spending money: our dear Brittany spaniel, Amy, had eczema caused by an allergy to fleas. I knew how expensive veterinarians were, but I hated to see Amy suffer. Sydney and Bill talked about our dog's problems to a vet, Dr. Cascinai, who offered to help.

As I drove with Amy to the appointment, I couldn't stop worrying about the cost. Dr. Cascinai smiled as I gave quiet commands to Amy in Polish. "Doesn't she speak English?" he joked.

"I don't know," I responded seriously, "but she won't respond to an English command."

After the examination, he told me that Amy would need frequent medicated baths, and that I would have to keep her standing still with medication on her skin for at least fifteen minutes. This would be no problem, I assured him; Amy was a very easy, obedient dog. The doctor gave Amy a shot, gave me a bottle of medicated shampoo and pills, and told me when to come back for the next checkup. I opened my purse and waited to hear the amount I owe him. "It will be four dollars," he said.

"But what is the total?" I asked, confused.

"That's all," he said, and smiled. I almost cried. Another Angel.

Teaching in the parochial schools was enjoyable and satisfying. I felt unquestionable appreciation and support from the students, nuns, and teachers—and unbelievable enthusiasm from the parents. My afterschool program was very popular, and I decided to start more classes in other places. Bill and Sid loaned me $4,000 to buy a set of tumbling mats.

I had another ace up my sleeve: Chris and Mary, who had begun learning gymnastics from the first day Duane and I started teaching. Even in the beginning, they took to the sport naturally. Children generally learn faster and better from another child than from an adult, and Chris and Mary were very likable and popular. I rewarded them with horseback riding lessons on the weekends, a pastime that brought back memories of my childhood in Poland.

And then there was music, which moves our emotions and spirits perhaps even more than our bodies. My childhood memory of my mother's piano playing never diminished. Frequently, when thinking about the harsh war years, I realized the music, dance, and songs had carried me through. Sometimes music made me weep, but even in crying there were tinges of happiness.

The day I learned of a piano on sale for fifty dollars, I immediately went to investigate. The offer sounded simultaneously too small for a good piano and too big for my budget. The upright piano was painted dull gray, but when I opened it and played, it had a good sound and a nice feel to its keys. I could not resist splurging on this incredible luxury. Somehow, I managed to move it into our miniscule house. We put it in my bedroom, the only space available. My double bed, a small dresser, and my prize possession, the piano, left barely any space for moving around, but I was happy nonetheless.

In the evenings, Chris and Mary started bargaining with me: "Zio, if you promise to play piano, we will get ready to go to bed soon ..." My children requested the most unprecedented list of compositions. Mary loved Beethoven's Sonata Pathetic, especially the first movement (I preferred the second). The other favorite was "Mack the Knife." In between came Chopin's Nocturnes and Mazurkas, and many popular songs, which I played without singing—Chris and Mary would have sung along instead of going to sleep.

On the fifth anniversary of our arrival in America, Thursday, September 28, 1961, I registered for my United States citizenship. I took classes and diligently studied government structure and the Constitution. When I was called to the San Francisco Consulate for my citizenship examination several months later, I had fun—and passed the exam with flying colors. Driven by reverence and love for my new country, it was my "credo" to learn everything about the Constitution and the U.S. government. My satisfaction at passing that exam in such a grand manner knew no limits. It was the least I could do for the country that had given me shelter.

Meeting Harley Stallman

Teaching gymnastic had its side benefits. One class in Palo Alto was composed entirely of children from a group of Stanford parents. In 1964, they invited me to their October Beer Fest, which was celebrated in one member's home on the hills above Peninsula. From my seat next to my friend Alberta, I noticed a young, tall, blond and blue-eyed man walking in. He got my attention. "Who's that?" I inquired. Alberta looked in the opposite direction and pointed laughingly at a woman. "There's his wife," she whispered

Later, while milling around amongst the home brew-testing crowd, I remember talking about people who show or do not show their emotions. "Hey Harley, Sophie says you have a mask on your face!" called out the man I was speaking with.

"She may be right," he responded, and gave a sad smile. A year later I learned how true our brief exchange was: on that day, Harley had signed divorce papers with his wife.

I saw Harley again when the same group of parents tried to talk me into starting tumbling classes for men. I tried one class—

and decided not to do it. The men were a danger to themselves. Several months later, however, I started adult gymnastics classes through the Menlo Park Recreation Department. Harley registered. The class was very small, but my supervisor and I decided to keep it going.

After one class, Harley helped me carry my mats to the car. "I'm surprised that the other fellows didn't come with you," I said.

"They're busy with their families," he said, his demeanor indicating that he himself was without a family.

"I guess you're divorced," I said softly, suddenly eager to help this novice with his newly-single status. "Did you start feeling like a fifth wheel around your friends?"

"Exactly!" Harley exclaimed, surprised by the accuracy of my remark.

"I have several divorced friends," I assured him, "men and women, who frequently stop by my house. If you don't mind the company of my two youngsters, a dog, and a cat that just had kittens, you're welcome to come by."

He came the next day, and the day after ...

Harley's visits to his parent's house became less and less frequent, which led to increasing inquires about his whereabouts from his mother. "Why don't you tell her that you're spending time with us?" I suggested.

His response was strange and ridiculously funny: "What should I tell her? That I'm dating a Polish divorcee with two children who works as a PE teacher?"

I realized then that Americans, at least in the Western states, had no idea what Europeans were like, especially those from Eastern Europe. Harley's parents had lived all of their lives in California;

the only foreigners they knew were the Mexicans who worked on Harley's grandfather's ranch. They would have no idea what to expect of me.

"Don't worry, you'll meet them soon enough," Harley added. And indeed, eventually the East came to meet the West. The children and I were invited for dinner at Gwyn and Carl Stallman's. Harley was relaxed; knowing what to expect from both Chris and Mary, he felt free to banter. The children responded jokingly, talked appropriately with Harley's parents, and showed off their perfect table manners with natural ease. I did not expect anything less, but Harley's parents were visibly surprised and impressed.

Soon I learned that the Stallmans came from Silesia. "Did the name originate from Stahle, which is steel in German, or stall, like a horses' stable?" I wondered. Harley started poking fun at the fluidity of European countries' borders: "You know, dad, now that I see how Silesia constantly moved back and forth from Polish to German hands, I think our forefathers might have been Polish!" Carl did not like Harley's idea, but kept silent.

But after these initial little games, what Harley politely called "pissing contests," our relations with his parents were wonderful. They accepted the children and me without question, and we appreciated our new family. I worked to involve them in our lives, and they appreciated my frequent invites to dinner.

A year later, on June 20, 1965, I walked into a friend's garden to the strains of my favorite Chopin ballad, following three flower girls who held bouquets of colorful daisies. On that beautiful sunny day, I walked out to join Harley and Chris, his best man, and Mary, my maid of honor. Standing between two flowering fuchsia trees was the minister. Unbeknownst to us—though evident from the smiling faces of our friends—Amy followed and lay down right behind me and Harley. She wanted to witness our vows, too.

A week after our wedding, we traveled to Oroville for Harley's brother, Hap's, wedding. From there, we drove to the end of the dirt roads in Trinity Alps to a horse ranch, where horses and mules took us to the Caribou Lakes in the high country. The six of us and Amy enjoyed a week of hiking and fishing with July snow all around. For many years, Chris and Mary would ask Harley: "When are we going for another honeymoon?"

The heavens must have smiled on us: shortly after our wedding, both our incomes started to rise. Harley, who worked for GTE Lenkhurt, was promoted to Chief Engineer, and my gymnastics program at Menlo Park Recreation Department started to grow by leaps and bounds. As a family, we settled comfortably in Harley's three-bedroom home. We liked this neat, close-knit neighborhood. All the houses were by Eichler Company; the front yards had lawns of the same size and shape, and the plantings against the houses differed only slightly from one home to another.

With summer passing, we lived our individually busy lives happily—until one Saturday morning, when my two beloved men had some sort of problem. As I drank my second cup of coffee, Harley walked by, muttering an epithet in Chris' direction. Shortly after, Chris burst in complaining about "your husband." Upset, I was close to crying. I went to the bedroom, composed myself, and decided to tell them: "Grow up, both of you, learn to live with each other and don't come to me to solve your problems!"

But where were they? The house was empty. Finally I looked in the garage, and there my boys were, standing side-by-side at the work bench, sorting the fishing gear. "Listen, you two," I started.

Two smiling faces turned toward me. "We're going fishing," they said in unison.

"Don't you ever..." But they didn't let me finish. They needed each other, of course. Chris needed a dependable, youthful father and Harley needed an older son and companion.

My gymnastic classes developed into a Peninsula KYS gymnastics team, which rose over the years from local competitions, to California State meets, to competitions at the national level. Mary, through her extraordinary ability and motivation, became our team's leader. In school, she was self-motivated, striving always for As. From the beginning, she approached gymnastics with the same passion.

By 1968, the sport of gymnastics was growing. So too did our team. In addition to teaching, coaching, guiding assistant coaches, and dealing with the recreation department—no easy task—I found myself writing press releases for television sportscasters and newspaper editors, hoping that they would send camera crews to promote our events, a primary source of the team's fundraising.

During her high school years, Mary became a great performer and an example to all our students. Whenever photographers from the press or TV came, they automatically focused on her. I let them dictate what pictures they wanted, remembering that they were doing *us* a favor.

I loved all my students. Through gymnastics, I believed they were becoming better people in every way. I never asked for more than I could get, and they gave back a great deal, receiving praises from me for honest efforts and good results. I loved looking into their eyes; they stared at me so intently, listening to every word of my accented speech and repeating it later with the same rolling R's and over-pronounced consonants.

The children's development and improvement were my signs that I was succeeding in my desire to do something for America in return for letting me and my children live here. I did not mind my work getting harder. It gave me enormous satisfaction.

In 1970, Harley and I took our first trip out of the United States. Ann and Hal were then teaching in Western Samoa, a country where temperatures varied between 78 and 80 degrees Fahrenheit, where people did not have refrigerators or need windows in their *fale*, which was more a shack than a house. The Samoans had very few cars, probably because there was only one road around the island and because everything rusted or mildewed instantly in the humid climate.

Harley and I enjoyed our three-week vacation, which we spent floating in the warm, shallow water amongst the most colorful fish. The minor dangers, such as having to avoid stepping on live corals, touching poisonous snails, or getting washed over the edge of the island's coral reef, added to our excitement.

Until then, Harley and I had perceived some countries as being better or worse, as more or less cultured. In Samoa, we learned that there are places in the world which are simply different.

The years passed. Chris was in the Navy. Harley, Mary, and I were making final decisions about where Mary would attend college. She wanted to study medicine, but she also dreamed to compete in the 1972 Olympics.

Unquestionably, our mother-daughter coaching schema had to end. A chance to make a U.S. Olympic team of six gymnasts (plus one alternate) was unspeakably small. The corresponding stress on the family would be too great. Eventually, Mary went to Long Beach College to work out with the SCATS team, home of Cathy Rigby, the best American gymnast at that time. When composed, the

U.S. Olympic team consisted of gymnasts drawn from the eastern United States. Mary was left disappointed—though another exciting event did occur.

In 1971, United Artists Studio was searching for a gymnast to perform in the James Bond movie, *Diamonds Are Forever*, with Sean Connery. They came upon a tape of Mary's Free Exercise routine in New York and started looking for her. To their surprise, Mary was in Long Beach, practically next door to their studios. When the studio called, Mary initially did not want to audition; she feared losing her amateur status and with it her chance to go to the Olympics. After a few telephone calls from the studio—and me telling her it couldn't hurt—she auditioned and got the part. United Artists scheduled filming for Mary's college semester break, and she enjoyed the days she spent in Las Vegas with Sean Connery and Paul Baxley, the stunt director.

Poland

As the years passed, I yearned to go to Poland again. With an American passport and an American husband, I finally felt secure enough not to worry about the Communists' arrests and the ongoing imprisonments of former AK members. I wanted to introduce Harley to my few living family members and friends, and to introduce Poland to Harley. My husband knew very little about the country, in part because it was difficult for me to discuss. As words came to me, the tears started pushing. After 27 years, I wanted to go to my old country, my old home.

We arrived in Warsaw, looking on in bewilderment. Soldiers with machine guns clustered, sharing space with hostile-looking government inspectors on the barricades between the foreign arrivals and the local population.

My cousin Wanda waited for us. She hadn't seen me since I was eighteen. When she spotted me, she started to shake her head, smiling and staring at me intently. When we came closer, she exclaimed, "I don't believe it! You look exactly like your mother; it's like seeing Ciocia Zosia's ghost."

Wanda was invaluable to us. Functioning in the chaotic Communist financial system was not so much difficult as peculiar. Foreigners were forced to exchange dollars at minimal value per every day spent in Poland. In contrast, the black market had a very high exchange rate, as dollars were the only available currency of stable value. Wanda supplied us with Złotys and Harley was like Alice in Wonderland, giving tips of single dollars instead of devaluated Złotys.

We organized a dinner in Europejski Hotel, an unaffordable luxury for most of the Polish population but cheap for us. At the head table, Harley enjoyed English conversation with Wanda and a few other English-speaking individuals; I, on the other end, reveled in speaking Polish. Everybody enjoyed themselves; Harley could not believe that the bill for the whole ten-person dinner came to the equivalent of ... $30.

We wondered through the rebuilt Warsaw. The historical buildings, like the old town, the King's Palace, and many others, were rebuilt identically to the originals. Harley was thus able to see the city in all its pre-1500s splendor, when the capital was moved to Warsaw from Kraków.

I also gave him a tour of the streets I recalled from my days fighting in the war. Harley appeared bothered, as he always is when I talk about the Uprising, something I still do not understand and he cannot or does not want to explain.

I corresponded with Ciocia Hala in Krakow; she knew roughly when to expect us, as she had no telephone. This was another peculiarity of life under the Communists: infrastructure was an oxymoron; there was only a confusing mess. Ciocia Hala knew that if anything changed, we would send her a telegram—which might well be delivered the next day.

We took a taxi to her apartment, and she saw us out of her second-floor window. We embraced and kissed; she pushed me away to take another look and then kissed me again. I introduced Harley, who gallantly kissed her hand, an old Polish custom she appreciated.

Hala led us through the dark entryway to the room she occupied with her husband, Wuj Janek (Uncle John). We had so much to talk about. My dear aunt prepared herself to keep us organized and to cover all the needed subjects systematically. For a while I translated for Harley, but eventually Uncle John showed him various military and historical memorabilia, many of which needed no introduction. They gesticulated and toasted each other with special vódkas prepared by Uncle John for our visit.

Thanks to my aunt and uncle, I saw the bed where Mother slept when she stayed with them. I was able to touch a few precious items she enjoyed, to hear more about my mother's last days in the fall of 1952, and her joy in getting pictures of the newborn Mary.

Dinner was delicious in spite of the fact that Ciocia Hala had to hunt for everything on the black market. In that respect, conditions had not changed much from the German occupation. The Soviets sent trains loaded with meats, butter, and cheese to Russia, while Polish stores made do with limited supplies.

We went back to the hotel with the list of places to visit next day. I could not wait to go to the Wawel Castle. Krakow is a pearl amongst ancient cities, many times invaded but never destroyed. Finally I would look inside the famous buildings the Germans kept closed against us Poles during the war. I knew what to expect, but wanted to see Harley's reaction.

Construction on Wawel Castle started in the twelfth century and finished during my favorite king, Kazimierz Wielki (Casimir

The Great's), reign in the 1300s. In the spectacular halls, the beautiful parquet floors made of Polish hardwoods caught Harley's attention first, followed by the pieces of furniture. "The Eastern Exhibit" was more impressive than we expected. It included all the treasures King Sobieski brought home after his victory in Vienna: tents, carpets, dishes, jewels, and armor. It truly evoked a feeling of history.

We reserved a special day in our tour to visit my mother's grave. It was in a very old cemetery; mementos of historical tragedies were scattered throughout the grounds. When we came to Mother's grave, I placed flowers I'd brought, lit candles, said a prayer, and thought of the last time I kissed her goodbye: twenty-seven years ago, as I was leaving my cousin's estate in Rzeki-Rivers; I couldn't tell her that Ann and I would be escaping from the oncoming Soviets.

During the days we spent together, Ciocia Hala told me everything about our family's history, including memories of my mother's early life and the stories I valued most: my parents' years together. Finally, the last day arrived. With our suitcases in the taxi, we talked "business." I would put dollars between pictures in a sealed plastic envelope, hiding the funds from the greedy censors. Aunt and Uncle walked us to the door, we kissed, and Ciocia tried to hold back her tears, but failed. "Why is she crying?" Harley asked me in an unsteady voice.

"I'm afraid I won't see you again," Hala sobbed.

Harley steadied himself and said, "Please tell Ciocia Hala that we will come back in two years. I mean it. It's not a maybe."

Harley kept his promise. In 1974, we flew to Munich, bought a BMW, and drove it to Krakow.

Home Sweet Home,
And a Time of Growth

The greatest pleasure of going on a trip is the return home. Within a year, we had bought a house whose gentle slope faced the morning sun. This was my first home. I loved it from the instant I set my foot in the door; years later, I realized that it loved me, too.

Like newlyweds, Harley and I found a new hobby: auction studios. While most people were buying light new furniture and wall-to-wall carpeting, we were ripping carpets from the hardwood floors and buying Oriental rugs and heavy wooden furniture. In the garden, we removed hideous ivy and other weed-like plants. With the exception of one plum tree, there was nothing worth keeping. My forefathers' land-loving blood enjoyed the possibilities.

Professionally, the time came to change, and I decided to quit gymnastics. My four children and Harley supported me—yes, four children. Mary married Jeff, and Chris married Lyn. Our new family was a wonderful blessing.

"You always wanted to have time to play tennis, to learn more about gardens," Mary reminded me.

"And I'd like earlier dinners and more weekends with my wife," chimed in Harley.

"But how can I leave my gymnasts without a good replacement?" I objected.

But eventually, problems with difficult parents and an uncooperative administration helped make up my mind. I quit in December of 1978. In January, I enrolled in horticulture classes at the College of San Mateo and did not stop until I'd taken all the courses available two years later. I'd long enjoyed using my hands—whether playing piano or ball, sewing or knitting. Now I "dug" into garden work.

Whatever I learned at school, I simultaneously practiced and applied at home. I practiced planting, propagating, graft and pruning, built retaining walls of wood, concrete blocks, and brick, and—in what became my specialty—I learned to install irrigation and drainage. The concrete block retaining walls and the brick planter boxes still stand, solid and professional looking.

Life was once more easy and good. I had plenty of time for tennis, for home improvement, and travel. And in another childhood dream fulfilled, my family and I were accompanied throughout our years in California by our best friends, our loving companions, our three Brittany Spaniels: Amy, who "spoke only Polish" and considered herself a ferocious guardian of little Mary; Juniper, Harley's best teacher, who taught him the art of unconditional love and how to hunt with a dog; and Gabby—who gave us the most of all. Why? Because the other two dogs prepared us to understand the secret wisdom of dogs: trust, faith, and love.

California is far from Poland, and it feels so long, long ago that I was a young teenager who had to live through five years of cruel war. Many young people today may not know where World War II was or why it was fought. For myself, I tried to forget but it's impossible. Those seemingly short five years left a sensitive string inside me, a string that reacts to the slightest touch with clear, painful vibrations. Truly, even mentioning it makes me cry. At that time, I had to learn to fight many battles according to the unwritten rules of war. The memories of those days taught me to differentiate between minutia and important matters, an ability that has served me for the rest of my life

As my mother used to say: there is nothing so bad that it cannot end with something good. My mentors and dear friends have never diminished in my memory. My dancing years with Mrs. Wanda left my old body supple and coordinated. Dear Ivo Gall taught me how to find the deepest thoughts and feelings in a character, imaginary or real. Even though I lost the range of my mezzo soprano singing voice, my memories of Czesław Zaremba are vivid and dear.

And my war experiences left another mark on me. My priorities and principles became simple and clear. I know my duty to God and my country and the importance of ethics and aesthetics. Above all, in matters big or small, those short five years set in stone my desire to always seek the complete unadulterated truth. Truth, which makes life so much easier.

The End

Acknowledgments

This book would never have happened if ...

I hadn't found a new, normal life in California, in the United States of America;

I hadn't discovered the "Life Stories" classes, taught by the patient and encouraging Sheila Dunec, and joined by the equally encouraging members of her class;

If my daughter, Mary Hiller, did not eventually decide to have my – by then abandoned – manuscript published;

If, after many trial and tribulations, we hadn't found Genevieve Gagne-Hawes, the most patient, efficient, encouraging, and timely editor ... in summary, my "Angel" editor;

Finally, looking far back into "the Alfa," the beginning of it all, if I hadn't been endowed with a special perspective on life developed long ago by my forefathers. It is all their doing!

CPSIA information can be obtained at www.ICGtesting.com
Printed in the USA
LVOW08s2155240516

489818LV00004B/187/P